The Journals of
William A. Lindsay

Dr. William A. Lindsay, circa 1830s

The Journals of William A. Lindsay

An Ordinary Nineteenth-Century Physician's Surgical Cases

Edited by
Katherine Mandusic McDonell

Indianapolis
Indiana Historical Society
1989

Publications in Indiana Medical History   Number 2

Library of Congress Cataloging-in-Publication Data

Lindsay, William A., 1795–1876.
  The journals of William A. Lindsay.

  (Publications in Indiana medical history; no. 2)
  Bibliography: p.
  Includes index.
  1. Surgery, Operative—Case studies. 2. Surgery—Middle West—History—19th century—Sources. 3. Lindsay, William A., 1795-1876—Diaries. 4. Surgeons—United States—Diaries. I. McDonell, Katherine Mandusic.
  II. Title. III. Series.
  RD34.L49 1989   617′.092′4   88-32003
  ISBN 0-87195-029-4

To my mother, Anna J. Mandusic
and in memory of my father, Sam Mandusic

Contents

Introduction

Early Nineteenth-Century Surgery

William A. Lindsay (1795-1876) was an ordinary midwestern physician who at times confronted extraordinary surgical problems. Although adept at surgery he, like other early nineteenth-century, country physicians, was neither exceptionally trained nor highly experienced. He made no major contributions to the field of surgery, and his minor surgical innovations went unnoticed among the larger surgical community. Nonetheless, Lindsay left behind a unique legacy: three journals which contain a wealth of information about surgical care in the rural Midwest.

During the early nineteenth century, general medicine and surgery were not yet separate professions. Most American physicians performed minor surgery in addition to diagnosing disease and prescribing treatment. Only in the larger eastern and European cities was surgery achieving independence. There, a few well-known surgeons were performing lithotomies, resections, artery ligations, and other complicated operations.[1] In contrast, most physicians treated relatively minor surgical ailments. Surgery in Indiana, where Lindsay practiced for several years, was equally unimpressive. In 1853 the members of the Indiana State Medical Society's Committee on Surgery noted: "there is nothing in Indiana surgery entitling it to be regarded as especially beneficial or skillful."[2] Account books, jour-

1. Richard Harrison Shryock, *Medicine and Society in America, 1660-1860* (New York: New York University Press, 1960), 132-33; John Duffy, *The Healers: A History of American Medicine* (1976; reprint, Urbana: University of Illinois Press, 1979), 129-34. Although eastern surgeons performed difficult operations, they did not perform them in large numbers. From 1822 to 1855, doctors performed an average of 6.2 amputations annually in the Massachusetts General Hospital (William G. Rothstein, *American Physicians in the Nineteenth Century: From Sects to Science* [Baltimore: Johns Hopkins University Press, 1972], 252).

2. J. S. Bobbs, George Sutton, and M. Bray, "Report of the Committee of Surgery," *Proceedings of the Fourth Annual Meeting of the Indiana State Medical Society, Held in the City of Lafayette, May, 1853* (Indianapolis: Elder & Harkness, 1853), 78.

nals, and case records of Indiana physicians confirm this observation. During the early 1800s, the surgical repertoire of most Indiana physicians included pulling teeth, treating minor wounds, setting simple fractures, reducing dislocations, and performing an occasional amputation.[3]

Most early nineteenth-century physicians performed major operations only in cases of absolute necessity.[4] Elective surgery remained rare. Patients who suffered structural disorders frequently allowed the situation to become severe before seeking professional advice.[5] One of Lindsay's patients, for example, waited three to four years before seeking relief from hydrocele. By that time his scrotum measured twenty inches in length.[6] Patients suffering from tumors had a tendency to let them grow until the sheer size hindered their day-to-day activities or the pain became too immense to bear.

The patient's reluctance to submit to an operation and the doctor's hesitation to perform one was understandable given the inadequacies of medical science. Prior to 1846 there was no anesthesia, and surgery was a grisly experience. Doctors often administered alcohol, opium, and other narcotics to allay the patient's sufferings, but these drugs did not render the patient insensible to pain.[7] Indeed, the patient's worst fears about an operation often were realized. Lindsay noted that an operation for retention of the placenta "was attended by excruciating suffering to the patient, and I felt sometimes fearful that she would be unable to bear up under it, and I was several times compelled to desist a short time owing to the exhausted and sinking exacerbations induced by the operation."[8]

3. Katherine Mandusic McDonell, "William A. Lindsay in Perspective," *Indiana Medical History Quarterly* 7 (June 1981): 13; Duffy, *Healers*, 129-30. Surgery was likewise limited in Europe. Most physicians there performed only minor surgery (Irvine Loudon, *Medical Care and the General Practitioner, 1750-1850* [Oxford: Clarendon Press, 1986], 73-85).

4. Paul Starr, *The Social Transformation of American Medicine* (New York: Basic Books, 1982), 156; Duffy, *Healers*, 131, 133-35; Rothstein, *American Physicians*, 250-51.

5. Owen H. Wangensteen and Sarah Wangensteen, *The Rise of Surgery: From Empiric Craft to Scientific Discipline* (Minneapolis: University of Minnesota Press, 1978), 3-10; Rothstein, *American Physicians*, 250-59.

6. Case of Frederick Daniels, Hydrocele, Lindsay Journal No. 3, June 4, 1839. See below, p. 98. The numbers 1, 3, and 4 appear on the front cover of each respective journal (hereafter, cited as Lindsay Journal) in the Indiana State Library at Indianapolis. The date appearing after the journal number, unless otherwise indicated, is the date the operation was performed, rather than the recorded date.

7. Rothstein, *American Physicians*, 250-51; Martin S. Pernick, *A Calculus of Suffering: Pain, Professionalism, and Anesthesia in Nineteenth-Century America* (New York: Columbia University Press, 1985), 71.

8. Case of Mrs. Mabbit, Retention of the Placenta, Lindsay Journal No. 3, January 17, 1835. See below, p. 77.

Forced to operate on a conscious patient, the surgeon had to be strong and often brutal, swift with the knife, and hardened to the patient's pleas for mercy. The patient's begging and screaming were disconcerting to even the most experienced surgeon.[9] Lindsay wrote about a young patient who faced an operation: "Having made known to him my views of his case & the necesity of an operation, I shall never forget the earnestness with which he emplored me not to operate on him. and he so far worked on my feelings & sympathies that it was with much dificulty that I could man my self up to the operating point."[10] In 1846 sulfuric ether was introduced as an anesthetic, but operating conditions remained primitive. Anesthesia itself was only vaguely understood, and its administration occasionally resulted in death. For this reason, and also because news of medical innovations spread slowly, some rural physicians did not immediately employ anesthesia.[11]

Without an understanding of germs and infection, even anesthesia could do little to lessen the surgical mortality rate.[12] Few suspected that germs present in the air, on the surgeon's hands and instruments, and on the patient's skin were responsible for deadly infections like gangrene and septicemia. Operators did not scrub their hands, sterilize their instruments, or disinfect the area in which they operated. Nor did physicians wear masks, operating caps and gowns, or rubber gloves. Instead, the nineteenth-century doctor operated in his street clothes, and after completing an operation, often wiped the bloodied knives and scalpels on his well-stained coat. The physician then placed the instruments back in their case for the next surgery. During the early decades of the nineteenth century, most operations were performed in the patient's home. The kitchen table served as the operating table, and the physician enjoined the patient's friends and relatives to assist in the operation.[13]

Lack of anesthesia and asepsis were not the only problems which limited surgery during the first half of the nineteenth century. In rural

9. Duffy, *Healers*, 130.

10. Case of Joseph Edgarton's Son, Skull Fracture, Lindsay Journal No. 3, September 5, 1835. See below, p. 66.

11. Rothstein, *American Physicians*, 252. Physicians evidently used anesthesia selectively. Some believed pain was beneficial for both the patient and the healing process. Therefore, anesthesia often was administered only in major operations (Pernick, *A Calculus of Suffering*, 35-58).

12. Paul Starr in his *Social Transformation of American Medicine*, 156, estimates the mortality rate of amputation patients in America at 40 percent. The death rate was actually higher in the large hospitals than in rural areas where surgery was performed in the patient's home.

13. Wangensteen and Wangensteen, *The Rise of Surgery*, 3-10; Duffy, *Healers*, 130.

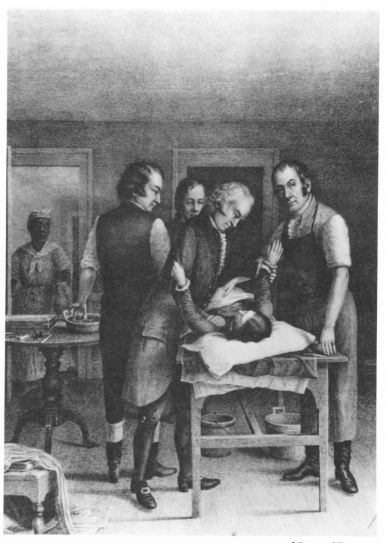

In 1809 Dr. Ephraim McDowell of Danville, Kentucky, performed the first ovariotomy. As with almost all operations performed during this time, the surgery was performed in the patient's or doctor's home on a sturdy table.

areas, doctors faced other difficulties. Travel was by horseback over rough and poorly constructed roads. Thus, an entire day might elapse before a physician reached the patient's side. In many accident cases, a patient died before receiving any surgical attention.[14]

Even when surgical care was accessible in country areas, many rural and small-town doctors lacked the training and experience necessary to perform difficult operations. During the early nineteenth century, medical students could not specialize in surgery. Surgery was part of the regular medical school curriculum, but most colleges devoted little time to the subject. The best surgeons had either trained in, or had access to, hospitals in large, urban areas. These hospitals, which admitted primarily poor patients, provided physicians with opportunities to see a wide variety of cases and to observe or perform a number of complex operations.[15] Although professors at large eastern schools recognized the need for hospital experience, few schools made clinical training mandatory. Medical school administrators insisted that required clinical instruction would lower enrollments. Professors at rural medical colleges believed clinical experience unimportant since rural communities lacked hospitals. These instructors failed to see the importance of clinical instruction in enhancing the physician's surgical skills or acquainting him with difficult surgical procedures.[16]

While few medical schools prepared students adequately for a surgical practice, many prospective doctors circumvented medical school entirely and established a practice after taking a few medical courses and serving an apprenticeship. Others elected an apprenticeship alone before opening a practice. Comprehensive, accurate statistics on the educational backgrounds of rural and small-town physicians are unavailable for the second quarter of the nineteenth century, but existing evidence suggests that formally trained physicians were a minority. Of 896 physicians practicing in 163 New England towns between 1790 and 1840, only one-third had graduated from medical school. In Litchfield County, Connecticut, located close to Yale and Berkshire medical schools, less than 20 percent of the practicing physicians held medical degrees.[17] Prior to 1840, perhaps three-fourths of midwestern physicians received only an apprenticeship training.[18] An inadequate medi-

14. Madge E. Pickard and R. Carlyle Buley, *The Midwest Pioneer: His Ills, Cures, and Doctors* (New York: Henry Schuman, 1946), 100-101.

15. Rothstein, *American Physicians*, 252-53; Duffy, *Healers*, 129.

16. William Frederick Norwood, *Medical Education in the United States before the Civil War* (1944; reprint, New York: Arno Press, 1971), 55, 400-401.

17. Barnes Riznik, "The Professional Lives of Early Nineteenth Century New England Physicians," *Journal of the History of Medicine and Allied Sciences* 19 (1964): 1-2.

18. Pickard and Buley, *Midwest Pioneer*, 120.

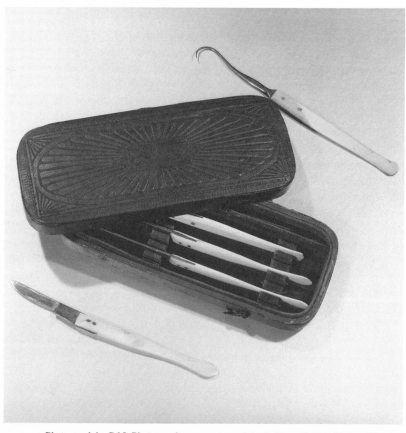

Photograph by B&L Photographers, courtesy of the Indiana Medical History Museum
A small, pocket case of surgical instruments containing small scalpels, forceps, and a tenaculum, circa late eighteenth-early nineteenth centuries. Often a small, pocket set of surgical instruments was all the midwestern physician possessed for performing surgery.

cal education meant that physicians were not only ignorant of many complex surgical procedures, but they were often unable to apply successfully what little knowledge they possessed. Many surgical patients undoubtedly died because of the ineptitude or inexperience of the attending physician.

Once in practice country and small-town physicians had few opportunities to further their surgical training. The sparse population of rural areas and the absence of hospitals afforded few occasions to observe or assist in difficult surgery. When these opportunities did arise, many of the physicians simply did not have the necessary instruments to perform complex operations. At the beginning of his career, one Indiana physician, for example, could afford only a toothkey (a device for extracting teeth), a few needles, and a pair of scissors.[19] Estate records of doctors in six Indiana counties reveal that less than half of the doctors who practiced prior to 1840 owned any surgical equipment.[20] Dr. Rufus Haymond of Brookville, Indiana, wrote in 1846 of an operation for the removal of bladder stones in which the attending physician owned only one pair of forceps. The doctor "tried some two hours to get hold of the stone" with his forceps. Before admitting defeat, he "got a workman to make a pair [of forceps] with handles. With this he succeeded in getting away *one* stone, but there was *another* which would not pass through the opening—He had therefore to put the patient to bed, and abandon the matter."[21]

Although poorly educated and ill prepared, rural physicians were occasionally called upon to perform difficult surgery. During the first half of the nineteenth century, chopping wood, sawing logs, riding a horse, driving a carriage, playing, or fighting resulted in life-threatening injuries requiring an operation. Difficult obstetrical cases, too, demanded surgical intervention. Lindsay's journals suggest that in these cases inexperienced physicians called upon their more seasoned colleagues for advice and assistance.[22] Yet, in these situations even the

19. Malthus Ward to Ezra Bartlett, November 27, 1815, as quoted in William Barlow and David Powell, "Malthus A. Ward: Frontier Physician, 1815-1823," *Journal of the History of Medicine and Allied Sciences* 32 (1977): 287-88.

20. McDonell, "William A. Lindsay in Perspective," 14.

21. Rufus Haymond Diary, April 21, 1846, pp. 37-38, Indiana Historical Society Library, Indianapolis.

22. Lindsay, as well as other doctors with whom he was acquainted, did not hesitate to call upon another physician for advice and assistance. Medical historian Charles E. Rosenberg, however, suggests that there was little cooperation among doctors because of the potential of another physician stealing patients. Although true of many urban physicians, it would appear that rural and small-town physicians relied upon each other to compensate for their own lack of experience and education (George Rosen, *The Structure of American Medical Practice, 1875-1941*, ed. Charles E. Rosenberg [Philadelphia: University of Pennsylvania Press, 1983], 6).

more experienced doctors like Lindsay had to reach beyond the limits of their knowledge to save a patient's life. These heroic efforts frequently ended in failure. Surgery therefore remained only a minor part of the general practice of medicine; and as with surgery, the practice of medicine was far from ideal.

Lindsay's Medical Career

Intense competition characterized the medical marketplace of the early nineteenth century. The dramatic rise in the number of medical school graduates contributed to the surplus of physicians. From 1800 to 1809, medical schools produced a total of 343 graduates. The number of medical school graduates produced each year continued to escalate. From 1830 to 1840, the number of medical degree recipients rose to 6,849.[23] The excess of formally educated physicians was only half of the medical profession's woes. The number of doctors with minimal or no formal education also increased. One physician, for example, found doctors in the western part of New York so numerous that "two are obliged to ride on one horse."[24]

Some self-trained practitioners were opposed to the accepted early nineteenth-century therapies of bloodletting and purging and offered their patients a multitude of alternative treatments. One of the largest dissenter sects during the early nineteenth century was the Thomsonians. Founded in the early 1800s by Samuel Thomson, a New Hampshire farmer, this sect argued that doctors were unnecessary since every person could be his or her own physician. Thomson therefore wrote his *New Guide to Health* in the nontechnical language of the common man. Thomson believed all disease resulted from the loss of body heat. Through a course of six botanic remedies, he maintained that the heat could be restored and the disease eliminated.

A number of other forms of alternative medicine including homeopathy, hydropathy, and eclecticism also emerged during the first half of the nineteenth century. Homeopathy, founded by Samuel Christian

---

23. John S. Billings, "Literature and Institutions," in Edward H. Clarke et al., *A Century of American Medicine, 1776-1876* (Philadelphia: Lea, 1876), 359, as cited in Rothstein, *American Physicians*, 98. Twenty-six medical schools were founded between 1810 and 1840. A few of these schools such as the Christian College of New Albany, Indiana, were not even authentic. The college president issued diplomas to the highest bidder forty days after the school was founded (Martin Kaufman, *American Medical Education: The Formative Years, 1765-1910* [Westport, Conn.: Greenwood Press, 1976], 40; Pickard and Buley, *Midwest Pioneer*, 141).

24. Malthus Ward to Ezra Bartlett, September 21, 1815, as quoted in Barlow and Powell, "Malthus A. Ward," 291.

Hahnemann (1775-1843), asserted that "like cures like." Since, for example, vaccinating a healthy person caused symptoms of smallpox,
Hahnemann derived from this a "law of similars": treating diseases
with drugs that in large doses reproduced symptoms of the disease to
be cured. Homeopathists administered their drugs, however, in infini-
tesimal doses, diluted to the extent that the patient ingested mostly
water. Hydropathy, as its name suggests, consisted of a variety of
water cures. Wet towel wraps, complete and partial baths, and a liquid
diet constituted the treatment. Eclecticism was founded by Wooster
Beach in 1829 as an independent movement, parallel to Thomsonianism. Beach borrowed from all medical systems. Although their cures
were mostly botanic in nature, the eclectics did not hesitate to employ
harsh remedies like bloodletting and purging if effective.

A variety of empirics, too, offered their services to the unwary
public. These doctors obtained their cures by hit-or-miss systems and
often proclaimed their abilities in newspapers. One type of empiric
specialized in the treatment of cancer patients with secret remedies.
Also practicing at this time were the unschooled root doctors, known
as Indian doctors, who used only indigenous roots and herbs to cure
disease. Moreover, many families relied neither on these lay healers
nor professionally trained physicians. Instead, in cases of nonsurgical
ailments, they turned to their own home remedies, which had often
been passed down from generation to generation. Others relied on
the many self-help, or domestic, medical books which were readily
available.[25]

Licensing legislation was ineffective in curbing the growth of alternative medicine, as well as the burgeoning numbers of entrants into
the medical profession. The public viewed most licensing laws as un-
democratic attempts by the medical profession to establish a monop-
oly.[26] This unabated rivalry adversely affected the individual
physician. Data pertaining to physicians' incomes indicate that urban
physicians were ranked in the lower middle class. The starting salary
for a physician in New York in the 1860s was $400 a year; the average
salary for a Massachusetts physician in 1850 was $600 a year. Country
doctors like Lindsay probably had the most uncertain incomes, and

25. Pickard and Buley, *Midwest Pioneer*, 169-239; Ronald L. Numbers, "Do-It-
Yourself the Sectarian Way," in *Medicine without Doctors: Home Health Care in
American History*, ed. Guenter B. Risse, Ronald L. Numbers, and Judith Walzer
Leavitt (New York: Science History Publications, 1977), 49-68.

26. For a history of licensing legislation in the United States, see Richard Harri-
son Shryock, *Medical Licensing in America, 1650-1965* (Baltimore: Johns Hopkins
Press, 1967); Joseph F. Kett, *The Formation of the American Medical Profession:
The Role of Institutions, 1780-1860* (1968; reprint, Westport, Conn.: Greenwood
Press, 1980), 1-31.

much of the pay for their services came in the form of produce.[27] With incomes so low, many physicians in rural areas pursued second, or even third, occupations to supplement their earnings.[28] Referring to this period in American medicine, historian Charles Rosenberg writes: "Economic security for a physician turned on his ability to attract and hold the loyalty of a sufficient number of fee-paying families." Unfortunately, as Rosenberg notes, "in every class . . . and in almost every location, the number of would-be practitioners outnumbered the supply of fee-paying families who might potentially employ their services."[29] It was in this atmosphere that Lindsay attempted to establish a lucrative practice of medicine.

Lindsay was born in Lincoln County, North Carolina, on December 24, 1795. After teaching school there briefly, he accepted a position in 1814 at the Dayton Academy in Ohio. While in Dayton, he began his medical career by apprenticing with a local physician. In 1819 he married Rhoda Allison Smith.[30] Her father, Peter Smith (1753-1816), a Baptist minister and root doctor, wrote the first medical book published in the Midwest: *The Indian Doctor's Dispensatory, Being Father Smith's Advice Respecting Diseases and Their Cure* (Cincinnati, 1813).[31]

In the early 1820s Lindsay moved to Lawrenceburg, Indiana, to practice medicine. He stayed there for two or three years and then attended the Ohio Medical College in Cincinnati. Lindsay never graduated; more than twenty years later, however, he received an honorary degree from the Starling Medical College in Columbus, Ohio. Upon leaving the Ohio Medical College in 1826, Lindsay practiced for a short time in West Alexandria and Germantown, Ohio, before setting up a stable medical practice in Richmond, Indiana, in 1829.[32] He announced the opening of his practice with the following advertisement:

27. Starr, *The Social Transformation of American Medicine*, 61-64, 84; Duffy, *Healers*, 297-98; Rosen, *The Structure of American Medical Practice*, 5-6.

28. Popular second occupations for Indiana physicians included postmaster, treasurer, legislator, surveyor, judge, minister, druggist, and merchant (G. W. H. Kemper, *A Medical History of the State of Indiana* [Chicago: American Medical Association Press, 1911]).

29. Rosen, *The Structure of American Medical Practice*, 4.

30. "Lindsay, Earl of Balcarras, Scotland," an unpublished genealogical account of the Lindsay family written by one of William A. Lindsay's daughters, in the private collection of Helen Louise Graham Silvey, Sacramento, California; Case of Rhoda A. Lindsay, Lindsay Journal No. 4, recorded October 21, 1840 (see below, pp. 141-42); "Obituary: William A. Lindsay," Eaton *Register*, May 11, 1876.

31. Pickard and Buley, *Midwest Pioneer*, 45-47; John Uri Lloyd, "Dr. Peter Smith and His Dispensatory," *American Journal of Pharmacy* 70 (1898): 1-9.

32. Matriculation records, 1825-1826, Special Collections Department, University of Cincinnati Library, Cincinnati, Ohio; *Catalogue of the Officers and Students of the*

Rhoda A. Lindsay

Dr. William A. Lindsay, after complimenting his friends for past favors, respectfully informs the public, generally, that he now considers
himself permanently located in the town of Richmond, Indiana. In the
practice of his profession, in the various branches of PHYSIC, SUR-
GERY and MIDWIFERY. He may at all times be found at his resi-

---

Starling Medical College for the Session of 1848-9 (Columbus, Ohio: Thrall and Reed,
Printers, 1849), 38. There is no indication that Lindsay attended any courses at
Starling Medical College. He was probably nominated for the degree by one of his
colleagues.

dence and Drug Store, when not on business, one door south of Samuel Smith's corner, and one door north of Achilles William's Saddler Shop . . . . A few young men who are qualified, will be taken as medical students.[33]

Lindsay, like many other doctors during this period, found it necessary to pursue other business enterprises to achieve economic security. During his stay in Richmond, he operated a large and prosperous drug firm. His inventory included a wide selection of medicines, paints, glassware, liquor, medical instruments, and "1001 articles too tedious to mention."[34] Although many physicians scorned the use of patent medicines, Lindsay quickly recognized the profitability of huckstering these packaged nostrums. In fact, his patent medicine business may have represented a significant portion of his income and given him a competitive advantage in an overcrowded marketplace. Included among his patent medicine inventory were Dr. Weaver's Celebrated Eye Salve, Porter's Vegetable Catholican, LaMott's Cough Drops, and Dr. Thomas White's Vegetable Toothache Drops.[35] He even developed and vended his own nostrum, "Dr. W. Lindsay's Vegetable Tonic," which he touted as excellent for general debility and malarial fevers. As with many of these patent medicines, Lindsay's product contained a secret ingredient (probably arsenic).[36]

Lindsay not only sold and manufactured packaged nostrums, but also produced his own "Oleaginous Gum Elastic Water-proof Blacking for Boots, Shoes, and Harness," advertised as a leather preservative "superior to any thing of the kind . . . yet seen."[37] In December 1833 he added to his repertoire of skills by offering dental services to the Richmond public: "Dr. W. Lindsey [sic] has prepared himself for cleaning and plugging the teeth, and keeps a Dentifrice Powder for preserving them, curing the scurvy, and correcting a bad breath."[38] Not all

33. Richmond *Palladium*, January 8, 1831.

34. Ibid., October 22, 1836.

35. Ibid., February 23, August 3, September 7 and 21, 1833, May 17 and July 21, 1834. For more information about the patent medicine industry during the early nineteenth century, see James Harvey Young, *The Toadstool Millionaires: A Social History of Patent Medicines in America before Federal Regulation* (Princeton, N.J.: Princeton University Press, 1961).

36. Richmond *Palladium*, October 22, 1836; Indianapolis *Indiana Journal*, August 5, 1837, May 26, 1838. One of the medical profession's major objections to these patent medicines was their secret ingredients, including mercury, arsenic, opium, and alcohol (Young, *Toadstool Millionaires*, 64-69).

37. Richmond *Palladium*, April 9, 1831.

38. Lindsay probably learned the rudiments of dentistry from a Mr. Frydinger of Dayton, Ohio, who specialized in making false teeth and was available for consultation at Lindsay's office in May 1833 (ibid., May 11 and December 28, 1833).

THE

INDIAN DOCTOR'S

DISPENSATORY,

BEING

FATHER SMITH'S ADVICE

RESPECTING,

DISEASES AND THEIR CURE;

CONSISTING OF PRESCRIPTIONS FOR

MANY COMPLAINTS:

AND A DESCRIPTION OF MEDICINES,

SIMPLE AND COMPOUND,

SHOWING THEIR VIRTUES AND HOW TO APPLY THEM

DESIGNED FOR THE BENEFIT OF HIS CHILDREN, HIS FRIENDS
AND THE PUBLIC, BUT MORE ESPECIALLY THE CITIZENS OF
THE WESTERN PARTS OF THE UNITED STATES OF AMERICA.

BY PETER SMITH,
OF THE MIAMI COUNTRY.

Men seldom have wit enough to prize and take care of their
health until they lose it—And Doctors often know not how to
get their bread deservedly, until they have no teeth to chew it.

CINCINNATI:
PRINTED BY BROWNE AND LOOKER,
FOR THE AUTHOR.
1813.

Indiana Historical Society
Title page from Lindsay's father-in-law's book, The Indian Doctor's Dispensatory . . . *(Cincinnati: Brown & Looker, 1813)*

Dr. WM. LINDSEY:

After complimenting his friends for past favors, respectfully informs the public, generally, that he now considers himself permanently located in the town of Richmond, Indiana. In the practice of his profession, in the various branches of PHYSIC, SURGERY and MIDWIFERY. He may at all times be found at his residence and Drug Store, when not absent on business, one door south of Samuel W. Smith's corner, and one door north of Achilles William's saddler shop.

He still keeps on hand a general assortment of

Drugs and Medicines,

including PAINTS and DYE-STUFFS, all of which he offers low for cash.

He has on hands, Dean's Gum Elastic Japan Varnish, for boots, shoes and harness, said to render leather water proof.

Likewise prepares (himself) an oleaginous Blacking, which renders leather water proof. And can with confidence recommend it to the public as a preservative of leather, superior to any thing of the kind he has yet seen. Tanners, Shoe-makers, Harness-makers, and all others, who wish to keep their feet *dry*, would do well to call and examine the article.

☞ A few young men who are qualified, will be taken as medical students.

Lindsay advertises the opening of his Richmond, Indiana, practice. (Richmond Palladium, *April 9, 1831)*

FRESH ARRIVAL.

JUST Received from Philadelphia a fresh supply of

Medicines, Paints, Drugs, &c.

Which are offered unusually low for cash, whole-
sale and retail; among which are the following,
viz:—

Carb. amonia, bals. copaiva, blue pill mass, a
London article, corrosive sublimate, lunar caustic,
cloves, calomel of English manufacture, ergot and
wine of ergot, flour of suphur, roll brimstone, gum
arabic, gum guiac, Russian isinglass, American do.
nutmegs, opium opt., orange peel sweet and bitter,
liquid ink, chalk pp'd., rad. rhei, do. pulv., sapo
castile, sulphate quinine 80 oz part French and
part English, spirits nitre dulcis., aqua ammonia
common and strong, sulphuric ether, sugar of lead.
borax refined, Chinese vermillion, white frostings.
dark blue smalts, prussian blue, chrome yellow,
chrome green, Turkey umber, terra de sienna,
stone ochre, sable pencils assorted, camel hair do.
do., toy paints assorted, fine water colors, indigo
span opt., pomatum, hair powder perfumed, otta of
roses, perfumery assorted, essential oils, dental instruments; gold foil, tin do compound syrup of sarsaparilla, fancy pungents assorted, soda powders in
tin boxes, vial corks, lancets best, gum elastic pes-
saries, glass do., sulphate zinc, extract of pinkroot fluid and concrete, tonic extract, extract of
cicuta, extract o beechu, oil of Lytta, seidlitz
powders, Saratoga do or Congress water, polishing
powder for cleaning brass and silver ware, &c
Judkin's ointment, toothache drops, White's and
Weaver's, eyewater Thompson's and Weaver's,
pinkroot, Weaver's worm tea an excellent article,
the red liniment for rheumatism, sprains, swellings
&c., gout and rheumatic drops, Dr. Jayne's car-
minative balsam, cough drops, do. lozenges, syrup
of boneset, ague syrup, syrup for diarrhœa or
bowel complaint, spirits of soap for renovating
soiled clothing and extracting grease spots, &c.
&c. tartaric acid, lemon syrup by the bottle or
gallon, super-carbonate of soda, capsicum, peruvian bark, lima, calyesia, red. yellow, &c; Griffin's
adhesive plaster by the case or yard already spread
for use, castor oil, sweet oil, copal varnish, leather
varnish, sperm ceti, spring lancets, La Mott's
cough drops, paint brushes of various numbers,
carb. magnesia calcined co., emery, vials assorted bottles, bottle corks, trusses of almost every
description, wafers, sealing wax fine, counter
brushes, indelible or marking ink, syringes in boxes large, do. small, spatulas, sucking bottles, glass
urinals, cupping glasses, apothecaries' weights and
scales in neat cases, surgical instruments, viz obstetric, dissecting, stomach pump, trephining,
pocket instruments, amputating, &c. &c. Shoe
brushes, Day & Martin's blacking, paste do, camphor 50 lbs, opium 10 lbs, opodeldoc liquid and
common. A general assortment of patent and
family medicines. Gum shellac, do. copal, ammoniac, benzoin, &c. &c. Benzoic acid, Iceland
moss, ipecac, jalap, cream tartar, gum dragon or
dragon's blood, balsam tolu, medicamentum or
Harlœm oil, red precipitate, do. white, Lee's pills
(of the stereotype label) by the dozen, linseed oil,
alcohol, caustic alkali, hydriodate of potash in oz.
do. iode or Iodine hermetically sealed, quicksilver.
lampblack, spanish brown, white lead by the keg
in oil, gum kino, uva ursi, red sanders, digitalis,
extract liquorice, gum elastic, do. myrrh, chamomile flowers, saltpetre, seneca oil, gum assafœti-
da, subcarbonate iron, do. soda, squills, bear's oil,
sponge, Huffman's anodyne, the various officinal
tinctures, solidified copaiva, gum gamboge, orris
root, blue vitriol, rosin, rad. mesereon, burnt alum,
Virginia snakeroot, Burgundy pitch, senna, rock
oil, annatto Spanish, lucifer matches, fancy mottled
wash balls, shaving soap, tooth brushes, nitrate bismuth, gum Senegal, &c. &c. And 1001 other articles too tedious to mention.

WILLIAM LINDSAY,
Main street, Richmond, Ind

An advertisement for Lindsay's drug firm in Richmond, Indiana (Richmond Palladium, *October 22, 1836)*

Lindsay's activities in Richmond were business-oriented; during his stay there he also began recording his most important surgical cases.

Although Lindsay occasionally had difficulty collecting fees, his medical and entrepreneurial endeavors in Indiana afforded him a comfortable living.[39] Unfortunately, his business sense was not as acute as his medical skills. In the summer of 1837 he invested his life savings in a specious get-rich-quick scheme. Lured by the prospect of earning over $20,000 a year, he naively joined Indianapolis physician George Stipp in a pharmaceutical and medical practice in the capital city. Less than one year after their joint venture, Lindsay dissolved the partnership and purchased Stipp's interest in the firm.[40] Undoubtedly upset by the takeover attempt, Stipp circulated reports among Lindsay's creditors of the unsound financial nature of the William Lindsay and Company drug firm. Stipp also accused Lindsay of counterfeiting and selling Dr. Gardner's Celebrated Vegetable Liniment, a popular proprietary medicine.[41]

Stipp's actions forced Lindsay to sell the drug company. A rancorous, public debate between Lindsay and Stipp followed.[42] Lindsay accused his ex-partner of embezzlement, noting Stipp paid personal debts with the drug firm's earnings.[43] Stipp countercharged that Lindsay was the one guilty of fraud and embezzlement, along with quackery and absence from duty. Stipp claimed Lindsay reneged on his promise to invest $4,350 in the drug business and instead "put in as capital an assortment of old Drugs, Patent Medicines, furniture and *'Davy Crocket Toothache Drops'* to the amount . . . [of] $1600." Moreover, Lindsay had kept the books during a six-week period and probably made alterations in them at that time. Stipp also complained of Lindsay's frequent absence from his drug company: "he was of no earthly benefit to the firm in any particular, never being willing to

39. Lindsay claimed that had he stayed in Richmond, his practice there could have netted him $1,000 a year. He probably exaggerated his income since physicians in large urban areas earned less than $500 a year during this period ("To the Public, and More Especially to the Creditors of the Late Firm of W. Lindsay & Co.," Indianapolis *Indiana Journal*, May 12, 1838).

40. "To the Public," ibid., June 17 and October 7, 1837, May 12, 1838.

41. "Counterfeiters Detected," ibid., April 21 and May 12, 1838. The sole proprietor of Gardner's Liniment was the firm of Glascoe and Harrison in Cincinnati, Ohio. Stipp accused William Lindsay and Company of reproducing this patent medicine without the permission of the Cincinnati firm. Stipp even went so far as to write a letter to Glascoe and Harrison informing the company of Lindsay's purported indiscretion.

42. "Notice," ibid., May 19, 1838. For an insightful analysis of this debate, as well as the debate itself, see Ann G. Carmichael, "The Lindsay-Stipp Debate," *Indiana Medical History Quarterly* 7 (December 1981): 6-19.

43. "Caution," Indianapolis *Indiana Journal*, May 19, 1838.

COUNTERFEITERS DETECTED.

W M. LINDSAY & CO., Apothecaries of Indianapolis, have been detected imposing upon the Public, a base counterfeit of the "GARDNER'S LINAMENT." The external appearance of their preparation is even calculated to deceive, being a *fac Simile* to the *genuine*. The only mode of detecting the counterfeit is the want of the signature of James C. Glascoe, of the firm of Glascoe & Harrison, written on the wrapper, and a stamp of the Lion and Mortar on the seal of the bottle.

The Genuine Gardner's Linament is prepared only by the subscribers, as the following certificate will show:

NOTICE—I hereby certify, that I have sold to Glascoe & Harrison the only Genuine Receipe for manufacturing "GARDNER'S CELEBRATED VEGITABLE LINAMENT," (as prepared by my husband, Jas. Gardner, who is now deceased,) and I also certify that none else have any knowledge of the receipe but them. They, therefore, are the only constituted and authorized proprietors.

                                MARY GARDNER.

The proprietors deem it necessary to state further, that there are many other preparations lately got up for a similar purpose as the said counterfeit, in order to deceive and mislead the public for mercenary views, by substituting analagoul names.

Indiana State Library

An advertisement placed by George Stipp accusing the William A. Lindsay Company of counterfeiting Gardner's Celebrated Vegetable Liniment (Indianapolis Journal, April 21, 1838)

either attend to practice or assist in the store." As if these accusations were not enough, Stipp suggested Lindsay was a quack. Lindsay not only manufactured a secret tonic, but readily endorsed and marketed other patent medicines. He also sold his drug business to a Peter Smith (not Lindsay's father-in-law), "an irresponsible individual, a jack of all trades, such as *root* doctor, preacher, cobler [*sic*], shoemaker, farmer and gun smith—an individual that is not nor never will be worth the powder that would blow the hair off his head."[44]

Although Lindsay's associates disproved the charges of embezzlement and fraud, some of the other allegations require further scrutiny. Lindsay was indeed absent from his Indianapolis drug firm on a regular basis. In November 1837 he traveled to the newly formed state of Arkansas to sell apples and apple trees. Stipp sarcastically summed up Lindsay's escapades: "Some time last Nov. '*an idea struck him very*

44. "To the Public, and the Creditors of W. Lindsay: 'Facts speak louder than words,' " ibid., May 26, 1838. Lindsay evidently huckstered packaged nostrums. Included among the property owned by the William Lindsay and Company drug firm were two horses and "a pedling wagon" (Case of *William D. Wygant* v. *William Buchanan, William Lippincott, William Lindsey* [*sic*], *George W. Stipp, Daniel King, and David Craighead,* Box 79, Supreme Court Appeals Cases, Archives Division, Indiana State Library, Indianapolis).

TO THE PUBLIC, AND THE CREDITORS OF W. LINDSAY.

"Facts speak louder than words."

THE false, libelous and slanderous publication, over the signature of "W. Lindsay," (a "surgeon of some celebrity,") in the Indiana Journal of the 12th inst., demand a few facts and passing remarks in self defence.

With W. Lindsay's private character, his prospects at Richmond, or any other place, I feel no disposition to meddle, as they did not appear upon the invoice that *he* exhibited, of his effects, that were put in the firm of W. Lindsay & Co., and therefore never meddled with, or thought them worth invoicing. And I would not notice him even now, were it not for the purpose of exposing his fraudulent transactions, and further, to convict him of willful falsehood, and vile slander.

His pathetic appeal to his creditors for indulgence, effects me not, and if they think proper, after all the evidence of fraud, that is manifest in the disposition *he* has made of the firm debts, I am sure I am contented. The communication separate from vanity, egotism, and falsehood is mere flummery, in which the public nor creditors can have any interest whatever. This man (W. L.) is surely his own worst enemy, and appears determined to make himself supremely ridiculous and highly notorious. The history of this (to me) unfortunate partnership, I feel well assured, will afford but a dry morsel to many, but to put things in their proper light, a short and succint statement may not be uninteresting to some. About one year ago at the *repeated, urgent* and pressing solicitations of W. Lindsay and his friends *I* was at an ungarded moment induced to give him an interest in my practice and Drug Store, upon the promise and belief that *he* would be able to put in a capital equal to my own, so soon as he could dispose of property sufficient. How well that promise was fulfilled the sequel will prove. W. Lindsay on the 3d day of last June put in as capital an assortment of old Drugs, Patent Medicines, furniture & '*Davy Crockot Toothache Drops*" to the amount as by himself invoiced of $1600 and drew from the concern since that time about $500 in *cash*, which was charged when known,'*blunders over the money drawer*, excep'ed. At the same time I had on hand in a new and well selected assortment of drugs, paints, &c. a stock at eastern cost and carriage of the value of $2,150. Cash put in by me since that time upwards of $1200, and house rent, boarding and other means, to the value of about $1000, making the amount of my investment about $4,350, and I have drew from the firm about $900, leaving a balance in my favor, over that of W. Lindsay of upwards of $2,350. You will perceive by this statement that all the interest W. L. had in the firm was only $1100. To have made his capital equal to mine, he would have had to advance the sum of $2,350, which it appears from his own *honest* confession *he* was neither able nor willing to do, for he frankly admits that he is not able even now to pay his private debts, which I have no doubt is *true*. That I have blended my private trancactions with the firm is true, so far as advancing money to pay firm debts and no further.

A public reply by George Stipp to Lindsay's accusations (Indianapolis Journal, *May 26, 1838)*

forcibly,' [(]and its well for his brains there was only one) that he could make money retailing *apples* and apple trees in the south part of the ARKANSAS territory and off he put on a wild goose chase with a cargo of appletrees and apples to make his fortune. In this hazardous business he employed what little individual capital and credit he had, much to the injury of prejudice of our joint business."[45] While aboard a steamboat on the Arkansas River, Lindsay cared for a smallpox victim. Shortly after leaving that boat to await another steamer, he suffered a mild form of smallpox. He recovered and continued his journey to Arkansas aboard another boat. Once passengers on that ship learned of his exposure to smallpox, they expelled him. His cargo, however, remained on the steamer, resulting in Lindsay's loss of $1,500, as well as his partner's goodwill.[46]

Stipp also was correct in accusing Lindsay of violating the tenets of regular, or orthodox, medicine. Lindsay did sell his own secret tonic and associated himself with a proclaimed botanic physician. He was not, however, alone in violating the tenets of orthodoxy. Even a few of the more prominent physicians during the late 1820s extolled the virtues of patent medicines.[47] Far from being a quack, Lindsay was by the standards of the time a competent, orthodox physician. Like many of his medical brethren in the early nineteenth century, he employed to varying extents the depletion techniques of purging, bloodletting, emesis, and blistering and believed that structural emergencies could be corrected by surgery. He learned through observation, however, that many suggested remedies were simply not effective. Thus, when suggested treatments failed, Lindsay abandoned them and employed any remedies which seemed to promise a cure, including those of sectarian practitioners.

Lindsay's surgical abilities gained him the respect of both his colleagues and his patients. He was often asked to consult with other physicians in difficult cases. His patients, too, respected his skill both as a physician and surgeon. In one case, he saved the life of an infant suffering from asphyxia. The parents of the child were so grateful that they named the child after him.[48] His concern for his patients seems genuine. His journals suggest that he maintained contact with them

45. "To the Public, and the Creditors of W. Lindsay: 'Facts speak louder than words,' " Indianapolis *Indiana Journal*, May 26, 1838.

46. Lindsay tells his version of the Arkansas adventure in his third surgical journal. The piece, entitled "A Case of Varioloid," is reproduced below, pp. 81-98.

47. Young, *Toadstool Millionaires*, 60-61, 65.

48. Case of Congenital Asphyxia, Lindsay Journal No. 1, Spring 1824, below, p. 10.

long after they left his care. Thus, Stipp's charges of quackery and the total dereliction of duty seem unwarranted.

Returning to Richmond after his disastrous year in Indianapolis, Lindsay opened an office at a local hotel.[49] His inability to resume a secure practice of medicine in Richmond probably was partially a result of the general economic conditions. From 1837 until the early 1840s, America was in the midst of a severe depression.[50] Apparently many of his patients could not afford to pay their medical bills, for Lindsay was forced to demand payment to meet his own debts: "The undersigned having made over to Irvin Reed, sundry notes, accounts &c those who are indebted will please call and make arrangements for payment or they will likely be placed in the hands of an officer for collection. Impervious necessity demands this course."[51]

Through 1840 Lindsay remained in Richmond, but from 1841 to 1849, little is known of his whereabouts. He probably spent these years in Ohio moving from town to town trying to establish a medical practice and to recover from his financial losses.[52] This was no easy

49. Richmond *Palladium*, September 22, 1838. Lindsay remained in partnership with Smith until at least mid-June 1838. On July 21, 1838, he sold his land at public auction (Indianapolis *Indiana Journal*, July 21, 1838). The William Lindsay and Company drug firm never became financially solvent. After Lindsay realized that he could not meet his obligations to creditors, he sold his stock of drugs to Dr. Peter Smith. Smith could not meet the firm's financial obligations and sold the company to William D. Wygant in June 1838. Wygant, too, tried to meet the firm's debts, but found this difficult since George Stipp had seriously injured the firm's reputation. Thus the firm was sold in 1838 to William Buchanan and Jesse L. Lippincott of Pittsburgh, and in 1839, to Daniel King. Wygant never received the money due him from his sale to Buchanan and Lippincott, so in 1840 he asked the Marion County Court for a restraining order to prevent King from paying Buchanan (Lippincott had died) until the firm's creditors were paid. King refused. No decision was made in the case until May 1846. By that time King had died, and the court ordered that the amount owed to Wygant be paid from Buchanan's estate, but since he was insolvent, that the amount King owed Buchanan ($1,402) be paid to Wygant from King's estate. The case was appealed and the decision reversed by the Indiana Supreme Court (*The Diary of Calvin Fletcher*, Gayle Thornbrough and Dorothy L. Riker, eds., 9 vols. [Indianapolis: Indiana Historical Society, 1972-83], 3:137-38, n. 60).

50. Glyndon G. Van Deusen, *The Jacksonian Era, 1828-1848* (New York: Harper Brothers, 1959), 116-17, 170.

51. Richmond *Palladium*, September 5, 1840.

52. Lindsay M. Brien, "Clan Lindsay," unpublished manuscript in the private collection of Helen Louise Graham Silvey, Sacramento, California, 23; "Lindsay, Earl of Balcarras"; "Obituary: William A. Lindsay," Eaton *Register*, May 11, 1876. Lindsay also practiced in Donnelsville, Clark County, Ohio, and was a justice of the peace in the county in 1849 (*The History of Clark County, Ohio, Containing a History of the County, Its Cities, Towns* . . . [Chicago: W. H. Beers, 1881], 718; *State of Ohio* v. *David Ewing*, report of the Justice of the Peace, Clark County, Ohio, March 8, 1849, and *Kemp Gaines* v. *George Agle*, Summons, Clark County, Ohio, July 14, 1849, both

Photograph courtesy of the Lindsay family
Lindsay's house in West Alexandria, Ohio. The house still stands and has several apartments in it.

undertaking since the number of physicians continued to increase and competition intensified.[53] Moreover, Lindsay had a large family to support. He and his first wife, Rhoda Allison Smith, had nine children before her death in 1840. His second wife of less than one year, Harriet Overton, died in December 1842, and he married Emeline Wilkinson in 1848. He had one son by his second marriage and five daughters by his third marriage.[54] His financial situation continued to deteriorate, and he was forced to declare bankruptcy in 1845.[55]

In 1849 Lindsay assumed the practice of Dr. William G. Lineaweaver in West Alexandria, Ohio.[56] Little is known of the extent and

in the miscellaneous papers of Dr. William A. Lindsay, private collection of Helen Louise Graham Silvey).

53. From 1840 to 1849 the number of medical school graduates was 11,128 (Billings, "Literature and Institutions," in Clarke, *A Century of American Medicine*, 359, as cited in Rothstein, *American Physicians*, 98).

54. Lindsay M. Brien, *A Genealogical Index of Pioneers in the Miami Valley* (Dayton, Ohio: Dayton Circle, Colonial Dames of America, 1970), 102.

55. Receipt of payment for fees in Lindsay's bankruptcy case, April 14, 1845, miscellaneous papers of Dr. William A. Lindsay, private collection of Helen Louise Graham Silvey.

56. *History of Preble County, Ohio, with Illustrations and Biographical Sketches* (Cleveland, Ohio: H. Z. Williams and Brothers, 1881), 328.

West Alexandria, circa late 1880s

The Archives, West Alexandria, Ohio

scope of his practice, since after 1855 his journal writing evidently ceased. The local newspaper in 1851 reported that Lindsay assisted in "a surgical operation of somewhat critical character" involving the removal of a tracheal tumor. In 1863 he amputated a leg of a patient at the Preble County Infirmary.[57] Also, while in the city, he became actively involved in the struggling local medical society, serving as its president during the early years of the Civil War. The war effort eventually curtailed the organization's activities.[58]

In 1864, at age sixty-eight, Lindsay enlisted in the Union army as a contract surgeon. His motives for doing so were probably less patriotic than economic since a contract surgeon received approximately $100 a month and had no military rank.[59] He began his army tenure in Indianapolis at Camp Frémont, which was in dire need of a physician. Located at this camp was the Twenty-eighth Regiment of the Indiana black troops.[60] During his stay in the army, Lindsay served at other camps and hospitals in Indianapolis including Camp Burnside, the Pest Hospital, and the Military Prison Hospital at Camp Morton. On December 24, 1864, the army transferred him to the Brown General Hospital in Louisville, Kentucky.[61]

57. Eaton *Democrat*, July 10 and 17, 1851; Eaton *Weekly Register*, June 23, 1864. In the July 10, 1851, article about this operation, Lindsay was not mentioned as one of the attending physicians. Dr. R. P. Nisbet of West Alexandria wrote a letter to the editor noting that Dr. Lindsay was "entitled to as much Surgical applause in the operation as Dr. Stratton [the physician credited with performing the surgery]."

58. Eaton *Weekly Register*, November 15 and December 6, 1860, May 16, June 6, and July 11, 1861, October 24 and May 15, 1862, October 22, 1863. At the November 1860 meeting of the Eaton Medical Society, Lindsay was elected one of three censors of the organization, and the next June Lindsay was elected president of the society. As president, Lindsay called regular meetings. He was reelected president on May 6, 1862. The war effort hurt attendance, and the organization's activities eventually were suspended. As late as 1869 the local medical society had not reorganized.

59. J. S. Bobbs to William A. Lindsay, March 25, 1864, Contract with a Private Physician, miscellaneous papers of Dr. William A. Lindsay, private collection of Helen Louise Graham Silvey. A contract surgeon was not considered an official member of the United States Army. These surgeons provided their own surgical instruments and were paid from $80 to $100 per month. In contrast commissioned medical officers earned $165 per month. Many contract surgeons had failed in private practice and joined the army for financial reasons (George Washington Adams, *Doctors in Blue: The Medical History of the Union Army in the Civil War* [New York: Henry Schuman, 1952], 174-75).

60. C. W. Forster, Assistant Adjutant General, Washington, D.C., to O. P. Morton, Indianapolis, Indiana, May 1864, Oliver P. Morton Collection, Archives Division, Indiana State Library, Indianapolis; J. S. Bobbs, Indianapolis, Indiana, to Colonel R. C. Woods, Louisville, Kentucky, March 26, 1864, and William Lindsay, Camp Frémont, Indianapolis, Indiana, to U. S. Surgeon General, Washington, D.C., April 24, 1864, miscellaneous papers of Dr. William A. Lindsay, private collection of Helen Louise Graham Silvey.

61. William Lindsay, Camp Burnside, Indianapolis, Indiana, to Surgeon General Charles S. Tripler, Columbus, Ohio, June 30, 1864; Lindsay, Pest Hospital, Indian-

After the war Lindsay returned to West Alexandria, where he attempted to reestablish a medical practice. With four doctors in the area, he found the task quite difficult.[62] On July 19, 1865, he wrote to the United States Surgeon General requesting a permanent appointment to a military hospital:

> Permit me to say to you, that since my experience in Hospital practice, & have returned home, feel reluctant to resume private practice, & should like much to obtain an appointment to some Hospital. and feel confident that from many years of experience in general practice & fourteen months in Hospitals, that I am capable of performing its varied duties, I will say, I think as well, as most surgeons with whom I have been associated in the profession & the Hospit'ls.[63]

Lindsay probably desired a hospital assignment for both professional and financial reasons. The elite among the physicians held hospital appointments, and certainly he hoped for an improved standing among his medical colleagues.[64] More likely, though, he knew that the practice of medicine in West Alexandria would not provide a sufficient income. Lindsay never received a hospital staff appointment nor did he ever recover from his economic setback in Indianapolis.

During the last thirty-five years of his career, medicine itself was changing. Those changes affected not only the type of medicine practiced but also the way in which it was practiced. In the early decades of the nineteenth century the causes of most diseases remained unknown, and physicians could offer their patients few effective remedies. The nineteenth century, however, witnessed many scientific advances. In the early 1800s French physicians began systematically studying disease through postmortem examinations. Their findings eventually led to the rejection of traditional remedies of bloodletting and purging. In the latter half of the century, Joseph Lister, Louis Pasteur, and Robert Koch advanced and refined the germ theory of disease. Surgery, in particular, benefited from the many advances oc-

---

apolis, to Tripler, Columbus, Ohio, August 31, 1864; Lindsay, Military Prison Hospital, Camp Morton, Indianapolis, to Tripler, Medical Director, Northern Department, October 21, 1864; C. C. Gray, Assistant Surgeon, United States Army, to Assistant Surgeon General's Office, December 24, 1864; Lindsay, Military Prison Hospital, Camp Morton, Indianapolis, to Tripler, Medical Department, Columbus, Ohio, October 21, 1864, miscellaneous papers of Dr. William A. Lindsay, private collection of Helen Louise Graham Silvey.

62. George W. Hawes, comp., *George W. Hawes' Ohio State Gazetteer and Business Directory, for 1859 and 1860*, No. 1 (Cincinnati: George Hawes, 1859), 528.

63. Lindsay, West Alexandria, Ohio, to J. Barnes, Surgeon General, Washington, D.C., July 19, 1865, miscellaneous papers of Dr. William A. Lindsay, private collection of Helen Louise Graham Silvey.

64. Rosen, *The Structure of American Medical Practice*, 11.

curring in medicine. While many physicians continued to practice medicine in a small-town or rural setting, the importance of the hospital as a training center for this new scientific medicine became apparent. Moreover, hospitals fostered the growth of specialization.[65] Lindsay was cognizant of many of these changes occurring in medicine, but whether he kept up with progress in the field cannot be determined since no case records from his practice during this period are known to exist.

Certainly his location in a small rural midwestern town did not foster advancement in the medical profession, encourage specialization in surgery, or offer opportunities for professional development. Furthermore, competition at the end of the century remained as intense as it had during the early 1800s.[66] To Lindsay, and other physicians who continued to minister faithfully to the ills of a largely rural clientele, the effects of this unrelenting competition were disastrous. Writing to his son-in-law in 1868, Lindsay noted that his "prospects for practice [are] exceedingly gloomy." He added: "It costs so much [to] keep a horse. Especially as in my case am not working enough by my practice to feed a horse. What shall I do? . . . Am greatly oppressed of course."[67] Lindsay died on May 7, 1876, in West Alexandria, with his major contribution to the history of medicine being the three surgical casebooks reproduced in this book.[68]

The Journals

Lindsay's surgical journals are valuable historical documents; few midwestern physicians left detailed records of the operations they performed. Lindsay recorded his most important surgical cases during twenty years of practice in four pocket-sized, leather-bound notebooks. Each is approximately one hundred pages in length. Although he recorded some of his case histories immediately, Lindsay wrote most of them several years after their occurrence. Moreover, he apparently wrote many of the histories in stages and probably reconstructed the details of each from earlier notes. He began writing in his casebooks on April 13, 1836, and continued until 1855. The majority of the

65. For more information about the changes occurring in medical science and practice, see Rothstein, *American Physicians*; Starr, *The Social Transformation of American Medicine*; Rosen, *The Structure of American Medical Practice*; and John S. Haller, Jr., *American Medicine in Transition, 1840-1910* (Urbana: University of Illinois Press, 1981).

66. Starr, *The Social Transformation of American Medicine*, 112; Rosen, *The Structure of American Medical Practice*, 12.

67. Lindsay, Ithaca, Ohio, to W. A. Matchett, June 11, 1868, miscellaneous papers of Dr. William A. Lindsay, private collection of Helen Louise Graham Silvey.

68. "Obituary: William A. Lindsay," Eaton *Register*, May 11, 1876.

Lindsay's three surgical journals

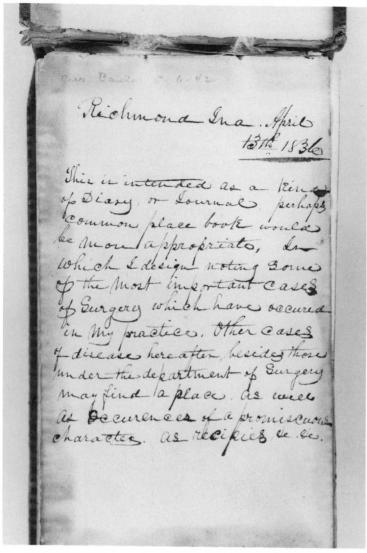

Lindsay's introduction to his writings in the front of his first surgical journal

cases in his notebooks date from 1822 through 1841, with only two cases recorded after 1841. In 1855 Lindsay recorded the last of these, which occurred in 1850. Numbers are stamped on the outside of each notebook. The second number, or volume, of his four casebooks is missing.

On May 6, 1942, the Indiana State Library in Indianapolis purchased Lindsay's three extant casebooks from a bookdealer in Crawfordsville. In 1976 a tour guide at Conner Prairie, an outdoor museum in Noblesville, recognized the significance of Lindsay's medical writings. Several years later while a research historian at Conner Prairie, the editor utilized Lindsay's casebooks in her research on early nineteenth-century medicine. Conner Prairie is a "living history" museum depicting central Indiana life in the 1830s, and the documents provided detailed information on early nineteenth-century medical and surgical procedures. Through her investigations the editor became more and more interested in Lindsay himself and discovered some of his later papers in the private collection of his great-granddaughter, Helen Graham Silvey, of Sacramento, California. The editor also met other descendants who shared her enthusiasm about Lindsay and his medical career.

The editor prepared a biographical sketch of Lindsay and transcribed and annotated approximately two-thirds of his cases for publication in the Indiana Historical Society's *Indiana Medical History Quarterly* 6-7 (March 1980-March 1981). For the *Quarterly* the editor grouped the cases by subject, with each issue containing a different set of operations. The March 1981 issue contained an analysis of his medical practice. All the cases in his three extant notebooks appear in the present edition, left in their original order rather than being arranged according to subject.

Editorial Method

The journals are here presented with their original spelling, capitalization, and punctuation, with the following exceptions. Lindsay's lower and upper case "J's," "S's," "A's," and "M's" are difficult to discern; in cases of doubt, these have been modernized. His other idiosyncrasies—he sometimes did not capitalize initial letters of sentences and occasionally used periods and commas interchangeably—are transcribed literally. Superscripts and interlineations have been brought down to the line. Underlined words appear in italic type. Words misspelled so as to appear to be the typesetter's errors are corrected by additions within brackets or by the device [*sic*]. Angle brackets enclose conjectures regarding illegible letters or words. Repeated words which are obviously slips of the pen have been silently deleted, while words or expansions of abbreviations within brackets are added by the editor. The first lines of paragraphs are indented, although Lindsay occasionally did not do so. Annotation is placed at the bottom of the page. Lindsay's notes, indicated by an asterisk, precede the editor's annotation.

The annotation enhances the reader's understanding of medicine and society and includes explanations of nineteenth-century medical practices, as well as archaic lay terminology. To reduce the amount of annotation, the editor has included a Short-Title List. The editor also has placed "Editorial Notes" in the journal text, prior to cases in which Lindsay's treatments deserve special mention. A Glossary of Medical and Pharmaceutical Terms defines modern, as well as archaic, medical terms and drug names. A Glossary of Proper and Place Names identifies local physicians and place names. Lindsay often misspelled medical terms and names. When his spelling of the term or name impedes recognition or location in the glossary, the correct spelling appears in brackets following the first appearance of the term.

The casebooks are transcribed and edited for those interested in medicine and medical, social, and local history. The introduction gives the general public a broad overview of the conditions confronting physicians rather than a complete history of early nineteenth-century medicine and surgery. For those interested in further reading on these subjects, the editor has included a bibliographic essay.

Acknowledgments

I am deeply indebted to a number of persons who assisted me in preparing this book. In particular, I would like to thank Ann G. Carmichael, M.D., Ph.D., associate professor of history at Indiana University, and Indianapolis neurologist Charles A. Bonsett, M.D., who initially encouraged me to publish this manuscript and throughout the preparation process provided invaluable guidance and editorial assistance.

I am grateful to several of Lindsay's descendants whose enthusiasm and support sustained me throughout the book's preparation. They also provided me with additional biographical information on Lindsay. Helen Graham Silvey, of Sacramento, California, the great-granddaughter of Lindsay and his third wife, Emeline Wilkinson, provided many documents on his Ohio medical practice. Eleanore S. Kilpatrick, of Troy, Ohio, and Carolyn L. S. Chapman, of Dayton, Ohio, both great-great-great-granddaughters of Lindsay and his first wife, Rhoda Allison Smith, shared information on him which they had obtained in various Ohio archives and libraries. Elizabeth Coulter, of Kempner, Texas, the great-granddaughter of Lindsay and Rhoda Smith, likewise provided information about her ancestor and additionally helped locate a portrait of Lindsay and his first wife. Moreover, these descendants, along with Jean A. Albright, Mary Anne Allen Baker, and William Lindsay Arnold, gave me permission to publish the journals.

The Indiana Historical Society has been most supportive of the book and has made possible its publication. In particular, I would like to thank Peter T. Harstad, Ph.D., executive director of the Society, for his suggestions on improving the quality of the manuscript, and Raymond L. Shoemaker, Ph.D., assistant executive director, for his support of the project. Thomas A. Mason, Ph.D., director of publications, provided invaluable editorial assistance and many useful suggestions on the organization of this documentary edition. Paula Corpuz, Kathy Breen, and Megan McKee spent many long hours proofreading the manuscript to eliminate imperfections, and to them I am especially grateful.

I would like to thank Steven M. Stowe, assistant professor of history at Indiana University, and Jay L. Grosfeld, M.D., professor and chairman of the Department of Surgery at Indiana University and surgeon-in-chief at Riley Hospital, for reviewing this manuscript prior to publication. Also, I am grateful to Mary A. Soule, M.D., and John E. Mackey, M.D., both of Indianapolis, who reviewed the illness of Lindsay's wife and provided a diagnosis for the case. Wilma James, a descendant of Lindsay's ex-partner, George Stipp, very graciously provided information on Stipp and his medical practice.

A number of organizations in some way provided assistance or support of this project. I would like to thank the Indiana State Library, Conner Prairie, the Arkansas History Commission, the West Alexandria Archives, the Ohio Historical Society, University of Cincinnati Special Collections Library, Ohio State University Library, Montgomery County Historical Society Library, and the Dayton Public Library. In particular, I would like to thank John L. Ferguson, state historian of the Arkansas History Commission, who helped me identify many of the towns and geographical locations in Arkansas. Audrey Gilbert of the West Alexandria Archives in West Alexandria, Ohio, provided me with early photographs of the town. Marybelle Burch, manuscript librarian at the Indiana State Library, originally brought Lindsay's journals to my attention and obtained permission to publish them from several of the descendants. John ("Scotty") Selch, newspaper librarian at the Indiana State Library, provided much assistance during my search through Indiana newspapers. David G. Vanderstel, Ph.D., and Dennis Kovener, both of the Conner Prairie Research Department, provided me with several documents on medical education. Jan Kehr and Libby Doss, interpreters at Conner Prairie, encouraged me to publish the manuscript. Ms. Kehr, who is also a registered pharmacist, provided information on some of Lindsay's medicinal preparations.

Finally, I would like to thank my husband, Edwin D. McDonell, without whose encouragement and support this book would not have been possible.

Short Title List

The following works appear at least twice in the annotations or the glossaries and are listed here in their expanded form:

Ashmore, *Arkansas*

Harry S. Ashmore, *Arkansas: A Bicentennial History* (1978; reprint, Nashville: American Association for State and Local History, 1984).

Bennion, *Antique Medical Instruments*

Elisabeth Bennion, *Antique Medical Instruments* (1979; reprint, Los Angeles: University of California Press, 1980).

Burns, *Principles of Midwifery*

John Burns, *The Principles of Midwifery; Including the Diseases of Women and Children* (London: Longman, Hurst, Rees, Orme, and Brown, 1814).

Cazeaux, *Treatise on Midwifery*

William R. Bullock, ed. and trans., *P. Cazeaux's a Theoretical Treatise on Midwifery, Including the Diseases of Pregnancy and Parturition and the Attentions Required by the Child from Birth to the Period of Weaning* (Philadelphia: Lindsay and Blakeston, 1863).

Conover, *Dayton and Montgomery County*

Charlotte Reeve Conover, ed., *Dayton and Montgomery County: Resources and People,* 2 vols. (New York: Lewis Historical Publishing Company, Inc., 1932).

Cooper, *Dictionary of Practical Surgery*

Samuel Cooper, *A Dictionary of Practical Surgery: Comprehending All the Most Interesting Improvements from the Earliest Times Down to the Present Period* . . . , 2 vols. (New York: J. J. Harper, 1832).

Cooper, *First Lines*

Samuel Cooper, *The First Lines of the Practice of Surgery: Being an Elementary Work for Students, and a Concise Book of Reference for Students*, 2 parts, 2d American ed. from 3d London ed. (Hanover: Justin Hinds, 1815).

Dale, "Arkansas and the Cherokees"

Edward E. Dale, "Arkansas and the Cherokees," *Arkansas Historical Quarterly* 8 (Summer 1949): 95-114.

Dewees, *Treatise on the Diseases of Females*

William P. Dewees, *A Treatise on the Diseases of Females*, 3d ed. (Philadelphia: Carey and Lea, 1831).

Donegan, *Women and Men Midwives*

Jane B. Donegan, *Women and Men Midwives: Medicine, Morality, and Misogyny in Early America* (Westport, Connecticut: Greenwood Press, 1978).

Dorsey, *Elements of Surgery*

John Syng Dorsey, *Elements of Surgery for the Use of Students with Plates*, 2 vols. (Philadelphia: Edward Parker & Kimber & Conrad, 1813).

Duffy, *Healers*

John Duffy, *The Healers: A History of American Medicine* (1976; reprint, Urbana: University of Illinois Press, 1979).

Dunglison, *Medical Lexicon*

Robley Dunglison, *Medical Lexicon. A Dictionary of Medical Science: Containing a Concise Explanation of Various Subjects*

	and Terms of Anatomy, Physiology, Pathology, Hygiene . . . (Philadelphia: Blanchard and Lea, 1856).
Eberle, *Treatise on Materia Medica*	John Eberle, *A Treatise on Materia Medica and Therapeutics*, 5th ed. (Philadelphia: Grigg and Elliott, 1842).
Gibson, *Institutes and Practice of Surgery*	William Gibson, *The Institutes and Practice of Surgery: Being an Outline of a Course of Lectures*, 2 vols. (Philadelphia: Edward Parker, 1824-25).
Gunn, *Domestic Medicine*	John C. Gunn, *Gunn's Domestic Medicine, or Poor Man's Friend, in the Hours of Affliction, Pain, and Sickness*, 8th ed. (Springfield, Ohio: S. and J. Perry and J. McReynolds, 1836).
Historical Reminiscences and Biographical Memoirs of Conway County	*Historical Reminiscences and Biographical Memoirs of Conway County, Arkansas* (1890; reprint, Van Buren, Arkansas: Press-Argus, 1967).
History of Dearborn, Ohio, and Switzerland Counties	*A History of Dearborn, Ohio, and Switzerland Counties, Indiana* (Chicago: Weakley, Harraman & Company, 1885).
History of Montgomery County	*The History of Montgomery County, Ohio, Containing a History of the County, Its Townships, Cities* . . . , 3 bks. in 6 pts. (1882; reprint, Evansville, Indiana: Unigraphic, Inc., 1971).
History of Preble County	*History of Preble County, Ohio, with Illustrations and Biographical Sketches* (Cleveland, Ohio: H. Z. Williams and Brothers, 1881).
History of Wayne County	*History of Wayne County, Together with Sketches of Its Cities,*

	Villages, and Towns . . . , 2 vols. (Chicago: Interstate Publishing Company, 1884).
Hodge, *Handbook of American Indians*	Frederick Webb Hodge, ed., *Handbook of American Indians, North of Mexico*, 2 vols. (Washington D.C.: Government Printing Office, 1912).
Hooper, *Lexicon Medicum*	Robert Hooper, *Lexicon Medicum; or Medical Dictionary; Containing an Explanation of the Terms in Anatomy, Botany, Chemistry* . . . , 2 vols. (New York: Harper and Brothers, 1843).
Jenkins, *Ohio Gazetteer*	Warren Jenkins, *The Ohio Gazetteer, and Traveler's Guide; Containing a Description of the Several Towns, Townships and Counties, with Their Water Courses, Roads, Improvements, Mineral Productions, &c. &c.*, 1st rev. ed. (Columbus, Ohio: Isaac Whitney, 1837).
Pickard and Buley, *Midwest Pioneer*	Madge E. Pickard and R. Carlyle Buley, *The Midwest Pioneer: His Ills, Cures, and Doctors* (New York: Henry Schuman, 1946).
Reminiscent History of the Ozark Region	*A Reminiscent History of the Ozark Region Comprising a Condensed General History, a Brief Descriptive History of Each County, and Numerous Biographical Sketches of Prominent Citizens of Such Counties* (1894; reprint, Easley, S.C.: Rev. Silas Emmett Lucas, 1978).
Rosenberg, *Cholera Years*	Charles E. Rosenberg, *The Cholera Years: The United States in 1832, 1849, and 1866* (Chicago: University of Chicago Press, 1962).

Rothstein, *American Physicians*   William G. Rothstein, *American Physicians in the Nineteenth Century: From Sects to Science* (Baltimore: Johns Hopkins University Press, 1972).

Scott, *Indiana Gazetteer*   John Scott, *The Indiana Gazetteer, or Topographical Dictionary: Containing a Description of the Several Counties, Towns, Villages, Settlements, Roads, Lakes, Rivers, Creeks, and Springs*, 2d ed. (Indianapolis: Douglass & Maguire, 1833).

Shepherd, *Biographical Directory*   Rebecca A. Shepherd et al., eds., *A Biographical Directory of the Indiana General Assembly*, 2 vols. (Indianapolis: The Select Committee on the Centennial History of the Indiana General Assembly in Cooperation with the Indiana Historical Bureau, 1980-84).

Shryock, *Medicine and Society*   Richard Harrison Shryock, *Medicine and Society in America, 1660-1860* (New York: New York University Press, 1960).

Smith, *The Indian Doctor's Dispensatory*   Peter Smith, *The Indian Doctor's Dispensatory, Being Father Smith's Advice Respecting Diseases and Their Cure: Consisting of Prescriptions for Many Complaints and a Description of Medicines, Simple and Compound* (Cincinnati: Brown and Looker, 1813).

Velpeau, *Elementary Treatise on Midwifery*   Alfred Armand Louis Marie Velpeau, *An Elementary Treatise on Midwifery, or Principles of Tokology and Embryology*, trans. Charles D. Meigs, 2d American ed. (Philadelphia: Grigg & Elliott, 1838).

Wertz and Wertz, *Lying-In*   Richard W. Wertz and Dorothy
                                       C. Wertz, *Lying-In: A History of
                                       Childbirth in America* (New
                                       York: The Free Press, 1977).

Wood and Bache, *Dispensatory*   George B. Wood and Franklin
                                       Bache, *The Dispensatory of the
                                       United States* (Philadelphia:
                                       Grigg and Elliott, 1836).

WPA, *Arkansas*   Works Progress Administration,
                                       Arkansas: A Guide to the State,
                                       American Guide Series (1941; re-
                                       print, St. Clair Shores, Michigan:
                                       Scholarly Press, Inc., 1976).

WPA, *Indiana*   Works Progress Administration,
                                       *Indiana: A Guide to the Hoosier
                                       State* (1941; reprint, New York:
                                       Oxford University Press, 1945).

Young, *History of Wayne County*   Andrew W. Young, *The History
                                       of Wayne County, Indiana, from
                                       Its Earliest Settlement to the
                                       Present. . . .* (Cincinnati: Robert
                                       Clarke and Company, 1872).

Chronology

This chronology was compiled using census records, newspaper accounts, miscellaneous papers of William A. Lindsay, his own family history as recorded in his journals, and his obituary.

December 24, 1795	William A. Lindsay born in Lincoln County, North Carolina, to Samuel and Eleanor (Wilson) Lindsay
1810 or 1811	Begins a teaching career in North Carolina
1814	Moves to Dayton, Ohio, to teach at the Dayton Academy
1815	Begins study of medicine with Dr. James Robins of Mad River, Ohio, and then with Dr. John Steele of Dayton, Ohio
1815	Meets Rhoda Allison Smith, daughter of Peter and Catharine (Stout) Smith
March 22, 1819	Marries Rhoda Allison Smith
February 27, 1821	Catharine Lindsay born
Spring 1821-Winter 1822	Lindsay teaches secondary school at Salisbury and Centerville, Indiana
Spring 1822	Moves to Lawrenceburg, Indiana, to practice with Dr. Ezra Ferris
October 24, 1822	Eliza A. Lindsay born
April 11, 1824	Mary Jane Lindsay born

1825-1826	Lindsay attends one term of lectures at the Ohio Medical College in Cincinnati, Ohio
April 8, 1826	LaFayette Lindsay born
1826	Lindsay moves to Germantown, Ohio, to practice medicine
Spring 1827	Relocates to West Alexandria, Ohio, to practice medicine
November 8, 1828	Rebecca Lindsay born
Fall 1829	Lindsay moves to Richmond to practice medicine and operate drug company
March 1, 1830	Eleanora Lindsay born
1832	G. W. Crawford becomes a partner in William Lindsay's drug company
April 19, 1833	DeWitt Clinton Lindsay born
1833	Lindsay joins local cholera board in Richmond
Mid-1833	Dissolves partnership with G. W. Crawford and continues to operate the drug company by himself
1834	Dr. Joel Bugg joins Lindsay in his pharmaceutical and medical practice
November 29, 1835	William W. I. Lindsay born
1835	Lindsay joins the Webb Masonic Lodge in Richmond
April 13, 1836	Begins journals
1836	Partnership with Bugg ends
1836	Introduces "Vegetable Tonic and Efficacious Remedy in Fever and Ague" to the Richmond public
March 1837	Introduces the tonic to the Indianapolis public
1837	Joins Richmond Antislavery Society

Summer 1837	Moves to Indianapolis to join Dr. George Stipp in medical and pharmaceutical practice
November 1837	Travels to Arkansas to retail apples and apple trees
Late December 1837	Aboard a steamboat, Lindsay attends a smallpox victim
January 7 or 8, 1838	Lindsay is removed from steamboat because of his exposure to smallpox. His cargo remains on board the steamboat
April 12, 1838	Dissolves partnership with Stipp
April 21, 1838	Stipp accuses Lindsay of counterfeiting Gardner's Celebrated Vegetable Liniment
May-June 1838	Lindsay-Stipp debate published in Indianapolis newspapers
May 19, 1838	Lindsay sells his drug stock to Peter Smith and sets up practice with him
June 1838	William D. Wygant becomes trustee of bankrupt William A. Lindsay & Company Drug Firm
July 21, 1838	Lindsay sells land in Indianapolis at public auction
September 22, 1838	Opens practice in a Richmond, Indiana, hotel
January 10, 1839	Edwin B. Lindsay born
October 10, 1840	Lindsay's first wife dies
1841	Lindsay moves to Dayton, Ohio, to practice medicine
1841 or 1842	Lindsay is reported to have moved to Donnelsville, Clark County, Ohio
1841 or 1842	Marries second wife, Harriet Overton
Late 1842	Charles Lindsay born

December 17, 1842	Harriet Overton Lindsay dies, possibly in childbirth
December 1843	Lindsay marries third wife, Emeline Wilkinson
1845	Declares bankruptcy
1846	Caroline Lindsay born
1849	Lindsay is justice of peace of Clark County, Ohio
1849	Moves to West Alexandria, Ohio, to assume the practice of Dr. William G. Lineaweaver
1849	Harriet Victoria Louise Lindsay born
July 1851	Lindsay assists in operation for removal of tracheal tumor
September 6, 1851	Joins the King Hiram Masonic Lodge in West Alexandria, Ohio
1851	Eaton Medical Society formed
1852	Mary J. and Flora B. Lindsay born
1855	Lindsay makes last entry in journal
1860	Eaton Medical Society reorganized
November 1860	Lindsay elected one of three censors for Eaton Medical Society
June 1861	Elected president of Eaton Medical Society
September 8, 1861	Helen Ada Lindsay born
May 1862	Lindsay reelected president of Eaton Medical Society
March 25, 1864	Becomes contract surgeon with United States Army
April 19, 1864	Reports for duty as assistant surgeon at Camp Frémont, Indianapolis, Indiana

June 30, 1864	Reports for duty as assistant surgeon at Camp Burnside, Indianapolis
August 31, 1864	Reports for duty as assistant surgeon at the Pest Hospital, Indianapolis
October 21, 1864	Reports for duty as assistant surgeon at the Military Prison Hospital, Camp Morton, Indianapolis
December 24, 1864	Transferred to Louisville, Kentucky, to serve as contract surgeon
1865	Resumes practice in West Alexandria, Ohio
1869	Becomes member of newly organized Preble County Pioneers Association
May 7, 1876	Dies at age eighty

Journal 1

Richmond Ina. April *13th. 1836*

This is intended as a kind of Diary, or Journal, perhaps common place book would be more appropriate, In which I design noting some of the most important cases of Surgery which have occured in my practice. Other cases of disease hereafter, besides those under the department of Surgery may find a place. as well as occurences of a promiscuous[1] character. as recipies, &c. &c.

Expulsion of Tape worm.

Philip Replogle's Son aged about 12. was called to him (in summer of 1825 or 1826). & found him complaining of much pain in Stomach & Bowels, some slight fever, considerable restlessness & general irritability, gave an emetic, next day found patient about the same, administered Cathartic Pills, composed of Aloes, scamony, Gamboage &c. On operating produced expulsion of a *Tape Worm* between 5 & 6 feet long.

1. Promiscuous: varied.   W.L.

[EDITORIAL NOTE]

The following is the first of six trephining, or trepanation, cases that Lindsay described. He recorded another case in this journal and four more in the third journal. Nineteenth-century physicians employed trephining primarily in cases of compression of the brain, a condition believed to be caused by a depressed skull fracture. An operation was deemed necessary if the depressed skull, bone fragments, or extravasated blood threatened inflammation of the brain's dura mater. To perform the operation, the physician shaved an area on the skull and detached a portion of the pericranium. He then applied a cylindrical saw to the skull and removed a circular piece of bone. The doctor next elevated the depressed skull, and, if necessary, dislodged the extravasated blood or pieces of bone. In extensive skull frac-

tures, the physician often removed several circular pieces of skull. Lindsay employed trepanation primarily in cases of depressed skull fracture, but also used it in a case of epilepsy in which he believed the seizures resulted from compression of the brain (see Case of Daniel Pucket's son, below, pp. 60-63) (Cooper, First Lines, 1:182-90; Gibson, Institutes and Practice of Surgery, 2:187-93; Dorsey, Elements of Surgery, 1:262-72).

George - man of color

Case lst. Fracture of the Crannium. This case having occured some years ago, the notice I shall now take of it, will be from memory.

This was a case in which, in common with the Physicians of Laurenceburg this state [Indiana] where I then was located as a Physician, was called in consultation. This unfortunate individual having been so imprudent as to address a Love Letter to a white girl; a young man then paying his addresses to her, undertook to chastise buffee [buffet] for the insult. And as the *argumentum ad hominem* was considered rather too mild in the case, *the argumentum ad baculinem*[2] was made choice of, which being applyed with a liberal hand, the results was a fractured scull. The fracture was in the Os Frontis, on the right, *I think*, laterel portion extending into the Parietal bone, There appeared to be some depression, accompanied by some of the usual symptoms, The particular state of the pulse, do not now recollect, one of the symptoms was an effort to vomit.[3] Drs. [Jabez and John] Percivals Father & Son were the principal operators. The operation was performed in the usual manner, at this late period have but a very imperfect recollection of appearences after a portion of the bone was removed. I think the membranes were not injured. This unfortunate individual was in a few weeks restored to apparent health, whether his faculties recd. any injury, is rather a matter of some doubt. at all events his *moral powers* did not seem to be *improved*. As he was some months afterwards convicted of *Arson*, viz of burning the Barn and Stables of *Col. Pike* [Major Zebulon Pike]. the venerable father of our lamented hero, Genl. Zebulon M. Pike. & George of course was sent to the work house. This case occured in the year of 1823.

W. Lindsay

2. The *argumentum ad hominem* and the *argumentum ad baculum* are fallacious lines of reasoning. The *argumentum ad hominem* is directed toward the person of an opponent rather than the substance of his arguments; the *argumentum ad baculum* is the use of force or threat of force to win an argument.

3. Nineteenth-century physicians noted that the symptoms of a depressed skull fracture included a slow but regular pulse, dilated pupils, stertorous breathing, loss of consciousness, and possibly nausea (Gibson, *Institutes and Practice of Surgery*, 2:185). Today, physicians observe these same general symptoms as indicative of a depressed skull fracture. Because the bone is pushed inward toward the brain, brain damage often accompanies this type of injury.

George   Man of color

Case 1st. Fracture of
the Cranium.

This case having occured some
years ago, the notice I shall now
take of it, will be from mem-
=ory.

This was a case in which,
in common with the Physicians
of Laurenceburg this State where
I then was located as a Physician.
was called in Consultation.
This unfortunate individual
having been so imprudent as to address
a Love Letter to a white girl;
a young Man then paying his

An entry in Lindsay's first journal

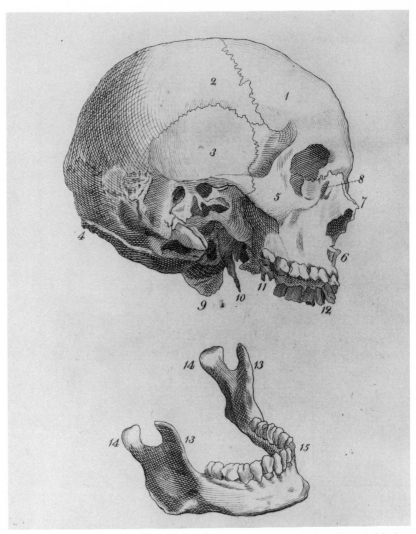

The various bones of the skull. Shown in the drawing are the frontal bone (1), the parietal bone (2), the temporal bone (3), and the occipital bone (4). (William Cheselden, The Anatomy of the Human Body, *1st American edition [Boston: Manning & Loring, 1795])*

[EDITORIAL NOTE]

The following case is the first of four hernia cases described by Lindsay. The other three appear in his fourth journal (see pages 147-49, 153-56). The treatment of this disorder depended upon whether the hernia was reducible *or irreducible. If the contents of the hernial sac could be returned to the abdomen by hand, as in the case of congenital umbilical hernia below, then the hernia was considered reducible. If the contents of the sac could not be returned by hand, the hernia was referred to as irreducible. If a stricture had formed over the opening where the irreducible hernia protruded, as in the three cases described in Lindsay's fourth journal, then the hernia was termed strangulated.*

Before attempting to return the hernial sac to the abdomen, the nineteenth-century physician employed a variety of remedies to relax the patient (e.g., bloodletting, warm baths, tobacco smoke enemas, applications of ice to the hernial sac, or the administration of opium and cathartics). Once the patient was relaxed, the physician tried to push the hernial sac back into the abdomen. Occasionally, the doctor advised the patient to wear a truss for a specified period of time. When these methods failed, the hernia was determined irreducible and an operation performed to return the contents of the hernial sac to the abdomen (Gibson, Institutes and Practice of Surgery, 2:366-77; Dorsey, Elements of Surgery, 2:1-6, 19-29).

Congenital umbilical Hernia[4]

Mrs. Maxwell was on the 22d. April 1836 delivered of a fine Female child whose Parturiant case I had the management as *Acouchier* [accoucheur]. The peculiarities of this case was that of an aggravated congenital umbilical Hernia, The protrusion of bowel within the calibre of the umbilicus was about that of a common sized orange, the convolutions of the bowel were pretty distinctly seen thro' the semitransparent Funis umbilicalis, which in this case was clustered with sacks of serous accumulation. on some parts of the cord at short intervals for the distance of about Six inches, which extended some distance beyond the ultimate protrusion of the Hernial sac, This being, with me, an unusual case, my friend Dr. Griffith was sent for before any attempt was made at reduction, the Dr. having arrived, on a slight examination of the case, unequivocally concurred with me in my diagnosis, with whose kind assistence without much dificulty succeeded in the reduction *Per Taxis*. After which a Ligature of narrow Tape was passed around the cord as close to the umbilicus as posable, (having first lubricated it with melted tallow.) the object of which, of course, was to prevent the posability of the bowel again protruding, to induce the adhesive inflamation or union by the first intention. & at the same time by the lubrication on the outside. guard if posable against too much inflamation.[5] After, also, passing a Ligature around the cord in

4. Lindsay was probably referring to an umbilical hernia present at birth. See Glossary of Medical and Pharmaceutical Terms, s.v. "Hernia, umbilical."

5. In most cases the nineteenth-century surgeon's major task was to eliminate

the usual place the now superfluous portion of the Funis was cut, a compress of Linen applyed over the umbilicus, secured by the abdominal bandage which finished the dressing (Dec. 5.) The foregoing case required Med. attentions during a period of something like 10 days. during the time much attention was necessary in keeping the Ligature properly adjusted. which had to be reapplyed several times, as the union of the rupture progressed, much suspense & anxiety of mind was experienced by the mother during the pendency of the cure. which was completed in about 14 days.

W. Lindsay

Case 2d. of Trephining which occured in the winter of 1822 & '3

The subject of this case was by the name of Moseby, a resident of Ky. nearly opposite Lawrenceburgh, where I then was engaged in the practice of Med.

Moseby, in company with a number of others. in a Public house[6] at the Town of *Aurora Ia.* 4 miles below Laurenceburgh, happened to get into an affray, being at the time a little intoxicated. The Landlord threw him out at the door, and then threw a mattock[7] at him before he had time to rise,—It was thought that the axe part of the mattock struck him, at all events the Crannium was found to be extensively fractured, which extended a little anterior from the joining of the Frontal & left Parietal bone, The fracture where the instrument hit him was probably about 2 inches in length, extending th[r]ough both tables & rupturing both membranes of the Crane.[8] from this point or deep fisure, were a number of diverging fractures. I attended this case in company with Dr. John Percival Such was the injury in this case that an operation was deemed necessary. several fragments, & spicula of bone with hair were carried by the blow within the Cranium, After some 2 or 3 months of confinement, Moseby recovered, & was considered not to have suffered any injury in his mental faculties. During the cure a great many spicula of bone were discharged from the *fisure* &

---

inflammation (characterized by abnormal redness, increased heat, or painful swelling) and promote normal healing, or adhesion of the severed parts (also known as resolution). Physicians believed that if inflammation did not result in resolution, then it could terminate with the formation of pus (suppuration), the growth of tumors, or the death of the surrounding parts (Dunglison, *Medical Lexicon*, 1:8).

6. Public house: an inn providing food, lodging, and liquor.

7. Mattock: an instrument used for digging and grubbing. It has an adze on one end and a pick or ax on the other.

8. Lindsay probably was referring to the dura and pia mater, two of the three membranes encasing the brain. The third membrane covering the brain is the arachnoid. See Glossary of Medical and Pharmaceutical Terms.

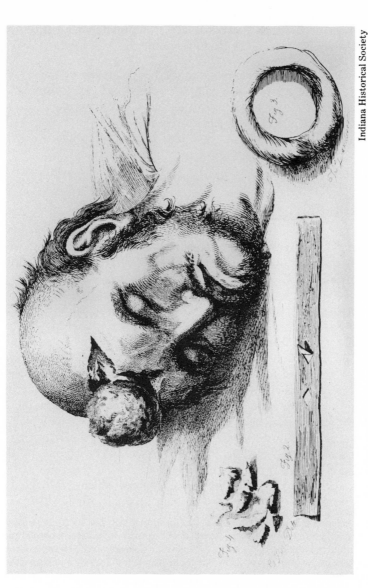

A case of fungus cerebri (Charles Bell, Illustrations of the Great Operations of Surgery, Trepan, Hernia, Amputation, and Lithotomy [1821; reprint, Pacific Palisades, Calif.: Pinecliff Medical Publishing Co., 1976])

Indiana Historical Society

inside the cranium. also a small portion of the substance of the Brain itself was lost, and Fungous cerebri, was found one of the difficulties attending the cure. which was treated by Compression & a part of the time by the applycation of the Red Precipitate.[9]

In the summer of 1822 was called to see a boy, aged about 15 years— son of _____ in case of simple fracture of the Os Humerus.— Having set the arm, applyed first the many tailed bandage,[10] over which simply 4 splints, & over these a roller,

In a few weeks my patient was quite recovered, & succeeded in preserving perfect symetry of the arm . . . .[11]

Diseased Testis

John Elliott—aged about 25, by occupation a Painter & chairmaker. called on me early one morning (In the spring of 1825) in extreme pain from an inflamed Testis. The history of his disease, or in what way induced is not now particularly recollected. The Patient had labored under syphalis, & Gonorrhoea, & think there was something like a sequale of the disease still remaining. but in what way treated am not informed.—In the present case, which was soon followed by a high degree of Fever, Bleeding, and cooling aperients, together in conjunction with soothing Emolient poultices were the Antiphlogistics resorted to, & I would add perseveringly. but the resolution which was anticipated or hoped for was not realised. supuration soon followed, and on making a puncture with the Abscess Lancet. a large quantity of supurative matter was discharged. So high did the inflamation & consequent fever in this case run; that the recovery of our patient, for a period of a week or 10 days, was despaired of. In the course of 3 weeks or thereabouts, swelling and inflamation had pretty much subsided. The discharge from the tumefyed part during this time, (from the time of its being Lanced,) had been copious, which, with the decrease of swelling & inflamatory symptoms gradually diminished.

9. Nineteenth-century medical authorities disagreed over the nature and treatment of fungus cerebri. Some believed that fungus cerebri was a growth of the brain which resulted from skull fractures or the removal of large pieces of skull. Other doctors believed the protrusion from the brain was not a growth but was either coagulated blood or brain tissue. Whereas some suggested either excising or applying caustics to the growth, others recommended applying soothing dressings to it (Gibson, *Institutes and Practice of Surgery*, 2:197-98; see also Journal 3, below, pp. 57-59).

10. Lindsay was probably referring to an eighteen-tailed bandage. See Glossary of Medical and Pharmaceutical Terms, s.v. "Bandage, eighteen-tailed."

11. Deleted from the text are two recipes: one for burns and hemorrhoids and another for hemorrhage. See Recipes from Lindsay's Journals, pp. 157-58 below.

In about 4 weeks the patient was able to walk about the room, tho' yet very feeble. what I consider most remarkable in this case; on the subsidence of the tumefaction, & swelling, the *Testis* was found still to be highly diseased, being in, what I supposed, a *schirous* [scirrhous] situation. which made its appearance in the form of a spungy or Fungous vegetation,[12] if the expression be admissible, which I treated with the red Precipt. for some time as an Escharotic. This application for some time, seemed, slowly, to promise a cure in the destruction of this sprouting state of the part. but by degrees again seemed to have become less efficient, & the Testicle still continued to shoot out, something like what I would term, luxurient granulations.[13] The Lunar caustic was next applyed without obtaining a much better result. At this stage of the case my next application was a highly consistent & concentrated extract of the sour, or sheep sorrel. (The botanical name of which dont recollect). A few applications of this, completely destroyed this organised schirrous part of the *organ*. & in a short time afterwards, my patient was dismissed as cured. & so long as I was acquainted with my patient afterwards he had no return of the disease. perhaps it would be in place to mention that this member was almost entirely destroyed, being but a very small portion remaining at the time my patient was dismissed. I have in conclusion to say that my reading does not furnish me with a parallel case: at least not in detail. My attention was called to this preperation of the sorrel. by a Mr. Watkins then a Teacher at Lawrenceburg Ia. where the writer of this article then resided. Mr. W. a gentleman of science informed me that this preperation of the sorrel was the secret preperation of a Cancer Doctor[14] who some years ago resided in cincinnati, & acquired some fame in that way. At the time, this preperation was a confidential matter. Mr. W. the last I knew of him was at the village of *Cleves* Hamilton Co. O. engaged to some extent in the practice of Med. & was

12. This growth was probably what nineteenth-century physicians would have classified as a later stage of scirrhosity. Scirrhus was defined as any hard tumor, prone to ulceration. It was believed the forerunner of cancer, and doctors noted that in its later stages the tumor would ulcerate, slough, and leave a large cavity in the skin. A hard fungus mass often filled this cavity (Gibson, *Institutes and Practice of Surgery*, 1:258-59). Although rarely used, the term today refers to a hard cancer.

13. In nineteenth-century parlance, granulations could be described as healthy and unhealthy. Healthy granulations were those which had a deep red color, rose evenly with the surrounding skin, and were prone to unite with each other to form skin. Unhealthy granulations, in contrast, were livid in color, had a languid circulation, rose higher than the surrounding skin, and were soft and spongy with no tendency to form skin (Hooper, *Lexicon Medicum*, 1:402).

14. Cancer doctors were untrained, having acquired their cures by trial and error. They frequently claimed they could cure all types of cancer (Pickard and Buley, *Midwest Pioneer*, 88).

a Justice of the Peace, Post Master &c. This *Ext*[ract] was prepared from the expressed Juice of the Plant. slowly reduced to the consistent state used, by being exposed to the hot rays of the sun in a Pewter dish. The Oxalic acid which the Plant is known to contain, is, undoubtedly, the active constituent in this preperation of the sorrel. My friend Dr. W. Mount now of the vicinage of Cincinnati, (once) saw the foregoing case with me.

Congenital Asphyxia

Such have I concluded to Nosologise the case now to be described.

In the spring of 1824 was called on as Accoucheur to Mrs. Jacob Fielding. nothing remarkable attended this parturient visitation, the presentation natural, duration about 5 hours. pains not very good, waters discharged early, no malconformation of Pelvis, had had several children all at the full period. Some *born dead* (still born), none survived the month (*if I mistake not*). Mrs. F. was of delicate stamina, The only circumstance that entitles this case to a place here, is the circumstance of resuscitation. after about (20 minutes) or a half hour's apparent suspension of the life of the Infant. means resorted to; warm bath (*Tepida*), friction, & occasional attempts at inflating the Lungs by blowing into the Mouth. probably the success of this case was owing in part to the great anxiety of the Mother (which prompted unusual exertion). As all symptoms of animation & life appeared to be extinct at birth, & for a considerable time afterwards, as above stated.

Such was the joy & satisfaction consequent on my efforts & success in this case that the Parents named their son for me. The last I knew of this family, were residing about 14 or 15 miles North of Laurenceburg, Ia. & W. L. Fielding then 2 or 3 years old was a fine, promising, healthy boy. This record being made several years subsequent to its occurence. do not recollect all the circumstances attending. with that clearness of precision that a recorder should!—however feel confident that I am substantially correct

Richmond Ia.   *W. Lindsay*

[EDITORIAL NOTE]

Complications resulting from gunshot wounds, fractures, tumors, and diseased joints often required the amputation of a limb. Yet, physicians performed amputation only if the injury threatened the patient's life. The timing of these operations was essential to the patient's full recovery. The amputation was to be performed immediately after the patient recovered from shock, but before inflammation occurred. When gangrene attacked a limb, the doctor postponed the operation until a line between the living and dead parts could be discerned. Even the slightest wait was deemed improper, however, if the rapid spread of gangrene threatened the patient's life.

Lindsay was undoubtedly familiar with the procedures for amputation since he attended several cases (see pp. 72-76). In amputating a limb, the nineteenth-century surgeon employed either the flap method or the circular method. In the flap method, the surgeon retained large pieces, or flaps, of skin to cover the stump. In the circular method, the physician separated the diseased muscle, flesh, and bone of the limb from the healthy portion by a circular motion of the knife. Then the doctor hollowed out about two inches of healthy muscle from the stump and used the remaining skin to cover the stump. After removal of the diseased portion of the limb, he removed any loose blood on the stump and tied the severed arteries with ligatures. Once all hemorrhaging had ceased, the physician brought together the loose pieces of skin to cover the stump. He then placed on the stump a dressing consisting of the broken fibers of flax, a waxy ointment, and strips of linen cloth. The physician secured this dressing in place by a bandage known as a Malta cross (Gibson, Institutes and Practice of Surgery, 2:509-42; Dorsey, Elements of Surgery, 2:250-52).

Femoral Amputation

Matthew Frank Aged about 28. years, In the month of July 1826 called on me for advice in case of an affection of the Knee Joint. Stated to me that some time previous when playing at Ball. felt, for the first time, pain in the part, by the time he consulted me his knee had become quite painful, & swolen, supposing his case to be something of a Rheumatic character, various applications were made during the summer, among which were Linaments, Epispastics, &c. consequent to which treatment, in conjunction with the internal use of the Gu[a]iacum, this affection of the knee became much better. During the following winter he again resumed his occupation. viz. that of a shoe maker. and was able to use the strap & Lapstone[15] with out much inconvenience. In the following month of *may*, I was called to visit my patient *at his own residence*, his knee at this time having become much worse, And was now confined to his bed. In a short time the knee became enormously swollen, & in spite of every thing done suppurated, the Left knee was the one affected & the matter seemed to point most prominently to the left & outside of the joint, where I Lanced it, but in a few days afterwards matter began to point to the inside of the knee, which I also gave exit to by the abscess Lancet. The discharge

15. Strop: a band of leather used for sharpening a knife or razor; lapstone: a stone or iron plate, held in the lap and used for hammering and shaping leather.

was very abundant, & remarkably fetid. mostly thin, & of a dirty bloody colour intermixed with white supurative matter, the pain still continued very excruciating, & by this time the bones had evidently become affected, including the whole joint, & some distence up the Os Femoris, having formed sinuses, as was evinced by the probe & the injection of milk & water, also a communication had formed between the external & internal parts opened by the Lancet. as when milk & water were thrown in by the P. syringe[16] at one opening, a part of it would be discharged at the other. so soon as I suspected the bones to have become thus extensively affected, Drs. Dubois & [John] Treon were called in council, & at a second meeting Dr. [C. G.] Espich of Germantown [Ohio] was also called.

Amputation was now determined on, & was performed about 6 inches above the knee. In about 3 or 4 weeks afterwards the stump had nearly healed & medical attentions dispensed with. and my patient was dismissed cured.

W. Lindsay

N.B. This case occured during my residence at Germantown Ohio, & I now make this record of the case Dec. 6. 1836 9 or 10 years afterwards, consequently at this lapse of time do not particularly recollect all the attendant symptoms of the case. but so far as here noted, altho' from memory, know I am substantially correct.

W.L.

N.B. In the foregoing case of M. Frank, on examination of the *Limb* after it was *amputated* the *heads* of the *Tibea* & *Fibula* were found much affected, corroded & carious as well as the articulating *head* of the *Femoris* [femur] with these bones, forming the knee joint. and as the patient had become much prostrated; to have restored him to health with an anchylosed [ankylosed] joint, would have required much greater demands on the constitution, (*and* the vis Medicatrix Natura) than could, reasonably, have been furnished, or could reasonably have been anticipated.

W.L.

16. Lindsay was probably referring to a pewter syringe. During this period, syringes primarily were used for the administration of enemas and the introduction of liquids or powders into body cavities and wounds. They were often heavy and cumbersome and made of pewter or silver. The endermic syringe for the injection of fluids into the skin was not used until the Civil War (Bennion, *Antique Medical Instruments*, 169-71).

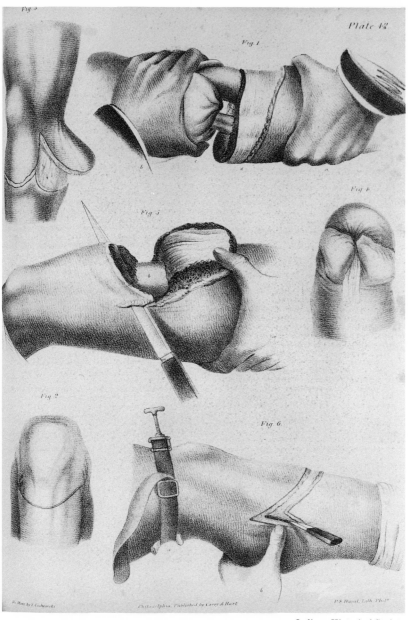

Drawing illustrating two methods of amputating the leg and thigh: the circular method (Fig. 1) and the flap method (Fig. 2) (Joseph Pancoast, A Treatise on Operative Surgery; Comprising a Description of the Various Processes of the Art, Including All the New Operations . . . [Philadelphia: Carey and Hart, 1844])

[EDITORIAL NOTE]

The treatment of hydrocele was one of Lindsay's specialties, and he recorded eleven cases of the disease. While most Indiana physicians charged five to ten dollars for hydrocele treatment, Lindsay confidently charged thirty dollars for his "permanent cure." Hydrocele, the collection of fluid between the testicle and its serous covering, or tunica vaginalis, was often treated by drawing off the excess fluid and administering harsh injections. Lindsay believed that "one bold incision" in the scrotum could effect a lasting cure.

Early nineteenth-century physicians speculated that rheumatism, urethral irritation, "a varicose enlargement of the spermatic artery," or blows to the scrotum were possible causes of hydrocele. To give the patient temporary relief, doctors punctured the scrotum and tunica vaginalis with a lancet or trocar. To achieve a more permanent or radical cure, some doctors either applied a caustic substance to the serous covering or removed part of the serous covering. A few physicians performed operations similar to Lindsay's, but the most common radical treatment was puncture and injection. In this procedure physicians drew off excess fluid by introducing a trocar through the scrotum into the tunica vaginalis. They then injected a mixture of wine and water and kept this mixture in the scrotum until a severe pain was felt along the spermatic cord. If fluid collected again, puncture and injection was repeated. When puncture and injection failed, some doctors followed the plan of English physician John Hunter (1728-1793). Hunter advised an inch-long incision in the tunica vaginalis and after evacuation of the fluid, filling the cavity with Indian meal or dough.

Lindsay treated hydrocele by the recommended method of puncture and injection during his early years of practice, but from experience concluded that permanent relief could be achieved by "laying the testes bare." His technique consisted of a five- to six-inch incision in the distended scrotum and a smaller cut in the tunica vaginalis to release the fluid. Lindsay's contemporaries believed hydrocele could be cured by causing the tunica vaginalis to adhere to the testicle. According to physicians, this effect could be achieved by inducing a high degree of inflammation in the scrotum. Lindsay regarded the incision method more effective than puncture and injection because of the high degree of inflammation caused by incision. He also considered incision more humane, since injection caused excruciating pain for several days. And he preferred "one bold incision" since the surgeon could then view the testes and perform a castration if they were diseased.

Today one-fifth of the hydrocele cases are attributed to tumors. Trauma to the scrotal area, mumps (virus orchitis), and nonspecific inflammations are responsible for the remainder. Although fluid can temporarily be drawn off by aspiration, surgery is preferred. By making an incision in the scro-

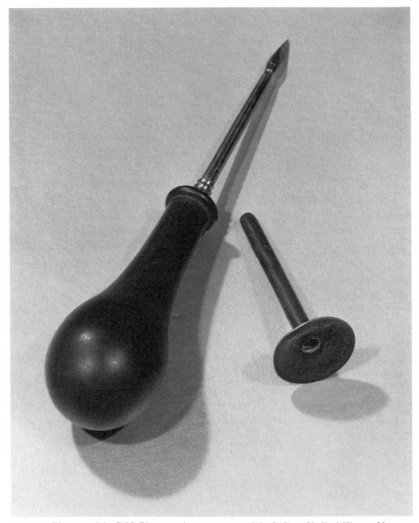

Photograph by B&L Photographers, courtesy of the Indiana Medical History Museum
A trocar, with cannula, circa mid-nineteenth century. The trocar was used in treating hydrocele. The doctor placed the cannula over the perforator, punctured the scrotum with the perforator tip, and then withdrew the perforator, leaving the cannula in the scrotum to drain the water.

tum, the physician can sometimes determine the cause of hydrocele. Although Lindsay had an imperfect knowledge of the mechanisms involved in the disease, he intuitively recognized the value of viewing the testes (Gibson, Institutes and Practice of Surgery, 2:434-39; Dorsey, Elements of Surgery, 2:102-10; Cooper, First Lines, 2:335-36).

Hydrocele *case 1*

Jacob Harry, aged about 42. On *consultation* (examination) found had been laboring under Hydrocele many years, which at this time had become aggravated, & the parts much enlarged. He had consulted with several Physicians, who left him in doubt with regard to the *Diagnosis* of his case, some had suspected Hydrocele, others Rupture, & protrusion of Abdominal viscera. Previous to this I had examined his case & satisfyed myself that Hydrocele was his disease.

Having called my friend Dr. J. H. Buel then of Eaton, [Ohio] on a careful examination he concurred with me in opinion.

Having explained to my patient the various methods of Operating, consented that I should take my own course: but wished to be operated on in that way which would promise the most certainty of a radical cure. For reasons which I design giving hereafter the operation of incision was determined on. Our incision was commenced tolerably high up & near the abdominal ring the Crus Penis, over the spermatic cord, and continued some 5 or 6 inches in length through the scrotum down to the Tunica vaginalis Testis, by the first stroke of the scalpel. The next cut was made into this latter coat, which discharged the fluid, about one quart in quantity, and laid the Testicle bare, which was found to be in a healthy situation. The dressing consisted of 2 or 3 stiches, and strips of Adhesive Emplas intervening, over which a pledget of lint, & a suspensary over all supporting the whole scrotum in the usual way attached to a bandage around the loins. In the course of about 3 or 4 weeks my patient had pretty well recovered, and since then has enjoyed excellent health, without any return of Hydrocele.

Mr. J. H. resides in Montgomery Co. Ohio.

Dec. 6. 1836   *W. Lindsay*

Hydrocele 2d. case

Joshua Bond aged about 60 years, having a few days previous on examination satisfyed myself that his case was that of Hydrocele, proceeded on the 13th. of May 1830 to operate, in which I was met as counsel by my friends Doctrs. W. Mount then of Eaton O., & J[ohn T.] Plummer of Richmond Ia. (my own place of residence,) whose friendly assistence hope ever to acknowledge.

In this, as the preceeding one of J. Harry the different methods of operating had been explained, viz. that of puncture, & that of Incision.

which as in the other case, was submitted to the judgment of the operators, wishing to be operated on with as much certainty of producing radical cure as posable.

I commenced the incision pretty well up towards the a[b]dominal ring, & carried the first stroke of the knife down near the bottom of the sac & scrotum, making the incision 5 or 6 inches long. something like a Quart of clear fluid was discharged. The transparent appearence described by our authors,[17] & so well known to those of the Profession who have had experience in this department of Surgery, was quite evident on darkening the room and examining the enlarged scrotum with a candle previous to the operation, & was one of the appearences present which enabled us to come at a Diagnosis of this & the foregoing case.

as an honest recorder I have to mention an untoward circumstance, viz. that of wounding the Testis by the knife in the operation. which was the occasion of some additional distress to the patient at the time; however, think this circumstance did not give any additional pain, afterwards during the cure. The dressing in this, as in the preciding case of J.H. was that of 2 or 3 stiches, with that of adhesive strips intervening.

In 4 or 5 weeks time my patient had nearly recovered. & is still living in the enjoyment of good health, not having had the least symptom of a return of his former disease now several years since the operation. and from my experience since in operations, feel confident that a radical cure has been produced or effected.

W.L.

Hydrocele Case 3d.[18]
Cellular

In Fall of 1830 was called to a Mr. Carson in consultation with Dr. W. Matchet[t] of Abington Wayne Co. Ia. who was laboring under very

17. One of the symptoms of hydrocele is a transparency of the scrotum. Lindsay's contemporaries recognized this condition as one of the early signs of hydrocele. Surgeons suggested placing a lamp or candle behind the scrotum to determine whether or not it was transparent (Gibson, *Institutes and Practice of Surgery*, 2:435; Astley Cooper, *A Series of Lectures on the Most Approved Principles and Practice of Modern Surgery* [Boston: Charles Ewer, 1823], 158).

18. From the description which follows, this case was probably not hydrocele since the patient's edema was generalized rather than localized. Hydrocele is the collection of water between the testicle and its serous covering, or tunica vaginalis. See Editorial Note, pp. 14-15.

considerable enlargement of the whole scrotum attended by swelling of both legs & feet. On examination gave it as my opinion that the patient was laboring under a collection of water within the cellular membrane of the Lower extremities. and that the scrotal enlargement was of that character. which was so enormously distended that he experienced great pain & restlessness. The general surface presented a glossey & shining appearence, attended by crepatus & pitting. Having stated my opinion to the Dr. The Patient & his friends, proceeded to puncture the scrotem on one side which gave immediate releif, by carrying off a considerable quantity of water, The particular symptoms attending this case am now deficient in its history; however, think by some great exposure in geting wet & wading in the water, supposed he had taken a violent cold, which was atten[d]ed by considerable fever, confining the patient to bed, being so unwell as to be considered dangerous by his friends. This singular development of an infiltration & engorgement of water within the cellular membrane as well as I now recollect came on suddenly, a few days after taking to his bed & I was called in a few days afterwards. Having conducted off the water of the scrotum; by the exhibition of aperient diuretic medicines the swelling in the lower extremities in a few days subsided, without any return of the scrotal cellular deposition. In the course of 5 or 6 days after the operation I again called, & found him doing well. And in 2 or 3 weeks afterwards, was able to resume some light labor on his farm— The exposure in the above case was occasioned by a trip to cincinnati with his waggon.

W.L.

Hydrocele case 4th.[19]

Aug. 9. 1831. was called to see son of a Mr. Fouts 15 years old, laboring under scrotal celular Hydrocele. The patient had been brot from a distance to the neighborhood of Richmond to receive my professional attentions. As regards the history of his case dont now recollect what his affection was traced to. The boy was a german by birth, had been of healthy constitution, and accustomed to labor on his father's farm. His lower extremities were somewhat Edematous, which in some degree was general of the whole surface of the body. On my first visit made a puncture into the scrotum & drew off a considerable quantity of water. 4 or 5 days afterwards, water had again collected in the scrotum, which I again drew off by puncture. The lower extremi-

19. As in the preceeding case, this was probably not hydrocele, since the patient's edema was generalized rather than localized.

ties continuing still to exhibit evident symptoms of cellular infiltration, next resorted to cupping the inside of each leg above the ancle which gave exit to a considerable quantity of water, being tinged by a small quantity of sanguineous fluid no doubt from the cuticular vascular system[20] only. I would here mention that my patient, was, when I first saw him, of yellow, Puffy, Cachetic, & exsanguinated countenance. and had regular exacerbations of fever every 24 hours. with some thing like an appyrexial [apyrexial] period of 18 hours duration.

Beleiving that there was considerable Hepatic derangement in this case, after my first operation, administered calomel & Jalap as a cathartic, & continued to keep the bowels open, which were inclined to torpidity, with Jalap & crem Tart. [cream of tartar] during the first 4 or 5 days. at the end of which time his exacerbations of fever had nearly subsided. about this time put him on a preperation of Carb. Ferri [*Ferri carbonas praecipitatus* or precipitated iron carbonate], in hard cider, The water continued to drean off or drip more or less for about 24 hours from the punctuers on the legs, made on cupping. & having introduced a small pledget of Lint, on puncturing the scrotum the 2d. time, kept it open 3 or 4 days; & until a slight degree of inflamation had taken place in the part. at this stage of the treatment there appeared to be some amendment. the Febrile Paroxysms having entirely subsided. The Edematous symptoms were much less evident. The Chalybeate was still continued. By the 10th. or 12th. day. the appetite which from the first had been better than might have been expected, now had improved. the expression of countenance had changed from the bloated cachectic, to that of returning health; the lips, the cheeks, & the skin, generally, put on a more healthful hue, & the eye had parted with its dulness, for that of expression & animation. at the end of about 18 days my Patient was taken home. The only change which had been made in the treatment, was when the preperation of cider before mentioned became disagreeable to the stomach, the sub. carb. Ferri [*Sub-carbonas ferri praeparatus* or prepared iron carbonate] was given in substence in 5 or 6 gr. doses 3 or 4 times a day—and when his stomach and appetite began to come up, directed Mustard seed ground, & Horseradish grated, to be used freely in good vinegar, as a condiment, or rather for seasoning, on his meat, & Beef steak. My Patient, so far as I have known any thing of him, has enjoyed since good health. It was something like a year afterwards his

20. Cuticular vascular system refers to the vessels and veins of the cuticle, or epidermis, which is the outermost layer of skin. The epidermis, however, is a nonvascular layer of skin, so Lindsay must have been referring to the corium, or layer of skin below the epidermis consisting of a dense bed of vascular connective tissue.

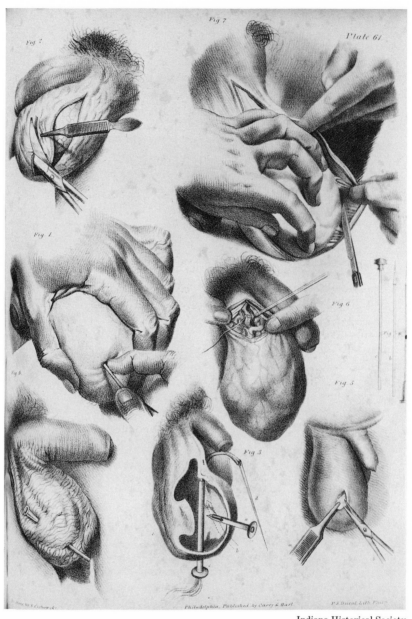

Indiana Historical Society

Drawings showing the treatment of hydrocele by puncturing the scrotum (Pancoast, A Treatise on Operative Surgery)

Father called on me to pay the Bill,[21] his son up to this time had enjoyed excellent health, and expressed much gratitude for my servises rendered in the case.

I forgot to mention that as an external application and Rubifacient during the continuence of scrotal & cellular infiltration, I prescribed the volatile Linament, with the addition of spts. or the ol. Terrebinth [terebinth]. to be bathed pretty generally over the whole surface two or three times a day. which as an adjuvant have reason to beleive had an excellent effect.

I would here observe that this & the foregoing case had, in some degree, similar symptoms; particularly in the scrotal infiltration. with regard to the general symptoms, the latter case was evidently more of the cachectic character than the former. The latter case I should have mentioned in the history of it, that the patient had been laboring under this disease some 2 or 3 weeks before he was brot to my neighborhood, for the purpose of being put under my care. what the previous treatment had been, dont now recollect what my information was on the subject, more than this, that when the scrotal enlargement had taken place, which I think came on suddenly, the Physicians of his neighborhood, professed to be at a loss as to its diagnosis, or real character, & recommended that he should be put under my care.

The operation of puncturing the scrotum, I feel confident, had an excellent effect in both cases. the infiltration & distention in both was so great, that nothing else, in my opinion, could have carried off the water, indeed was it so great in the former case, that the skin must have given way in a few days, had the operation not been performed, could the patient have survived so long.—As it regards the cupping in the latter case, am well satisfyed as to the good effects of this also. And altho' these operations are deemed hazardous by some of our writers on the subject, so far as my experience goes, must say that there is little danger in the majority of cellular infiltration. I have performed the operations of puncturing, scarification, & cupping on many patients during my 14 or 15 years practice, and in no instance has *gangrene,* or any other untoward symptom resulted. The reasons advanced, as every medical man knows, are, that when *cellular dropsy* or infiltration takes place there is so much debility, or want of tonicity[22]

21. It was not unusual for bills to be paid as long as a year after medical treatment. In country areas, where cash was scarce, doctors' bills were paid in produce and services (Duffy, *Healers,* 178-79).

22. The theory of tonicity, or the proper tension or firmness of an organic tissue, was formulated by Friedrich Hoffmann (1660-1742). Hoffmann believed that living fibers had a *tonus,* or life force, with the ability to expand and contract. This *tonus* was believed regulated through the nervous system by a fluid, or "nervous ether," concentrated in the brain. When the *tonus* was normal, the body was healthy (Dun-

on the surface & within the cellular tissue that the healing process may
not be sustained, & that there is danger of gangrene & mortification,
direct, or the result of inflamation. That such may have been the
result, in some few cases of dropsy of the cellular structure have no
doubt. but where such results have taken place I should presume the
operation must have been delayed too long. Under great prostration
of the powers of life. & almost within the Articulo Mortis,[23] *when
Death was shaking his fist under the nose of the Patient*, and under
circumstances when any treatment would have been unavailing.—I
once had a patient which (who) had been laboring a long time under
a[s]*cites*, or Abdominal Dropsey, attended, when I was called, by general infiltration of the cellular membrane. even the head, <&?> scalp,
participated in this affection, producing much distortion, & enlargement of the head & face. the eyes nearly, or quite closed in consequence. her legs almost as large as her body should have been, & her
bodys corrisponding with the lower extremities. & the other members,
in this awful sight of human wretchedness. This was a Female 13 or 14
years of age. during some months attentions on her, I tap[p]ed the
Abdomen several times, drawing off some 2 or 3 gallons at a time, The
legs were also taped or scarifyed with the lancet at different times, &
ran water like a sugar tree. much to her relief for the time being.
which in some instances continued discharging for a day or two, in no
instance was there any untoward, or unpleasant symptoms attending
the healing of the punctures & scarifications. And would just add,
altho' foreign to the subject under discussion, that at one time. this
patient had become so much better after the water had been drawn
off, under the exhibition of chalybeate medicine, (Sub. Carb. Ferri) in
conjunction with the squill and Digitalis, that strong hopes were entertained of her recovery. She had gained so much strength as to be able
to walk to a neighbour's house. if I mistake not several times, her
countenance had much improved, her cheeks had began to put on the
bloom of health, & her before distorted frame, began to resume its
once gracefulness, and symetry. but on returning from a pedestrian
excursion in which she visited a near neighbor was caught in a shower
of rain, and was immediately taken worse, seemed to have taken cold,
& in a few days afterwards, died suddenly.

   If there be any danger attending the operation of puncturing the
legs, or any part of the surface of a dropsical patient, as deep as the
cellular tissue, it could only be in crouded hospitals, surrounded by a

glison, *Medical Lexicon*, 864; Arturo Castiglioni, *A History of Medicine*, trans. and
ed. by E. B. Krumbhaar [New York: Alfred A. Knopf, 1941], 584).
   23. *Articulo mortis*: the moment of death.

putrid, or tainted atmosphere. & during a very unhelthy season of the year.[24]

Dec. 12. 1836.   *Wm. Lindsay*

Hydrocele, case 5.

Sept 20. 1831. was called to operate on Benj. G. Moore 45 or 50 years of age for Hydrocele of one side. Having invited my friend Dr. W. Mount then of Eaton. to whom I acknowledge myself under peculiar obligations. proceeded to examine the case, which being a well marked one of simply Hydrocele. made an explanation to the patient of the various methods which had been practiced by authors on the subject. our patient consented that any operation we migh[t] prefer, should on his part be submited to, but seemed rather to prefer, that of simply drawing off the water with the Trochar, & the injection of such fluid as we might prefer. We proceeded immediately to the operation, & succeeded without any difficulty in drawing off the water, which we followed by the injection of the tepid fluid (dont now recollect which was made use of, wine & water, or Brandy & water,) keeping it within the scrotum until considerable pain, & some sickness, were induced. This was the first time I had operated, or witnessed an operation in this way. & was induced from the good authority on the subject, to hope it would have been successful. and for a period of something like 4 or 5 years was of the impression such was the fact. but some 2 years ago am informed that water had again collected, & was drawn off by a Physician of his immediate neighborhood. what was the success of this 2d. operation, or what is the present state of the case, am not informed. as I have not had an interview with the Patient or Physician on the subject. but am compelled from the result of this case, & some others which have since presented, that, the operation in this way is much less certain of producing a permanent cure of Hydrocele than that of the operation of laying the Tunica vaginalis, or the sac containing the water, freely open with the knife. In another place, at the close of these cases, coming within my practice, I design giving my views, on the subject of operating for the radical cure of Hydrocele, more *in extenso.*

Richmond Ia   *W. Lindsay*
Dec. 17. 1836

24. Many doctors believed "bad" or "tainted" air caused disease. According to these "miasmatists," effluvium in the air, resulting from unsanitary conditions, or the existence of marshes, caused epidemic diseases such as cholera and yellow fever. During the unhealthy season of the year, or the summer and fall months, the atmosphere was believed more likely to become tainted or filled with effluvium (Duffy, *Healers*, 44; Rosenberg, *Cholera Years*, 75-77).

Case 6th. Hydrocele

———————— Reynolds, Aged 65 or 70, by profession an Indian Doctor[25] having some time previous consulted me concerning his case, pronounced it Hydrocele. He informed me on the 1st. interview that he had been laboring under this disease many years. Supposed it was of syphalytic origin, had consulted, as he informed me with several Physicians who had given various opinions with regard to what might be his disease. & himself was quite at a loss to det[e]rmine what was its true character, but by some was supposed that his case was Rupture. My Diagnosis was soon made out, considering it a case of, simply, Hydrocele, & that well marked. The patient resided 25 or 30 miles distent from me. On the date above I was called to a case of Surgery in his neighborhood, where Reynolds met me, & requested me to call on him on the next day before I left for home. which I accordingly did. As the man was so far distent from my residence operated by simply drawing, off the water, having no syringe or necessary preperations for injecting fluid as recommended, by our Authors on the Subject. This was on the 14th. Sept. 1832 Some time during the following winter my Patient called to see me at Richmond, my residence, Hydrocele having again returned. I now operated on him in my own office by drawing off the water, & throwing up whiskey, it being an article of which he had some fondness, or prepossesions for, when administered in a diferent manner. My patient in a half hour after being operated on, set out on foot, as I afterwards learned, designedly, for his residence, as before stated 25 or 30 miles distent. but on the road, about 3 miles from Town, having called on an acquaintence, the pain from the operation was such, that, he was compelled to take up lodgings, & was under the necessity of remaining a week or ten Days. being very busily engaged myself at that time in attending to other cases of practice did not again see him during the period that the inflamation continued but the next day after the operation, on learning his situation, sent out an experienced nurse[26] to stay with him, who as instructed, gave me daily information how his case was progressing.

25. Indian doctors were self-proclaimed physicians who primarily used the natural or herbal remedies employed by the Indians. Not all of these cures, however, were derived from the Indians. A number of the treatments had their origins in ancient Egypt, China, and India. Many of the Indian doctors only practiced medicine part time, as did Lindsay's father-in-law, Peter Smith (see Introduction, p. xviii). Others established full-time practices, competing with the regular or orthodox physicians for patients (Pickard and Buley, *Midwest Pioneer*, 36-37).

26. During this period, there were no professional nurses. Protestant and Catholic religious orders provided nursing care in private hospitals; untrained women and men cared for the sick in city-owned hospitals. Secular nursing developed in the mid-nineteenth century as a result of the efforts of Englishwoman Florence Nightingale

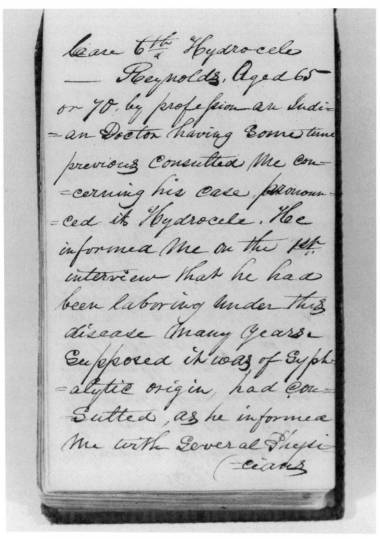

A page from Lindsay's first journal

who during the Crimean War tried to upgrade the quality of hospital care. In the United States the first attempts to train women as nurses came in the 1850s, but these efforts were sporadic and eventually interrupted by the Civil War. During that conflict, large numbers of female nurses worked in field hospitals. Although Dorothea Dix, superintendent of nurses in the Union army, did much to upgrade the image of nursing, professional nurses' training was not instituted until the 1870s (Duffy, *Healers*, 279-83). Thus, in this case the nurse to which Lindsay referred would have been untrained.

In his case the inflamation appears to have run about the necessary height, to produce an obliteration of the sack containing the fluid viz the Tunica vaginalis Testis. I think him radically cured.

as it regards what may have induced the disease with him, presume the cause which he himself suggested since his cure, viz. that of syphalis is a matter of doubt. That he had once been laboring under this latter disease is quite probable, having many years ago lived with the cherokee or Creek Indians.[27] & since my acquaintence with him, among the negroes, having a blackey for a wife. The fact is among the many cases which have come under my notice, have generally been unable to trace Hydrocele to any particular cause. with absolute certainty.

Richmond Ia.   *W. Lindsay*
Dec. 17. 1836

Hydrocele case 7.

T. Johnson Esqr. now Prosecuting Aty. for one of the Judicial Districts of this state, consulted me during the summer of 1832 with regard to his case. He informed me that some 2 or 3 years previous he had been operated on by a Physician of cincinnati. Dr. [William] Judkins I think, a small incision, (having taken no notes, of the preceeding history of the case, this is given from recollection only) had been made, with a view of inducing the adhesive inflamation. I think no fluid was injected. Mr. J. informed me that the Dr. assured him, or at least flattered him that he was cured, & so dismissed him, How long it was before fluid was again collected have now forgotten what was my information on the subject. but think it was only a few weeks. From my supposed success in Moores case, the 5th. case before reported, (as will be seen by refering to it was fallacious) and from Orthodox authority[28] on the subject: concluded to operate by simply drawing off

27. Before their removal through various treaties in the 1830s and 1840s, the Cherokee primarily occupied a large portion of the southern Alleghenies in western North Carolina, northern Georgia, eastern Tennessee, and northeastern Alabama. They were highly educated and in 1820 adopted a form of government similar to that of the United States. The Creeks were the largest Muskhogean tribe and received their name because of the numerous creeks and streams in their country. They occupied a large portion of Alabama and Georgia along the Coosa and Tallapoosa tributaries of the Alabama River and on the Flint and Chattahoochee rivers (Hodge, *Handbook of American Indians*, 1: 245-46, 362).

28. Orthodox authority refers to regular or orthodox medicine. Orthodox physicians were the largest group of practitioners during the early nineteenth century. They had formal training in medicine, based their therapies on observation rather than trial and error, and believed structural disorders could be corrected by surgery. During the early nineteenth century, they employed to various extents the depletion techniques of bloodletting and purging.

the fluid & injecting. explaining to my Patient its posable failure, but in case of which, my confidence in the operation by way of incision, which could be performed at any future time, if necessary. The anticipated adhesive inflamation did not follow, consequently in the course of a few weeks the *re*collection of water within the scrotem was the result. In the spring of 1833 Mr. J. came to Richmond & again was operated on. In operating this time I resorted to that of incision by the knife, The degree of inflamation which was anticipated did not follow, & by artificial means, such as irritating & stimulating dressings were resorted to, with a hope of inducing the state of things, wished for. & indeed flattered myself that my efforts had been crowned with success. but after a period of a few weeks the result shewed that my sucess was only partial, having produced adhesion in about one half the extent of the sack. The following May or June my Patient put himself again under my care, On operating this time I was more successful having made a more extensive incision,* & thereby brot on a higher degree of adhesive inflamation. It is now more than 3 years since the last operation, and I think there has been no return of Hydrocele. The fact is, such was the degree of inflamation, that I am induced to hope that the sack is completely obliterated. In this case there was some unusual enlargement of the spermatic cord; & am of the opinion some unnatural enlargement of the Testis also. if not schirrosity. Admitting this state of things to have been the fact. may this not account for the unusual difficulty in the case?** I suggested my opinion of this matter to the patient of the unsound state of the *organ*, who admited that such were his own fears. & suspicions. he admited that the Testis had at times been somewhat painful, & that this unpleasent feeling extended up the cord.

The foregoing cases comprise about the amount that have been operated on by me with the exception of *one* (Two) other, which, owing to the peculiar situation of the testis, & its appendages, on making an extensive incision, for the purpose of drawing off the water, with a view to a permanent cure, terminated in that of castrotomy; I will give it a place hereafter.[29]

It is remarked by Dorsey[30] in his Surgery, that the method of operating by incision, was so cruel, he would not describe it. beleiving that

* at least more extensive in a comparative point of view. in proportion to the extent of the sack now less.
** or was it that the incisions were not sufficiently extensive?

29. See Case of Samuel Woods, below, pp. 34-35.
30. John Syng Dorsey (1783-1818), a well-known Philadelphia surgeon, was the first American to ligate the external iliac artery. He taught anatomy and surgery at the University of Pennsylvania and was a surgeon on the staff of the Pennsylvania Hospital. His *Elements of Surgery* was first published in 1813.

the operation by the stylet & Trochar, with the injection of wine, or Brandy & water, was much less painful, & promised in the general, as much success. or at least, the circumstance of having an opportunity of repeating the operation of Taping at pleasure, in case success should not attend it, was sufficient to give this method of operating in Hydrocele the preference & I am inclined to beleive that this is the opinion of Physicians generally, of the present day.—The result of my practice has been such, as to give me but little confidence of producing a permanent cure by it. *puncture* and when successful, my experience warrents me in saying, it is owing to the adhesive inflamation induced (a fact of general admission).—That the inflamation necessary to the obliteration of the sack containing the morbid accumulation of fluid in Hydrocele, must run as high in the operation of puncture, as that of incision,* is, to me, so evident, as not to require argument or proof. Let what operation may be performed, there is much judgment required of the operator to *know* (determine) how high it should be carried, & how to graduate it. this requires a discrimination which can only be obtained by practice & experience in operating. The inflamation can, in my opinion, be more judiciously & successfully graduated in operations by incision, than by puncture. That the operation of incision may be more painful, perhaps is true. however, my experience will not allow me to admit that there is much difference.—The sickness we are directed to induce by the injection of the wine, or Brandy & water is distressing:—it is recomended to keep it up until a disposition to fainting comes on. In this the patient must suffer as much, as from the operation of incision. besides, incision gives the surgeon an advantage in another respect. viz, that of examination of the Testicle itself. this appears to me a consideration of much importance. it is highly satisfactory to the operator to know that the organ is sound & healthy. & if diseased, to know posatively of what character. And if admited that the organ may be so diseased as to require the extirpation of a portion, or entirely, either from the disease of the testicle or the spermatic cord, the operation of incision should undoubtedly have the preference. That such has been the case. as stated in the outset of these remarks, my own practice has furnished me one case at least.**

In further support of the doctrine, of giving the operation of incision the preference, shall now advert to a case of Hydrocele in which I was consulted; a case too, in which I might have operated, & should have

---

* Making allowance for the difference (& additional) inflamation consequent on the incision as a simple incised wound.

** See S. Woods case record commenced page 63 [p. 34]

operated, had not a brother Esculapius[31] succeeded in geting it out of my hands.

It was in the spring of 1834 a Mr. Johnson of the Society of Friends.[32] who resided about 25 miles beyond Indianapolis, came to our place, to consult with me & others respecting his situation. Previous to calling on me, however, he had called on Drs. N.[33] & D.[34] of our Town who, on examining his case pronounced it Hydrocele. This I was not apprised of until having given my opinion of his case, & not until he had learned what my *Fee* for the operation would probably be. Having learned that the applicant was in moderately good circumstances, on being asked by him what my charges would be, proposed to operate on him for the sum of $30. but in case success should not attend my operation, proposed to operate until a cure was effected without further charge. He then informed me of having consulted with my Brother chips,[35] & that one or both of them proposed to operate on him for $5 or $10; at the time giving the preference to the operation of puncture. I gave him my reasons for preferring the operation of incision, as he was anxious to be operated on in that way which would promise the greatest certainty of cure. He insisted on me operating for $25. which he prefered giving me, rather than be operated on by either of the others at their pitiful low fee. & observed from what he had learned of me as an operator, he would pay me $25. "as cheerfully, as eat his dinner," making use of his own expression. but as my feelings were excited, told him the sum proposed was the least cent I would take, provided my operation should be successful.

So the patient passed off from me, and was operated on by simple puncture & injection. But the result was unsuccessful. fluid soon collected again. & I have had some intimations that the case may yet come under my care.—

Perhaps I should not have indulged myself in some of the foregoing remarks. but having been much persecuted on the score of liberal or high charging, have concluded to indulge my feelings a little. and while on the subject would remark further, that I have never refused to

31. Aesculapius: the Greek god of medicine.

32. Society of Friends: the Quakers. Numbering approximately ten thousand by 1816, Indiana Quakers had mostly come from Virginia, the Carolinas, and northern Georgia and initially had settled in the Whitewater Valley, especially near Richmond. They opposed slavery, tax-supported schools, and military service (R. Carlyle Buley, *The Old Northwest: Pioneer Period, 1815-1840*, 2 vols. [1950; reprint, Bloomington: Indiana University Press, 1983], 2:474-76).

33. Possibly Dr. Samuel Nixon. See Glossary of Personal and Place Names.

34. Possibly Isaac V. Dorsey. See Glossary of Personal and Place Names.

35. Brother chip: a person of the same profession or trade; in this case, a fellow physician.

attend to an operation, because the patient was unable to pay me a liberal bill. On the contrary I have operated in various cases *several times* gratuitously, where the unfortunate patient was poor. But in all cases where the circumstances of a patient are such, as to justify being charged a liberal bill, I have always practised on the principle, that the dignity of the profession requires it.

When the foregoing remarks were commenced* by me, I forgot that I had another case, of simply, Hydrocele, not yet repoarted. otherwise this case now alluded to, would have been given first; which will now commence on the 58th. page [see below, p. 32]. and the complicated case of Hydrocele in which it was considered advisable to perform the operation of castrotomy, will follow next in course; the same adverted to in pages 45 & 46 [see above, p. 27].

Richmond Ia   *W. Lindsay*
Dec. 17. 1836

Before closing my remarks on the subject of the most preferable method of operating, intended to have said something on the subject of external applications. among those which I have given a trial, have the most confidence in the Iodine, & the Muriate of Am[m]onia (Sal. Amoniac). In cases of infants & young children should have considerable confidence in these, Since closing my remarks on the last page, recollect a case of a child at the breast laboring under Hydrocele which was cured by a saturated solution of the Mur. Amon. in vinegar which was a case in which I was consulted. I also once treated the case of an adult, in which, as I supposed, there was a collection of water within the scrotum, accompanied with some pain & swelling of the Testes & spermatic cords. This man some years previous, had contracted syphalis. for which he had been under treatment by two other Physicians before calling on me. He being a married man, his wife also contracted the disease, which may in part account for the disease being very obstinate to cure, both were under my care for a considerable time, before their diseases yielded to medicine, various forms & combinations of Mercurials, with adjuvants, were exhibited during the process of cure. It was some months after this man was dismissed, as was thought cured, he called on me in the situation above described. whether it was from a sequele of the disease still *hanging* (lingering) about the system, or from the circumstance of his having taken pretty freely of the Mur. Hydrarg.[36] during the treatment of his syphalis

---

* on the subject of the most preferable method of operating.

36. Lindsay was probably referring to hydrargyrum. See Glossary of Medical and Pharmaceutical Terms, s.v. "Mercury."

which had not been completely drained off, am at a loss to say. The reason I make this last suggestion, is, that in some work which I have read, perhaps Matthias on the Mercurial disease,[37] similar effects are mentioned, supposed to have been occasioned by this preperation of the mineral being exhibited too freely, or too long continued. The *Iodine* in this case, as an external application in the form of ung[uentum] I made use of, after some soothing applications had been resorted to, to releive the pain & inflamation accompanying. In the course of a few weeks the *Hydrocele* disappeared, the testes and appendages were reduced to their natural sise, and up to this time, being about 5 years since, no symptoms of this affection has again returned. In confirmed cases of Hydrocele, or those of long standing. So far as my experience goes, have no confidence, whatever, in the *above* (foregoing) Med. or any others of which I have knowledge, in the whole Materia Medica.

In giving a description of 7th. case of Hydrocele, viz that of T. Johnson Esqr. I might have mentioned one or two other facts not there detailed, which are the following. The collection of fluid was inconsiderable, The operation in cincinnati had I presume to some extent destroyed the sac containing the secreted fluid. & the first two operations performed by myself it appeared to me had a similar effect, the scrotum after the collection of fluid each time seemed to be less in volume, & the water to occupy a diferent position. The first time I operated the fluid extended up the greater part before the Testis, along the Spermatic cord pretty high up, at the 2d. operation was confined more to the lower part of the Testis, & at my 3d. & last operation adhesions were such as to confine the fluid entirely in front, & only about one half the volume as that of the preceeding operation. My incisions were not sufficiently extensive in either operation to allow me a view of the Testis, the volume of the fluid secreted was so inconsiderable at the 2d. & 3d. operations as to require only a small incision to traverse the whole length of the sac. I mentioned in another place that I suspected that the Testis & cord were somewhat enlarged, had my incisions been made of sufficient length, this matter could have been determined with more certainty. and had the incision the first time been thus extensive, beli[e]ve a cure of Hydrocele would then have been effected.

---

37. Andrew Mathias, *The Mercurial Disease: An Inquiry into the History and Nature of the Disease, Produced in the Human Constitution by Use of Mercury with Observations on Its Connection with the Lues Venera,* first published in London in 1810. The mercurial disease refers to mercury poisoning. See Glossary of Medical and Pharmaceutical Terms, s.v. "Calomel."

The result of this case has more confirmed me in the opinion than I was previously, of the propriety of an extensive & bold incision in operating with a view to a radical cure of Hydrocele

Dec. 20. 1836   *W. Lindsay*

N.B. *Dr. Thomas*, formerly of *Paddy's run* either of Butler or Hamilton Co. Ohio,[38] As I am informed, operated by the extensive bold incision, and believe him to have been a very successful operator.

Hydrocele case 8.

John Clark aged about 45, was operated on by me Dec. 28. 1833. for the disease of Hydrocele of the left side, He had been laboring under this affection several years. On examining his case, & describing the operations of Incision & puncture, made choice of the latter. The collection of fluid in this case was considerable. he was of the impression that the disease was induced by hard lifting, The disease had been attended by pain in the small of the back, left loin & side. weakness of the back was associated with the pain in the side, & sometimes accompanied with pain in the left Testis & spermatic cord. but so far as could be ascertained by an external examination the organ itself with its appendages had the appearence of being sound & healthy.

After drawing off the contained fluid, & in injecting a preperation of water & proof spirits tolerably strong, not being much diluted. my assistant unfortunately let the Trocar slip from its position,[39] so as to cause a part of the injection to be forced within the cellular tissue. or at least the result was such, that this state of things were my suspicions—The patient spent a very restless night, as he informed me the next morning when he called on me at my office. On examining his case found the scrotum in several points had risen up with dark vesicles, containing a fluid, secreted immediately under the cuticle. And it was evident that gangrene had taken place which in a few days run into mortification & sloughing of a portion of the scrotum in the immediate neighborhood of the puncture. Swelling of the Testis & cord soon followed attended by considerable pain & suffering, as might have been expected. However the patient under the influence of a false delicacy continued to keep his situation and suffering from his Brotherinlaw and friends with whom he had taken boarding for a week

---

38. Paddy's Run is in Butler County, Ohio. See Glossary of Personal and Place Names.

39. It was not unusual for the trocar to slip from its position and puncture the cellular membrane of the scrotum. The well-known Philadelphia surgeon William Gibson (1788-1868) claimed that such accidents happened even to "first-rate surgeons" (Gibson, *Institutes and Practice of Surgery*, 2:438-39).

or two, & persisted in coming to my office to be dressed, however at last I prevailed on him to make his situation known to his brotherinlaw, when I visited him for the future until he became better at his lodgings. On discovering the situation of his case the following morning after the operation, immediately made an application of soothing applications & the light bread poultice. varied as the symptoms & indications seemed to point out from time to time, until the sloughing process had thrown off so much of the scrotum as had taken on the gangrenous vesication, described at the first dressing. My patient with the exception of his hydrocele & its effects as already mentioned, had been of a robust & athletic constitution, had been accustomed to hard labor, at least in his early life being one of the early setlers of the country. The result of the gangrene and mortification, as might have been expected, induced considerable debility & prostration, altho' he managed to keep up appearences for a while as if there had not been much the matter with him, as a means of counteracting the gangrene & mortification, in a few days prescribed nine, Barks [nine-bark root] & the diluted sulph. acid. (*Elix*[ir] *vit*[riol]). This unfortunate result was unexpected as new to me. that such, or similar results are described by our books, was fully aware, but feel confident there have but few such results been the fortune of surgeons in this country. such a result should, & no doubt would have been avoided, had the necessary precaution been used in keeping the Trocar within the sack or Tunica vaginalis. This I trust will ever be a lesson to me in future operations should I operate on this plain. And such a result will be carefully avoided. My patient suffered more, infinitely, than he would have done had he been operated on by incision. and was much longer under treatment, being something like six weeks before the swelling of the Testis & cord had subsided, & the scrotem had so far sicatrised [cicatrized] as to discontinue my attentions. and when I review the rough ground traveled over in his case, feel rejoiced that the result was no worse. during a considerable period of the treatment of the case. the Testis was bare, partly protruding between the ragged edges of the opening made in the scrotum consequent on the sloughing. & the edges of the wound were very difficult to *approximate & sicatrise.*

However had the satisfaction of being successful in curing my patient completely. My patient was a widower at the time I operated on him. But soon after recovering, was married in pursuance of a previous *espousal*, & the result has given favorable testimony of his powers being unimpaired, in the performance [of] the animal functions[40] as his

---

40. In the journal, Lindsay had originally written "family functions" but pasted a piece of paper over it and replaced it with "animal functions."

wife in due time presented him with a fine pledge, as the result of their weded, & mutual love.

Dec. 21. 1836
Richmond Ia   *W. Lindsay*

Hydrocele & Castrotomy

Saml. Woods age <68?> or 65 years had been laboring under Hydrocele a number of years. On the 21. Sept. 1831 was called in consultation with my friend Dr. W. Mount, now of the vicinity of Cincinnati. to consult on the above case. having previously examined his case had satisfyed myself that it was a well marked one of Hydrocele. which was also the opinion of Dr. Mount on examining the case. The patient having made up his mind to submit to an operation. we proceeded to operate by incision. On cutting into the Tunica vaginalis, which gave exit to a large collection of fluid, the Testis exposed to view, we found to us an unusual appearance. viz. that of a number of small sacks which on cutting into them were found to contain a fluid similar in appearance to that which was contained within the tunica vaginalis Testis, these on an average probably contained one half oz. of fluid, which were thickly clustered by bases or pedicles attached to the spermatic cord at its connexion with the Testis. also some scattering sacks were on a more minute examination of the case found attached some distance up the cord, having made up our minds, on finding this state of things that the removal of the Testis would be proper to a radical cure, our patient readily consented to its removal which we proceeded immediately to do, having dressed our patient & put him to bed, left him in moderately good spirits, in the hands of a nurse. On returning home in the afternoon Dr. Mount returned to Eaton, & I rode out to see a patient 4 or 5 miles in a different direction from the place of the operation above described. On returning home in the dusk of the evening, a messenger had just arrived from my patient, Woods, with the inteligence that he was "bleeding to death." The fact of the case was this. Shortly after leaving, Mr. W. regardless of our instructions to remain in bed & keep still, he got up, walked out thro' the dining room into the kitchen, & sat down,—Shortly after taking his seat at the kitchen fire, the ligature around the Spermatic Artery gave way, & hemorrhage in a dripping stream was the result. Mr. W. being somewhat credulous, in the efficacy of the *powwowings* of some self confident ignorant old women, who are found in every neighborhood, & make loud pretentions to stopping blood and many other things, equally ridiculous & extravagant, he sent one of his family to one of these

"Endors"[41] living not far distant. The messenger having made known the object of the embassey, was ordered to return & bring the exact age of my patient. day, month, & year. but behold after all this far-rango, he continued still to bleed on apace. It was then that a runner was next sent after myself. The hemorrhage had commenced probably about two oclock, & I did not get there until after dark, the patient was 3 miles distant from Richmond. On removing the dressings, found that the blood had coagulated, & distended the scrotum to an enor-mous size, besides much blood had been lost which had made its exit in a stream. My patient was now weak and almost exhausted from the loss of blood. I found I had a difficult task to perform, The coagula had become so moulded & impacted, that to remove it was indeed a very difficult task, the more so in consequence of having to perform it by candle light. however at length I succeeded in finding the artery, & again secured it firmly with the silk Ligature. To my patient, this second operation of taking up the spermatic artery, was far more tedi-ous & painful than that of the operation of the removal of the Testis; and to myself far more perplexing. my patient now dressed, & in bed the 2d. time was more careful afterwards, in attending to instructions, and without any other untoward circumstance was again on his feet in about three weeks, though not restored to his former health & strength under 5 or 6 weeks. Mr. W. has since paid the debt of nature. but had no return of *Hydrocele* he lived 3 or 4 years after this opera-tion. Whether it was the most judicious course to remove the Testis, there no doubt will be a difference of opinion. I beleive my reading does not furnish a similar or a parallel case. The removal seemed to us to be the most preferable, to a radical cure of hydrocele in this case, and after this lapse of time, & much reflection, beleive I have nothing to regret, or to charge myself with, unless it be that of securing the Spermatic Artery so badly. perhaps the ligature might have been in some way faulty, or in its application not well adjusted. as any one on reading the foregoing, must have learned the situation of things, which, in our opinion, called for the removal of the Testis, I scarcely deem it necessary to add here, that it was owing to the Hydatid State or appearence of these sacks which clustered around the cord as before described. Our fears were, that they would serve as a nucleus to re-produce, at no very distant period, a return of Hydrocele.
Dec. 21. 1836
Richmond Ia.   *W. Lindsay*

---

* Mrs. Thomas Craft

41. Endor: a witch or "woman with a familiar spirit" consulted by Saul in the town of Endor (I Samuel 28:1-25).

Castrotomy—Sol. Harris—

Sept. 23. 1831. was called on to see the above. Found him laboring under extreme pain, enlargement of the right Testis, accompanied by a high degree of inflamation. On making enquiry into the history of his case, learned that some 2 or 3 years previous, had had *syphalis*, (or perhaps only Gonorrhoea). and, as was supposed, had never been completely cured. From the information recd. by my patient, was at a loss in determining satisfactorily, whether he had during all this time been laboring under a *sequele* of his former disease, or *Gleet*. But be this as it may, this my patient, had been under the care of an empiric who was treating his case as a case of Syphalis. What the treatment was, had no opportunity of knowing. as his *cure all* of a Quack made pretentions to the knowledge of a specific, unknown to the less fortunate regular faculty.[42] My opinion was, that the bad state in which I found this fellow, was induced by improper treatment. by the exhibition of highly stimulating Diuretics, & heating injections thrown up the urethra. With a view of counteracting the high degree of swelling & inflamation, of the Testis, made use of the Lancet, cooling aperients, and as an external application the most soothing emoluents; such as the Slippery Elm in combination with Bread & Milk poultises, This plan was pursued until the 27. or 28th. of the month, without any abatement of the swelling, or the *pain* attending. The agony of my patient was such, at times, as induced him earnestly to request me to operate on him by the removal of the organ, This was his determination on sending for me. which he continued still to urge every day until the date above mentioned, when I (somewhat reluctantly) consented to gratify him in his earnest intreaties. There was nothing difficult in the operation, more than might be expected in any other case attended by as high degree of enlargement of the Testis & Spermatic Cord. accompanied, as this was, by a very high strung *sensibility*, & great exaltation of the excitability of the system, & of the organ itself. It was with the hope of countervailing this high toned exaltation, that my treatment was mainly directed, fearing that this state of the nervous system, might defeat the benifits, of an operation, in hastening that fatal termination of the case to which it appeared to be portending.—Perhaps it would be in place here to make a remark or two on the subject of determining the *proper time to operate* (operations, generally, is meant,), in cases which the propriety of an operation is admited, sooner or later to be imperatively called for, To the novitiate in surgery this must be an important consideration, involving much responsibil-

42. Regular faculty: regular or orthodox physicians. See p. 26, n. 28 above.

ity. That there have been many cases, in which an *illtimed* operation has been entirely unavailing, is undoubtedly true.* operations may be illtimed, in being performed *too soon*, as well as *too late*. A discriminating judgment, associated with experience is indispensible in order to arrive at a proper knowledge of this matter. It is difficult to learn, or acquire it from books. of course for *ourself* to undertake to record any thing like special or correct principles, on this difficult subject might be considered presumptuous. Without reference to what my reading has been, would say, we must draw our decision, from all the circumstances of the case. For instance if an extremity be mangled, badly lacerated & broken, & in short so injured that an amputation, is plainly, & inevitably called for, I would say operate immediately, if you are then called. but in cases where the surgeon cannot be had until the system shall have taken on a high degree of excitement. nervous irritation, & perhaps great febrile action, my experience would say, first try and tranqualise the nerves, wait until the febrile diathesis shall have in some degree spent itself, watch nature closely, see if She (*vis Medicatrix natura*), is making any attempt towards drawing a line of demarcation between the living and the dead, or in other words between the mutilated part of the Limb, & the sound part, wait until the stomach shall have shewn symptoms of resuming its orderly action, the illimination of nutrition from proper nourishment, not forced on it, but now called for, & in addition to this state of things, u[n]til the general system shall have begun to acknowledge its debility. & ask the assistence of Tonics, manifested by the powers of life shewing a disposition to come up. Now is a favorable time to operate. thus assisted by nature, amputate without further delay. Should this favorable opportunity be neglected, until the system begin to sink under her long & heavy weight of infirmity, and great violence done her, ten chances to one you are too late; an operation now would be almost certain to hasten the awful catastrophe, & approaching dissolution! It would be cruel to operate now under such circumstances. you must now relax the sternness of the operator & surgeon, and act the part of a tender affectionate friend, let your treatment now be directed to the object of soothing, & palliating the sufferings of the patient during the little time of existence now left.[43]

I might instance, or suppose many cases, other than that of the foregoing, which perhaps may not unaptly apply to amputation in gen-

* Imperatively called for & which if performed in the right time, would have been attended by complete success.

43. For a discussion of the proper time to amputate, see Editorial Note on case of Matthew Frank, above, pp. 10-11.

eral. but must decline the task here, not having time nor room.—As regards the foregoing case of Castrotomy would just add, that I was not assured as well as I should like to have been, that the operation might not have been dispensed with.[44] I have only to say as a matter of encouragement, that my patient in a few weeks recovered from the operation. has since enjoyed much better health than he had done for several years previous. Having conversed with him frequently since, expresses his opinion unequivocally, that the operation saved his life. For 4 or 5 years he continued to reside in this place, during which time his wife had 2 or 3 children. Perhaps the interogatory *est femina chasta?* might arise, her husband so far as I have had an opportunity of knowing, was unsuspicious of her in this matter. What our Physiological writers say on the procreative powers of man thus circumstanced, have forgotten what has been my reading on the subject. My patient resided, the last I knew of him, at Connorsville this State, in an adjoining County. In *blood* has been a little amalgamated, & by occupation, for the last few years, a barber.

Dec. 24. 1836
Richmond Ia.   *W. Lindsay*

On reviewing the foregoing remarks on the subject of determining the proper time to operate, I mean in operations generally, and particularly in that of amputation, I should have remarked that the indications & symptoms as distinctly & strongly laid down, will perhaps rarely occur. however I *expect* (design) hereafter to record a case of Amputation, performed by me some years ago in which the situation of the patient, run very nearly parallel to the symptoms which I detailed in the foregoing, as indicating the proper time to operate.[45] And it was this case which was, (more particularly than any case furnished by my reading) portrayed in my mind's eye, & from which the symptoms & indications of the proper time to operate were drawn up.

Operation of *Adipose Tumor Reuben Grimes*. Aged about 40. was called to operate Sept. 30. 1831 had a Tumor on the shoulder of many years standing, was of Adipose character. was gradually increasing in sise, operated by making a Longitudinal incision of about 5 or 6 inches

44. In the text, Lindsay crossed out the following: "not having much experience in it. Suppuration, Mortification, seemed or was thought to be threatened. which <might?> exaltation of the organ was still kept up, portending as was feared, to this result after the general irritation, *Phlogistic* (consequent) fever had in a good degree yielded to the treatment, or had exhausted itself in the system."

45. Perhaps Lindsay was alluding to the "case of a common laborer, on the farm of Mr. W. Woods" (performed on December 18, 1831), recorded in Lindsay's third journal, below, pp. 72-74.

in length. through the skin. was found to be incisted [encysted], which I dissected out without any difficulty. The Tumour probably weighed 8 oz. dressed by taking a couple stiches & Adhesive Strips intervening & outside. On the 4 or 5 day dressed again & the last time. wound healed completely by the first intention. This Tumor was situated over the Deltoid Mussle, which I cut into a little in operating, but did not produce any injury or lameness in the shoulder. This I must confess was rather awkard of me. & should another case similar present. should be more careful not to be guilty of the like blunder.

I forgot to mention that my friend Dr. W. Mount then of Eaton O. was present at the foregoing operation, whose friendly assistence and advice shall ever gratefully acknowledge.

Jany. 7. 1837   W. *Lindsay*

I would here mention that the cases which shall be recorded in filling up the balance of this note book, will be cases, some of them of little importance. however consider them of such as to entitle to a place some where. Another fact would mention that they do not appear in the order of time, in which they occurred, but intending to record some importent cases of Amputation, Trephining &c which would take up more room than the balance of this record book will accommodate, have concluded to reserve them for another place.

W.L.

[EDITORIAL NOTE]

The following is the first of several cases which Lindsay diagnosed as cancer. As his journals reveal, the nineteenth-century physician's understanding of cancer was limited. During the period in which Lindsay practiced, doctors distinguished two stages of cancer: the occult and the open. The occult stage, commonly known as scirrhus, was defined as a hard and insensible tumor, with little or no discoloration of the surrounding parts. When scirrhus spread to the surrounding tissues, the growth became malignant, or open. During that stage, the tumor became unequal on the surface, painful, and purple. After ulcerating, it emitted a blood-tinged pus and serous discharge. Cancer was believed to attack any part of the body, but the eyes, tongue, glands, skin, tonsils, bladder, rectum, prostate, breast, and reproductive glands especially were prone to it.

For many years, physicians had believed that cancer, even in its incipient stages, was a constitutional disease, and therefore they recommended the internal use of arsenic and hemlock. By the nineteenth century, however, cancer was defined as a localized disease, with metastatic properties. Thus, the necessity of removing the cancerous growth became apparent. The tumor was removed by either excision or the application of caustic substances such as red precipitate or arsenic. If cancer, or what doctors called sarcoma, affected the bone, an amputation was performed. Some cancers, such as uterine cancer, were considered inoperable. Although a few partial hysterectomies were performed in large urban areas, most women suffering from uterine cancer were placed on bland diets rather than being subjected to an operation.

Most nineteenth-century physicians believed cancer was curable if discovered before metastasis occurred. Unfortunately, since most cancers were not diagnosed in their early stages, the prognosis for cancer patients was bleak. Given the technology of the period, internal cancers were difficult to diagnose. Undoubtedly, many persons ostensibly cured of cancer may not have even had the disease. While metastasis of cancer was recognized, it was not completely understood. Also, the patient may have suffered a return of cancer, but died of another disease (Gibson, Institutes and Practice of Surgery, 1:258-64; Dorsey, Elements of Surgery, 1:392; Cooper, Dictionary of Practical Surgery, 1:226-35).

Levi Antrim Cancer of the Lip.

Previous to coming under my care, had been under the care of several Physicians, had been laboring under the disease 25 or 30 years. had now arrived to the advanced age of about 70 years. Among those who had treated his case had been under the care of a Dr. [A.] Hindman for the last three months, a professed cancer curer, & had undertaken on the condition of no cure no pay. Treated him with a secret med. which in its effects was very severe. having some nights walked the floor with the pain induced as he informed me without being able to sleep. at length Hindman pronounced him cured. but in a few weeks the cancer was again *vegetating.* A law suit now ensued. the Dr. brot suit for his fee which Antrim refused to pay. On trial H. plead that he would yet cure him if A. would again submit to treatment. The J.P. decided against the Dr. giving for reason in his verdict that he (H) had had sufficient time to cure in, & that it was unreasonable that his patient should longer submit to being punished & tormented by his Escarotics particularly as he the Dr. had at one time pronounced him (A) cured.

Previous to calling on this *Dr. Cancer,* I had been consulted, & gave it as my opinion that the knife promised the best prospect of cure. & that I would undertake his case should he think proper to submit to the treatment proposed. But having met with much encouragement from Dr. H. concluded to give him a trial first. The result of which has just been detailed For many years my Patient had worn a black patch confined by ribbon around the head. And as the cancer was seated on the upper lip, was a matter of much public notoriety. The cancer which

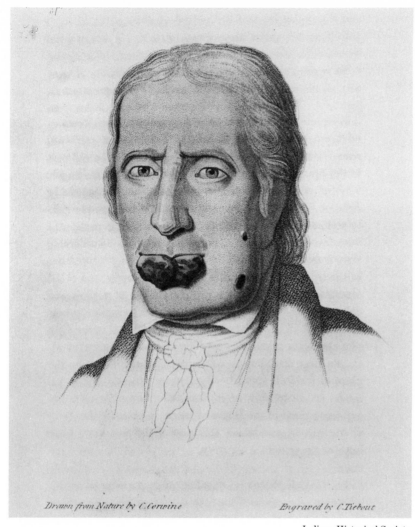

Drawn from Nature by C.Corwine   Engraved by C.Tiebout

Drawing by C. Corwine of a man suffering from cancer of the lip (Gibson, The Institutes and Practice of Surgery, *vol. 1)*

was situated on the left side of the *Labia Superiora* between the left Angle of the mouth near the left nare of the nose occupied nearly the whole substance of the Lip. So that in the operation, I cut a piece out through & thro making a fisure similar to the letter v inverted (ʌ) which made a fisure in the part of ghastly and formidable appeerence. which was made more frightful from the Hemorrhage produced from cutting the Superior Labial Artery which bled profusely, having in an instant filled the patient's mouth & throat so as to threaten strangling and suffocation. I must acknowledge myself that the hemorrhage was so great as for a moment almost to disconcert me. to see my patient strangling from it, & at the same time streaming down his bosom, greatly to the injury of his linen and clothing. However I succeeded without any difficulty in taking the artery up, & securing it with the silk ligature.

In 5 days I dressed my patient for the 2d. & last time. the incision having completely healed by the first intention. and am happy in having it to say with little eschar or sycatrix. & as in bringing the wound together by a stich & Adhesives in so doing smoothed a wrinkle which existed from age at either Angle of the mouth, the Symatry of the part was rather improved than otherwise. Antrim paid my bill of $5. with much satisfaction.

I would in conclusion remark that in the cou[r]se of a year or two my patient went to the St. Joseph Country in the northern part of this State. Since which my Brother Chip Dr. Hindman circulated a repourt that the cancer had again returned, which altho' I did not beleive in the correctness of the repoart must say occasioned me much vexation & anxiety. But to set the matter at rest I addressed a letter to Mr. Antrim on the subject who informed me that his cancer had not returned, & he had no fears that it ever would. at the same time authorised me to make any use of his letter I might deem proper.

Mr. A. informed me that his father died with cancer, & had been treated by *Dr. Rush*.[46] This is a matter of some doubt with me whether or not the disease may not be constitutional. in his case. However have no fears of cancer ever reappearing in the part operated on as I am confident of having removed it *en mass*. and should it Hydra like make its appearence on some other part, I am not responsable. & should have nothing to charge myself with.

Jan. 7. 1837   W Lindsay

Jacob Coalman laboring under Tumour of the Breast which I presume was of scroulous character. called on me in the summer of 1828. The Tumor of the left breast as large as a hens Egg. On examining it found it to contain supurative matter. which on being opened discharged freely. But little of the previous history of the case is now

46. Lindsay was most likely referring to Benjamin Rush (1745-1813), the prominent physician of the previous generation. Rush had received his medical degree from the University of Edinburgh and pursued postgraduate studies in London and Paris. Upon returning to America in the 1770s, he taught chemistry at the College of Pennsylvania. He revived the practice of bloodletting, and his views on medicine and disease affected the practice of medicine for almost three generations.

recollected. The tumor or abscess, continued to run something like a year, and during a considerable part of the time was an extensive sinus ulcer, having formed sinuses to a considerable extent under the Pectoral Muscle and deep as the Ribs, being located between & over the 2d. 3d. & 4th. Ribs. The sinu[s]es ran in various directions, & had 2 or 3 outlets near the connexion of the Ribs with the Sternum which could not be followed with the Probe owing to the circuitous direction which they took, but were known to be connected, by throwing in. milk & water, or injection with the P. Syringe. The discharge was generally very thin, & frequently abundant. various treatment was used during the pendency of the case, internally & externally. As an external treatment sometimes Emoluent Poultises soothing applications, such as simple cerates & digestive unguents [simple digestive ointments] were tried, at other times irritating & stimulating dressings were tried, and discouraged with all these sometimes endeavored to produce a healthy change of action by cutting into the ulcer with the knife, sometimes trimming out a part of the ragged and indolent edges of the sinu[s]es, hoping by this means to change it into the nature of a simple incised wound all of which did not seem to produce any immediate good effect. As internal medicines, The Carb[onate of] Iron. & the veg[etable] Tonics were alternated & becoming discouraged with these, the Iodine was tried to some extent, also Mercurials as a part of the routine were resorted to & for a long time apparently with the same unsuccessful results. After having nearly exhausted the materia Medica. the *Arcenic* [arsenic] was injected & applied in powder. this was attended by some u[n]pleasant consequences, producing much swelling of the surrounding integuments, and much tenderness & soreness, at the same time attended by much distress, and irritation of the general system. so much so that the effects were deemed somewhat hasardous at one time. This last treatment after these unpleasant symptoms subsided seemed to have been singularly beneficial. As the ulcer not long afterwards completely healed up. And beleive the cure has been permanent.

Jany. 7. 1837   W. Lindsay

[EDITORIAL NOTE]

The following is one of several cases of wound management. The major goals in the treatment of wounds were first to suppress the bleeding and then to approximate the wound's edges. The ancient practice of cautery had been abandoned by the early 1800s; the most commonly employed permanent method of suppressing hemorrhage was tying the artery with a silk thread or leather ligature. After grasping the torn vessel with either artery

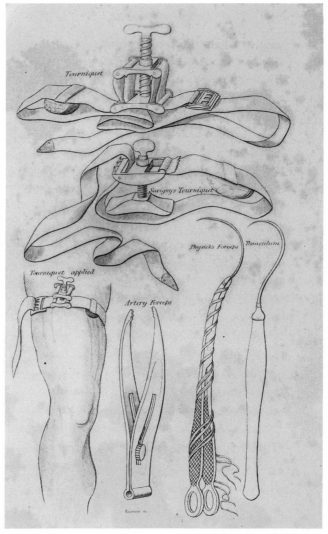

An illustration of the types of tourniquets, forceps, and tenaculum used in nineteenth-century wound management (Gibson, Institutes and Practice of Surgery, vol. 1)

forceps or a sharp, hook-shaped instrument known as a tenaculum, the physician placed a ligature around the vessel. To close the wound, physicians applied linen strips, spread with a resinous ointment, or adhesive plaster (see Glossary of Medical and Pharmaceutical Terms), over the wound. These strips of linen were commonly known as "adhesive straps." The surgeon completed the dressing by covering the adhesive straps with *another piece of linen. For more extensive wounds, doctors recommended the use of sutures or stitches.*

Adept at wound management, Lindsay employed the recommended ligature and adhesive straps for simple wounds and used stitches for more extensive wounds. He also recognized that bleeding quickly exacerbated the patient's condition and therefore saw the necessity of rapidly controlling the hemorrhage (Gibson, Institutes and Practice of Surgery, 1:67-78; Cooper, First Lines, 1:67-72; Dorsey, Elements of Surgery, 1:42-48).

Splitting Foot with the *Axe* Son of Jacob Delawta.

Mr 27. <1827?> was called to this boy 12 or 15 years old who had by an unlucky stroke of the axe cut thro the great Toe of the left Foot partly within the upper joint. the axe passing up between the Metatarsal bones of the 1st. & 2d. Toes. splitting the foot on the upper side up to the Instep, & on the under side about 2 1/2 or 3 Inches, was but little hemorrhage, dressed by 2 stiches below & 4 above with strips of adhesive intervening, passed one around the great toe, & several quite round the foot, & lapping over the ends on the upper side. In this case was a complete union by the first intention, had completely united & sycatrised in about 14 days & soon after was able to walk without use of crutch. being little lameness.

Had the bone not been cut, as it was quite off, or through & through, there would have been nothing in this case worth recording. but when the fact of so complete a union of the bone as there must have been in comparatively so short a time, have considered the case of sufficient interest to give it a place with other ordinary ones: This case occurred during my residence at Germantown O. and I now make the record nearly 10 years afterwards

Jany. 9. 1837   W. Lindsay

N.B. Last fall year ago had a similar case, occurred in Richmond, present residence in the person of a man by the name of Gipson <Leas?>. This case differed in not being cut so extensively, was not quite divided through the sole of the foot. and in dressing concluded to trust to the Adhes. Emplas alone, in this case was not so successful as the one above detailed. the failure I attribute to the neglect of the suture, or not making use of the stiches, consequently failed in keeping the cut so completely approximated as in the other case. The diference of age, probably had likewise something to do in the matter.

W.L.

Peter Albaugh's child. having got a sprig of cedar Top in the Esophagus. 23d. Mr. 1827 was called in great haste 5 or 6 miles to extract it.

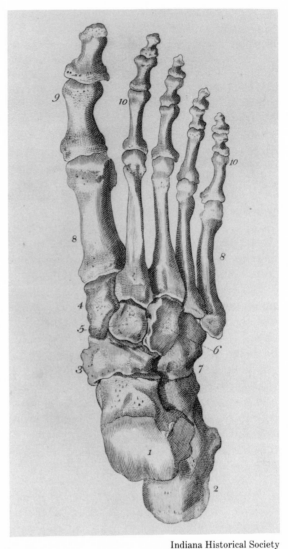

Indiana Historical Society

A drawing representing the bones of the foot. On the diagram, number 8 shows the five metatarsal bones to which Lindsay refers in the Case of Jacob Delawta. (Cheselden, The Anatomy of the Human Body)

The child at the breast, found it unable to suck or swallow, any fluid. The parents, mother particularly very much alarmed. On examination could just see with much difficulty the upper point of this substance, which from its peculiar formation & nature, was imposable for the child ever to have swallowed, or eject. I succeeded in my first attempt in dislodging & extracting, by means of the dressing curved Forceps, to the very great gratification of myself, Mother & friends. I dont recollect that I have ever been more caressed, or that a trifling circumstance ever in my practice was the occasion of more satisfaction & rejoicing.

Jany. 9. 1837
Richmond Ia.   *W. Lindsay*

Wm. Klinger. Extirpation of Tumour from his left Side.

Operated on him 30th. Dec 1828. The Tumor was about the sise of a hens Egg, was pendulous, or loosely situated under the skin. In *operating* unfortunately cut into it (the sack), altho, believe it was completely incisted, & think I missed it much in thus evacuating its contents, which was of about the consistence of cream or healthy puss [*sic*].[47] which emited a remarkably fetid odour. The operation gave a great deal of pain, in healing found it very troublesome, & tedious requiring a time of 6 or 8 weeks, had I succeeded as I should in dissecting it clean out with its inveloping membrane, presume I should have succeeded much better in effecting a cure. I am at a loss to give this tumor a name, perhaps that of *Melicerous* may be appropriate. and as regards diathesis, perhaps *Strumous*, in character. The period of cure was attended by much pain & suffering to the patient, produced much loss of flesh & consequent debility. This much have the satisfaction of stating that the cure so far as I have had any opportunity of knowing has been permanent.

W.L.

Mr. Clemmer's Son case which had strong symptoms of *Lock Jaw* or *Tetanus*. In Month of Mr. 1829. was called to see this young man who from Being engaged in making spickets or spiles out the Elder, by runing out the pith with a heated spindle of a big spinning wheal.[48] unfortunately ran the spindle through the hand between the Thumb & forefinger in the thick part of the hand, the Iron spindle lodging against the skin on the back of the hand. What improprieties he was guilty of, or how he had been treated the first few days have forgotten this part of the history of his case, it was about 2 or 3 weeks after the injury I was called in, when I found him with strong symptoms of

47. Healthy suppurative matter, or pus, was white and described as having the consistency of cream. When cold, it had an offensive odor. Unhealthy suppurative matter, in contrast, consisted of globules and flaky particles floating in a transparent fluid or pus (Hooper, *Lexicon Medicum*, 2:222-23).

48. Large wheels were used for spinning wool, small wheels for spinning flax.

Tetanus or Lock Jaw. The hand had been in a high degree of inflamation. was much swolen, & the ha[n]d had put on the appearance of
gangrene. The nervous system highly affected, severe pain extended
up the arm, extreme pain in the head—& back some stiffness of the
Jaws, occasional spasms, a general listlessness. Twitching of the mus-
sles of the face, attended by a difficulty in speaking, & articulation.
The hand had become benumbed, the puncture in the hand discharging
a thin bloody, & very offensive matter, The wrist was highly inflamed
& it seemed as if nature was about to effect a seperation in the carpus
between the arm & the hand. On my first visit I made a puncture quite
through the hand which as before stated had extended in the first
injury, nearly through the hand, the skin only remaining unabraded
over the puncture on the back of the hand. I ordered a poultice of
Elm[49] Peruvian Barks, Charcoal & East [yeast] prepared in a decoction of Dogwood, Slipery Elm, & Oak Bark[50] which was afterward
changed for the light bread & milk. In this decoction made as hot as
could well be borne, had the arm from the elbow down & hand immersed from 15 to 30 minutes frequently repeated. This seemed to
give great relief to the pain & appeared also much to relieve the
spasms before described. for a day or two, the hand still continued of
the leaden & gangrenous appearance, & on my 2d. visit took my Instruments, & remained all night with my patient, expecting that an
amputation of the hand would be necessary, The next morning symptoms appeared rather more favorable, having put my patient on the
free use of wine & decoction of the barks, in as large portions as the
stomach would bear, about the 3d. day from my first attentions. The
inflamation of the wrist had come to supuration, & was lanced. this
being a healthy discharge, seemed much to releive the whole arm. by
this time the unhealthy discharge from the puncture or place of injury
in the hand had nearly ceased discharging the puffy swelling had much
subsided, and the dead gangrenous appearence began to change for
that of a more healthy one. In the course of a few days more the
inflamation at the carpus had pretty much subsided. & the suppuration
soon was now very trifling which in a few days more subsided altogether. By this time the young man had began to improve in every
respect, the nervous & feverish excitement had given way to a more
healthy action of the general functions. & in something like 2 weeks
he was again able to sit up & walk a little about the room. I would
again remark that the bath as described heated as hot as could be

49. Lindsay's poultice most likely consisted of the barks of the slippery elm. See
Glossary of Medical and Pharmaceutical Terms, s.v. "Elm, slippery."
50. Lindsay possibly used either white oak bark or black oak bark in this decoction. See Glossary of Medical and Pharmaceutical Terms, s.v. "Oak, black or white."

borne, in which the hand & arm was frequently immersed for a considerable time, seemed to have an excellent effect. and in my practice since have frequently resorted to the hot bath, in cases of a high degree of inflamation and severe pain, either of the arm hand or foot. The particular preperation, or composition of the bath, think is a matter of less importance than the Temperature. myself am much troubled with corns on my Toes, which occasionly on becoming irritated inflame & produce the most acute pain & sufering. In these cases the hot foot bath gives more relief than the best emolient & soothing Poultises. In Felons or Whitlows of the fingers & hand have seen much benifit from it. And were I called to treat a case of inflamed nerve or Tendon, threatening Tetanus, should have great confidence in this as a very important means of releiving my suffering patient. The bath should be used so hot as to counteract the pain of the injured part. so hot as scarcely to be endured at first.

I had forgotton to notice that so soon as the wrist had supurated & was lanced, in a short time omited the poultises. & the hot bath was not longer necessary. for the poultice I now substituted as an emb[r]ocation & linament, a saturated preperation of Sweet oil[51] with camphor. This is an excellent embrocation, being soothing and anodyne. and I generally use it in cases where poultises have been necessary, after suppuration has been brot about. as well as a linament in many cases of inflamation & pain, where no supuration is induced or anticipated.

Richmond

Jany. 10. 1837   W. Lindsay

A Case of Phlebitis

P.S. While practising at West Alexandria O. some years ago was called to see the wife of a Mr. *Philip Hewit*, who during Parturition a few weeks previous had been bled in the arm.[52] which by the time I was called the vein had taken on a high degree of inflamation. The whole arm had become greatly swolen, & highly inflamed. The place in which the vein had been opened, had began to discharge a thin watry like fluid, along the course of the vein a distinct red streak seemed to mark the state of the inflamation. The whole system was now much affected

---

51. Although sweet oil could be any edible oil, it generally referred to olive oil. See Glossary of Medical and Pharmaceutical Terms, s.v. "Oil, olive."

52. Doctors often bled pregnant women. Healthy, pregnant women were not bled, but when disease threatened or labor was protracted or difficult, bloodletting was performed immediately and often resulted in phlebitis, or inflammation of a vein (Dewees, *Treatise on the Diseases of Females*, 195-96).

by this state of affairs. a high degree of Fever, which was marked by irregular exacerbations. accompanied by great nervous irritability. how far her fever was complicated with Puerpural [fever] am unable to say, but am of the opinion that Phlebitis or the inflamation induced by the venissection was the great & proximate cause[53] of the fever, consequent on the peculiar inflamation of the arm & vein. The whole system was peculiarly affected. the legs for instance seemed to be affected by a Rheumatic excitement, but might say more properly nervous or neuralgic. The pain of one particular limb or part of the body was so great and *accuto* (acute) that she could scarcely bear the weight of the bed clothes. & her position of recumbency could only be altered by the assistence of a nurse, & with all the care posable, in altering her position, she would cry out indicating the most acute suffering. So very cautiously & tenderly was the assistence obliged to be given in helping her to change her situation from one position to another, however trifling, several minutes was generally occupyed in effecting it. but when I commenced this case my principal object was to further instance the beneficial effects of the hot bath. In conjunction with emoluent poultises, a strong decoction of the *Hop*[s] (Humulus Lupulous) prepared qu[i]te hot in a bread Trey so as to admit the arm from a little above the elbow to be completely immersed, a period sometimes of 15 or 20 minutes & frequently repeated had a decided excellent effect in releiving the arm of its high toned pain & inflama-tion. before the inflamation could be repelled or had run its course. Supuration took place at *Two* or *three* points on the arm below the point of the bleeding in the hollow of the elbow, These points of supur-ation were small rising up a little like a Phlegmon. which when the matter was first discharged, did not continue to discharge longer at this point. As evidence that the arm was the cause of the feverish action, & Neuralgic distress before described when the arm began to amend, all these symptoms began to subside, & so soon as the arm was well all other bad symptoms had become exhausted, having worn themselves out & run their course.

53. According to the medical authority of the period, a proximate cause referred to the one underlying cause common to all diseases. The earliest and most persistent theory of disease was humoral pathology. For centuries physicians believed that an imbalance in the body's four fluids or humors was the one condition common to all diseases. In the seventeenth and eighteenth centuries, many physicians believed that spasms of the nervous system were responsible for disease. Thus Lindsay's reference to phlebitis as the proximate cause of the patient's fever was incorrect. Phlebitis would have been the exciting, or external, cause of the fever. More precisely, phlebi-tis was responsible for causing the spasms in the nervous system (Shryock, *Medicine and Society*, 49-53; Hooper, *Lexicon Medicum*, 2:209).

Having commenced this case under the head of a Post[s]cript. merely intending it as an instance of additional evidence of the good effects of the hot levigation, or emersion of a painful limb or part from severe swelling & inflamation, would say, induced from whatever cause. it was not my design to have given any thing like a detail of the case or of the treatment. would here remark that the Metastasis of the disease was followed up as it appeared in various parts of the body, & treated *per indication* without particular reference to the first cause of her disease, As before observed the whole system suffered much the general character neuralgic & a circumstance worthy of a passing notice was set on a highly nervous temperament. In general terms I would remark that various soothing & Anodyne Medicines were re- sorted to in the treatment. The various secretions required attention & were treated as above stated on the plan of indication. The liver & stomach suffered considerably. and required their usual appropriate medicines. when the knee, ancle, or foot took on the metastasis of the nervous irritation, The hot bath, soothing linaments, & applications, all members of the same class or family were all given a trial in turn, on the plan or principal of giving relief On the plan of counter irrita- tion. vesication was to some extent made use of. & for the time being generally promised a benifit to the patient. but the *hydra* character of the affection was such that it was no sooner repelled in one point than it would [a]ppear at some other point. as a change of medicine, as an anodyne & tranquiliser of the nervous irritation, after giving the opi- ates, & camphor a trial, the cicuta Ext.[54] was in the form of Pill made trial of, which were attended with apparently for the time being with some good effect. The opium & camphor combined generally gave rest & tranquility for a night. & until the combination had spent itself, & perhaps until the bowels from becoming torpid required, moving off. It was 3 or 4 weeks before this nervous irritability had exhausted itself. and it was not until about this time that, Tonics in their effects promised any advantage. The system had very much run down, the prostration of the powers of life was such that recovery was for a considerable time a matter of much doubt. her friends generally con- sidered the case a hopeless one, & myself was unable to hold out much encouragement. and if *Phlebitis* be admited was her disease. I had little to encourage me among my community of authors. & as regards my then experience, nothing. being the first of the kind opertunity of

54. Probably Lindsay was referring to the extract of cicuta, a term which nine- teenth-century physicians incorrectly used to apply to hemlock. See Glossary of Med- ical and Pharmaceutical Terms, s.v. "Hemlock."

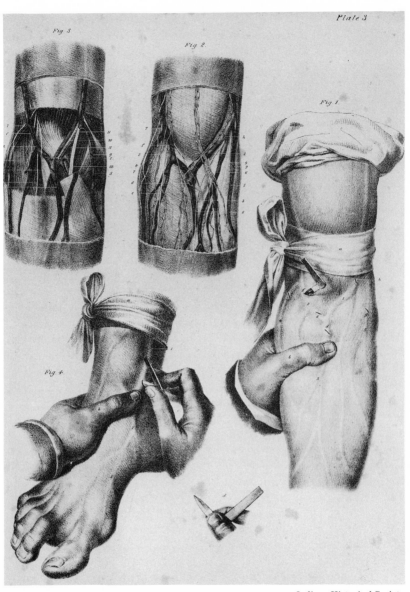

An illustration showing bloodletting, or phlebotomy, from the arm and the foot. Bloodletting was a commonly employed remedy during the nineteenth century. (Pancoast, A Treatise on Operative Surgery)

seeing had presented. & I might add it is fortunate for humanity such cases are of rare occurrence.

The foregoing case occured late in the fall of 1828.

Richmond, Jany. 11. 1837   W.L.

Mrs. Badon Case of *Phlebitis* In Summer of 1830. Treated this case in conjunction with my friend Dr. J. T. Plummer. It is my intention to give quite a brief notice of the above case. And should not notice it [at] all, only for its similarity to the foregoing case of *Mrs. Huit.* She like Mrs. Huit had been bled during her accouchment, which was quite protracted & difficult. The accouchment was managed by Dr. J. T. P. but owing to the difficulty of the case council was considered necessary, when I was called in. The bleeding was in the arm, appeared to be called for, & no doubt was well enough performed. The geting up during the first week or 10 days appeared fine, had been out in the garden, & had commenced spining at the little wheal,[55] being a hard working industrious woman no doubt left her room too early. The orifice from the bleeding, had not got quite well, but the soreness was so trifling no attention had been paid to it, until after she had been in the garden & took her seat at the spinning wheal. Soon after the arm began to be a little painful & the orrifice to shew a slight appearence of inflamation. A day or two afterwards the arm had become considerably swolen and the orifice began to emit a thin discharge. At the termination of about 2 weeks from her parturition I was called in, & found her in great distress & agony from the state of the arm, Fever had supervened. great nervous irritation pervaded the general System. In this as the foregoing case the arm ran into a high degree of inflamation & the pain was of the most acute character. To the general & local treatment in the course of a week after Dr. Plummer & myself were called in. the arm began to shew some symptoms of amendment. Our treatment had been the warm bath to the arm, frequently repeated, & Emoluent and soothing Linaments. Soon after the arm had began to shew symptoms of amendment one of her legs began to take on swelling, inflamation, & severe pain of the nuralgic or Rheumatic character. The usual treatment for Rheumatic & Neuralgic affections were resorted to,[56] & after a few days continuence. this Leg having become much better. the other leg, was taken in turn & ran about the same round of swelling & suffering as the first. & in like manner

---

55. On the small spinning wheel, see above, p. 47, n. 48.

56. As in the previous case of phlebitis, Lindsay probably used anodynes and narcotics such as opium and camphor for the disease's nervous character and liniments and stimulants for its rheumatic character.

Photograph by B&L Photographers, courtesy of the Indiana Medical History Museum
A thumb lancet, circa early-to-mid-nineteenth century. This instrument was commonly used for bloodletting.

yielded to the treatment now strong hopes were entertained that our patient was about to get well but delusive hope the arm a 2d. time took on inflamation & ran about the same round as before, & as before appeared to yield to the same or similar treatment as before. Again we flatered ourselves that the disease had worn itself out, and that our patient was in a hopeful way of recovery, but again vain delusive hope. when it was thought our servises could in a few days be dispensed with about this time, by a metastasis the lungs & breast was the next point of attack by this potent hydra. The Pleura & lungs seemed now the seat of the disease and such was the severity of the attack, in the now great debilitated state of the system, in a very few

Photograph by B&L Photographers, courtesy of the Indiana Medical History Museum
Spring lancet with case, early-nineteenth century. This instrument was used for bloodletting.

days our patient terminated her severe & protracted sufferings in death.

What the Puerperal irritation had to do, in this and the foregoing case, am at a loss to determine. and in what manner, or what was the bearing of the Parturient period on the venissection. with me is inexplicable speculation. That the venissection at another time, & under other circumstances, would have run into a development of Phlebitis. is with me a matter mantleed [*sic*] in doubt & uncertainty. So far as I have read have no recollection of a parallel case.

Richmond Jany 11. 1837   W. Lindsay

Journal 3

Lindsay's second journal is missing.

John Jays son, Fracture of the scull and Trephining Nov 8. 1831.

I was called to see this Boy at this date, in consultation with my old friend Dr. [Clement] Ferguson. who had been called in first. Mr. J. resides near [New] Paris [Ohio]. This call being made in the night the operation was performed same night.

During the day this young man who was probably about 15 years of age, was Kicked by a horse, on the side of the Head, the whole force of the injury was recd. on the upper part of the Ear & in the Temporal Bone. The upper portion of the Ear was cut off, most the whole of the *Os Tempora* was fractured, besides a portion of it drove in on the <brain?> rupturing bothe the Dura & pia Mater. The necessity of an operation was of course apparent and imperatively called for. The patient was in a kind of comatose, mutering delerium. and during the operation of the Trephine and the subsequent use of the raspatory in removin[g] sever[a]l fragments & spicula of bone, was almost insensible, and quite unconscious of pain, or of what was going on. The pulse was rather weak & slow, showing, or at least corrisponding with other symptoms of cerebral oppression.[1]

After having operated depleted, & moved the bowels by degress [degrees] the pulse rose, sensation & consciousness by degrees gradully returned, at the end of two or three weeks, symtoms of amendment & of recovery were quite flatering, however shortly after this, spongy granulations, or *Fungus cerebri* began to take place, and after all our prospects of recovery, our hopes proved to be fallacious. every effort was made to correct & suppress this morbid growth of the cerebral substence, by means of the compress & astringents, and when these failed the knife & escarotics were resorted to—but in 24 hours

1. Probably Lindsay was referring to a depressed skull fracture, with cerebral edema due to the extravasation of blood within the skull (See Journal 1, p. 2, n. 3, for symptoms of a depressed skull fracture).

Anatomical drawing showing the dura mater of the brain by W. A. Ashton, Franklin County, Indiana, circa 1850s

we almost invariably found that a fresh portion of this mushroom production, had sprung up, soon after this state of things had taken place
our patient began to loose ground, and at the termination of 5 weeks
he was releived of all his sufferings by death. This was the 2d. case I
had seen of Fungus cerebri, The other case was that of Moseby, whose
case is repoarted in the 1st. Manuscript volume [above pp. 6-8]. In his
case this spongy growth was stubburn, but at last yielded to compression, astringents, and at last to the application of the Red precipitate.
In Moseby's case the os Frontis was the part in which the injury had
been made. it will be recollected that Moseby recoverd. That fractures
of the Temporal bone are more fatal than of the Frontal, we are ad-
monished in our works on surgury.[2] But I have never seen a patient
apparently mend faster than young Jay did until Fungus cerebri took
place. and altho injuries of this part are almost universally fatal according to some authors, In this case notwithstanding the depression
& fracture was so very extensive, had the membranes not been ruptured, this young man would undoubtedly have recovered.

I should have mentioned that Dr. Whiterage,[3] & Dr. [James] Knox
(the latter then a student) both of New Paris also were present at the
operation and rendered me all the assistence in their powers

Friend Charles Osburn's Case of fracture of sons Head. Injyry [*sic*] of
the os frontis. operation Nov. 9th. 1833. at Economy [Indiana] 20 miles
distant from Richmond.

History of the case, some days previous to the above date young
Osburn with two or three other boys while in the woods amusing
themselves among the timber, one of the boys engaged with the axe
by accident struck young Osburn in the forehead, the latter having
inadvertently, and unobservingly of the danger, placed his head within
the range of the stroke of the axe while the former was busily engaged
in cutting at a stick of timber. The corner of the edge hiting on the
forehead in the edge of the hair probably about one inch on the right
side, from the central line of the top of the head.

My friend Dr. T. T. Butler then of Economy being called, on examination of the case discovered that the cut had cut some distence thro'
the bone & fractured the scull. And from the agrevated symptoms of

2. The works of surgery to which Lindsay was referring could not be located.
Fractures to the frontal bone are not necessarily more fatal than those of the temporal, but since the frontal bone is thicker than the temporal bone, a fracture can
result only from a severe blow to that area.

3. Either Dr. John or Dr. Peleg Whiteridge of Preble County, Ohio. See Glossary
of Personal and Place Names.

the case was of the opinion that an operation was necessary. On the same day I received the call I set out for Economy & got there just before nightfall. In this case there was no want of consciousness, nor did there appear to be as yet much cerebral derangement. However a high degree of fever, considerable degree of pain in the head attended by some derangement of the stomach, seemed to call for a critical examination of the injury—on cutting down, and dissecting back the integuments it was evident that there was some portion of the scull depressed, and that there was some considerable fracture.

Assisted by Dr. Butler I applyed the Trephine operating by candle light. The operation was attended by considerable pain, but the patient bore up under it with considerable fortitude. I left the case the next morning under charge of Docr. Butler. For several days Inflamation and Fever (accompanied by extensive swelling of the forehead & face) continued to keep up with considerable severity. and it was considered that the patient during several days could not survive, however, by prompt & close attention of Dr. Butler, during which he had the room darkened, and confined the patient to a strict antiphlogistic treatment, this unfortun[ate] youth in a few weeks time perfectly recovered and has ever since enjoyed good health. and is possessed with a promising intellect.

Son of Danl. Pucket Trephining Dec. 31. 1831. History of the Case.

This young man from an early age had been afflicted with something like Lunar Epileptic Fits[4] which of late years had become very alarming, had considerably affected his intellect, These fits now lasted a week or more, and during that time probably would have from 20 to 30 spasms. when a period subsided he was left in a weakly debilitated situation and for something like another week generly lay in a comatose stupor, gradually geting over this and rousing up he would probably enjoy a few days some what rational, or at least was more so than at any other period, but at the end of another week about, he would commence a period of restlessness during which he became very talkative, irritable and quarrelsome, and so unmanageable that the mother & sisters were in continuel dread when his father was absent, requiring harsh treatment from his Father to keep him in subjection,

This was something like the routine of his symptoms, being accompanied by a constant distress in the head, so very distressing that he

4. In the nineteenth century, lunar was a synonym for lunatic. By lunar epileptic fits, Lindsay may have meant epileptic seizures accompanied by mania, or temporary insanity (Dunglison, *Medical Lexicon*, 528).

at times would plead with his friends to bore his head with an augur in hopes that the operation would give exit to a collection of fluid or matter which would give him alleviation,

From the success of an operation being performed on an acquaintence of the family, viz that of Trephining many years ago in the state of N.C. by a surgeon at Salem of the Moravian Society,[5] which case was, as was represented, very similar to the case of this young man now under consideration. The Father and some of his friends brot this young man to me wishing me to operate on him, if I should think the operation would promise any reasonable prospect of a cure, or amendment. at the same time citing the N.C. case, and to the individual himself an Elderly friend by the name of Kersey residing in the neighborhood of Milton [Indiana] this County. I gave the Father and friends no encouragement, as I had too little experience to form an opinion on the propriety of the operation. I knew, & so informed them, that Dr. Dudley[6] & perhaps some others had operated under certain circumstances, had been successful, and recommended the operation as being justifyable and correct, in cases in which Epilepsey could be pretty satisfactorily traced to a depression of the scull, which, in some cases, was said to have been from injuries of infancy, or youth, inducing years subsequently, & continuing unabated for years, or for lifetime. In others, operations had proved Epilepsey had, on operating, been cured and found to have been induced by spicula of bone, growing from the inner table of the cranium, & shooting downward or inward on the brain, being thus the cause of great irritation.

On examination of his case I could see nothing like a depression from previous injury or any other cause, but that in the point he complained of such great distress, It might be posable that a spicula of bone was penetrating the cerebral substance. The young man was now taken home for the present, but after some time His Father and friends again brot the young man with them to consult me on the subject of an operation. I had taken it upon myself in the mean time to pay Friend Kersey a visit who had been operated on by the Salem

5. Moravians: a German-speaking Protestant sect opposed to war. The sect arose in eastern Bohemia in the sixteenth century. During the first half of the eighteenth century, some of its members emigrated to Georgia and Pennsylvania, where they did much missionary work among the Indians. In 1766 they established a community at Salem, North Carolina, which later merged with the town of Winston to form Winston-Salem.

6. Possibly Dr. Benjamin Winslow Dudley, a noted surgeon who taught anatomy and surgery at Transylvania University in Lexington, Kentucky, during the early nineteenth century (Robert Peter, *The History of the Medical Department of Transylvania University* [Louisville: John P. Morton & Company, 1905], 15-26).

Surgeon of N.C.—And after a consultation concerning the case by a committee of the society of friends, who concurred in the experiment of an operation, I very reluctenly consented to operate.

The point which the young man complained of, as being the seat of this distress, was in the right parietal, rather between the sagital suture & the organ of cautiousness as held, or located by Phrenologists.[7] On removing the piece by the Trephine no spicula of bone existed there, neither was any morbid or unnatural appeerence discoverable.

The wound was dressed in the usual manner by bringing the scalp up, & approximating its edges, in juxta position by means of a few stiches assisted also in the interstises by the Emplas Adhesivum [adhesive plaster]. The wound had united completely by the 5th. day by the first intention, but The patient was soon after the operation manafesting symptoms of his wrestless, loquatious, and ungovernable exacerbations approaching; & in a day or two was so frantic that he was with dificulty kept in bed, or from escaping from the room. Epalepsey in the course of 6 days came on—And a few convulsions terminated his sufferings.

This turned out to be truly an unpleasent case for me, & I was indeed sorry that I consented to operate, however, it must be recollected that all hopes of curing the young man by the usual or any other medical treatment was hopeless he was a source of great distress & dread to his Family. his sufferings beyond description, & now almost entirely an idiot. It must likewise be recollected that his Father & relatives had submited the propriety of an operation to the church, which, had been under the deliberations of a special committe; which committe had repoarted favorable, & recommended an operation. I

7. Phrenologists believed the skull was divided into thirty-seven different regions, each representing a certain human characteristic such as hope, wonder, firmness, and cautiousness. An enlargement, or "bump," on the cranium implied that the individual was endowed with an excess of the particular faculty or characteristic whereas a depression meant a lack of that trait. The section for cautiousness was located above the ear (O. S. Fowler, *Fowler's Practical Phrenology: Giving a Concise Elementary View of Phrenology* [New York: Fowler and Wells, 1853], 33-35, 54, 44-45).

Phrenology, or the science of the mind, was developed in the late 1790s by Austrian physician Franz Joseph Gall (1757-1828) and popularized by his colleague Johann Gaspar Spurzheim (1776-1832). Phrenology became popular in England in the 1820s and in America during the 1830s. Its advocates included many well-known physicians, who established phrenological societies throughout America in the 1830s and 1840s. During the same period, itinerant phrenologists traveled to towns and villages across the country to preach their new gospel (John D. Davis, *Phrenology: Fad and Science, A Nineteenth-Century American Crusade* [1955; reprint, Hamden, Connecticut: Archon Books, 1971], 1-45).

would willingly have left this case unrepoarted, but considering it a duty to repoart my unsuccessful, as well as successful cases, could not consistently omit giving it a place. The record here made I know to be substantially correct, & is as faithfully recorded as my successful ones.

Case of Joseph Edgarton's Son, Fracture of scull and loss of Brain,

Operation Sept. 5. 1835, History of the case.

This boy was about 10 years old. was run over by a horse in the door yard,[8] The injury was in the right Temporal Muscle. The Physician first called was Dr. Trout of Germantown [Indiana] this County 14 or 15 miles west of Richmond near where Mr. J. Edgarton then resided. On the 9th. day after the injury I was called with instructions to take my case of Trephining Instruments[9] along with me. On arriving there I found that the fracture was considerably extensive, and was informed that a considerable quantity of Brain had been discharged from the wound, during the time that had elapsed since the injury.

I took my friend Dr. Swain with me as I passed thro' Centreville. and Met Dr. Trout the attending Physician at the place. Having cut down & dissected back the scalp & Temporal muscle. it was evident that the fracture was extensive, and that a portion of the scull some what more extensive than the cork of the shoe, which it was beleived had knocked down the scull, was buried in the Brain. as it was evident that some portion of the cerebral substance was anteriour, and which filled up the fisure,

I proceeded to remove a circular piece of the scull of the Os frontis, from the opening thus made, and was enabled by means of the raspatory & forceps[10] to remove the depressed portions of the scull, which consisted of several pieces, During the removal of which, a quant[it]y of Brain was removed also, probably amounting to a Table spoonfull or thereabouts.

Notwithstanding the great delay & number of days that had elapsed, the boy had not shewn any delirium or stupor, I think he had complained of some Gastric derangement. as well as some fever. The

8. Dooryard: the yard surrounding the door of a dwelling.

9. A complete set of trephining instruments would have included two or three trephines, or cylindrical saws (ranging from one-half inch to one inch in diameter), a Hey's saw or semicircular saw, a lenticular (an instrument with a hollow, semispherical head which was used to depress the brain, remove pieces of bone, and trim the edges of the skull), two elevators, one pair of trepan forceps, a brush for cleaning the saws, a probe, tenacula, sponges, crooked needles, and a scalpel (Gibson, *Institutes and Practice of Surgery*, 2:187-88).

10. Doctors used a special type of forceps in trephining operations. Trepan forceps were double-edged and used to grasp small and large pieces of bone.

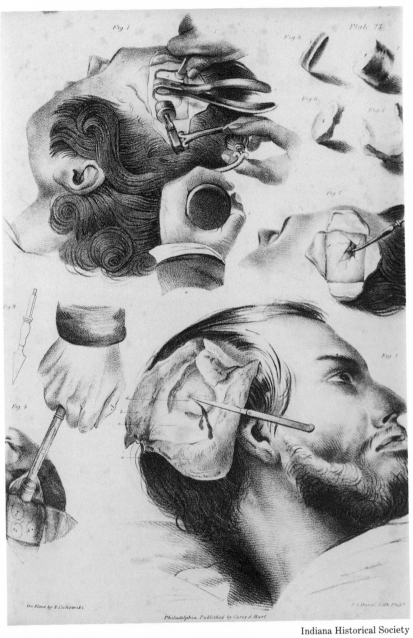

Drawing illustrating the operation of trephining (Pancoast, A Treatise on Operative Surgery)

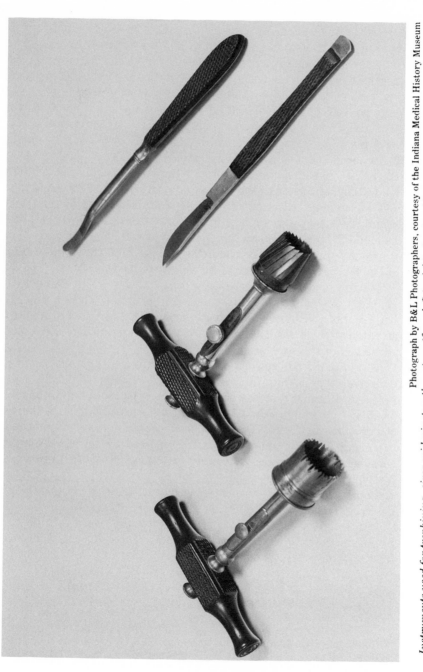

Photograph by **B&L Photographers, courtesy of the Indiana Medical History Museum**

Instruments used for trephining, circa mid-nineteenth century (from left to right): two trephines, a small scalpel, and raspatory

boy was as sensable of his situation as any boy could have been expected to be of his age & inteligence. and by the by he was a smart little fellow. Having made known to him my views of his case & the necesity of an operation, I shall never forget the earnestness with which he emplored me not to operate on him. and he so far worked on my feelings & sympathies that it was with much dificulty that I could man my self up to the operating point; I had a son at home near his size & age,[11] and could not help anticipating what my feelings would have been, had this unfortunate boy been my own son thus emploringly pleading with me not to operate on him. His feeling Mother left the house unable to see the operation her son so much dreaded, while his Father lay Sick with the Fever[12] in another bed in the same room. But I was much encouraged in the operation which I so reluctently commenced, by the manly resignation & fortitude of my patient, when he found the operation was commenced & would be performed.

Having operated and finished the dressing I left the boy in the care of Dr. Trout who had subsequently charge of the case.

In a few weeks he had recovered, I have never seen a case get over an injury & an operation of the kind so well. & in so short a time, and Dr. Trout is undoubtedly entitled to much credit for the u[n]remitting attentions which the patient received from him during his recovery subsequent to the operation.

The loss of brain did not seem to be attended by any bad consequences either in retarding his recovery, or injury of faculties after recovery. I cannot discover that his intellect has suffered in the least. The boy is now (more than 3 years since the operation) in the immediate neighborhood of Richmond, I have seen him several times since the operation. The quantity of scull removed by the operation was considerable, & of necessity has left an extensive surface unprotected by the natural bony covering,

I must not omit here to mention that my friend Dr. Swain as well as Dr. Trout rendered me important servises in the operation.

The extent of scull removed in the operation were I to be more precise or definite would say it would have equaled some thing more than a Twenty five cent piece had the irregular extent been brot into

11. Lindsay's son, LaFayette, was born on April 8, 1826 (Lindsey M. Brien, *A Genealogical Index of Miami Valley Pioneers* [Dayton: Dayton Circle, Colonial Dames of America, 1970], 102).

12. The patient here most likely was suffering from a malarial fever or ague, which was prevalent during this time of the year. Malarial fevers were so common in newly settled areas of Indiana that many considered ague a natural part of frontier life, rather than a disease (Pickard and Buley, *Midwest Pioneer*, 16-17).

a circle. In the operation the *Temporal artery* had to be taken up b[e]ing cut in dissecting up the integuments.
Mr. 10th. 1839
Richmond. Ia.

Operation July 18th. 1833

Of taking up the right Radial Artery 18 days after one of its branches were wounded on the back of the hand. Case of John Mackey of Preble County Ohio.

History of the case as I learned it from the paytient [*sic*] himself and Dr. Ferguson who was first called to him, was, that by some accident which is not now recollected the branch of the radial artery on the back of the hand between the second joint of the Thumb & the Third Joint of the first finger. Mackey, on wounding it, managed by such applications as his family, & assisted by some of his neighbors, were capable of making, after the loss of considerable blood, to stop the hemorrhage, Burnt allum[13] & Coperas or Sulp. Ferri [*Ferri sulphas* or iron sulfate] in solution were all tried probably, and what more am not informed, but finally was stoped by cording the *wrist*. in this way the family and patient got along with it during a week or about that time, The artery always breaking out again in some hours after the hemorrh[a]ge being thus treated & commanded.

Dr. F. after attending some days on this man had him brot to his own house. But notwithstanding every astringent & every application that could be made, the bleeding was sure to return again if not sooner at the farthest the next day, or so soon as sufficient reaction took place.

On the 18th. day after the accident Dr. F. sent his then student, now Dr. [James] Knox, to get me to go with him to Paris to see what I could do for his unfortunate patient. On arriving at Dr. Fergusons I was much astonished at the paleness and the weakening effects consequent on this severe depletion, The Bleeding had been stopped some hours which had occured on that day, and which was so alarming when Dr. Knox set out for me, the blood that the patient supposed he had lost, do not now pretend to recollect precisely, but think it was several gallons, the blood was now said to have become very pale, and he no doubt had lost more blood than he had in his system when in health, but new blood* being all the time furnished to some extent, must have

---

* Thro' the process of nutrition and the medium of eliminating the lacteals.

13. Lindsay was probably referring to powdered alum. See Glossary of Medical and Pharmaceutical Terms, s.v. "Alum, powdered."

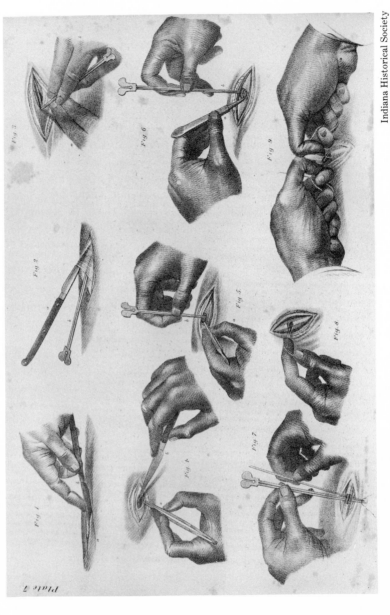

Drawing illustrating the general procedures for ligating arteries (Pancoast, A Treatise on Operative Surgery)

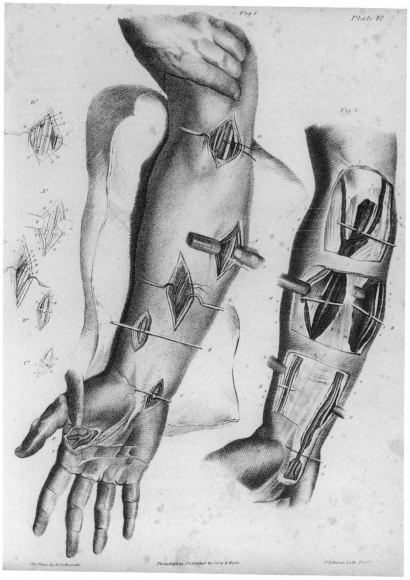

Drawing illustrating the ligation of arteries in the arm. Fig. 1, B shows the ligation of the inferior third of the radial artery. (Pancoast, A Treatise on Operative Surgery)

been the means of keeping him alive. The hemorrhage frequently kept up until arrested by *ad deliquium animi*.[14] The various applications which had been made to the wound & the effect of resorting so frequently to the ligature or cord around the *wrist*, had been the means of swelling the hand & wrist very much indeed. The wounded place over the wounded artery had the appearence of approaching gangrene. And the ligature had had such effect in denuding & chafing the skin and flesh on the wrist where it had been applyed that it could not be longer bourne.

I said the patient had become very pale, such was his palor & blanched appearence that the term exsanguinated would well have applyed to his appearence and situation. And during the operation which I performed on him, he was unable to sit up. but remained reclined, as I found him on arriving there on a palate on the floor. I operated by making an incisi[o]n about two inches long the cour[s]e, & immediately over, the Raidial Artery in the wrist. having laid it bare I passed two ligatures around it at about an inch apart & then bissected the artery, and finished the operation by applying adhesive strips across the incision so as to approximate the edges of it, leaving the Ligatures hanging out.

The operation was completely successful. In due time—I think about 3 weeks from the period of the operation his arm was well and he [was] fast recovering from the debility induced by the loss of Blood. Mr. 10th. 1839
Richmond Ia.

Operation on Mr. Beard Esqr. of Dark[e] Co. O.

Case of Sarcomatous Tumor of the nose, or som[e]what such affection, which seemed to have produced a spongoid cancellated state of a large portion of the bones of the face as well as nearly the whole of the nose. Operated Nov. 23d. 1831 History of the Case—This diseased Tumour of the nose had been slowly developing for several years. and when I saw him first a short time previous to operating on him, had grown out on the centre of the nose, or rather to the left side, of the volume of about an English walnut. of a red cherry colour, which was solid and unyielding to the sense of touch & pressure. For the last few months it increased much faster than it had done previously. and had so grown downward or inward, as to almost entirely to obstruct breathing thro' the nose,

I think several years previous to this he had been operated on by a Dr. Thomas, since decd. who was an English surgeon of some notoriety

14. *Ad deliquium animi*: to fainting.

Indiana Historical Society
An illustration of a man suffering from a cancerous tumor of the nose (Robert
Liston, Practical Surgery: With One Hundred and Thirty Engravings on Wood *[Phil-*
adelphia: James Crissy, 1838])

& considerable merit, & who resided on Paddey's run either in Butler
or Hamilton Co. O.

In the operation as performed by me on the date above, I was met
in consultation by Drs. Ferguson, Whiterage,[15] and Knox. I made an
attempt to lay back the skin by dissection, and then remove[d] the
tumefyed portion, which I did so far as seemed prudent. but on cutting
'round the tumour, what, from a superficial vi[e]w, seemed to be its

15. Either Dr. John or Dr. Peleg Whiteridge of Preble County, Ohio. See Glossary
of Personal and Place Names.

boundery, and cutting down and dissecting it out, it was then evident the malar bones of the face, extending up into the cribiform plate of the nose were all in a morbid spongoid condition, The mallar portions were yielding on presure giving way under presure with a kind of elasticity. The portion of sarcoma or spongy exostosis[16] when removed, presented, on a close examination, to be composed of diverging ossific or cartilaginous radii, diversifyed, with fleshy substance somewhat after the growth of the pith, or cortical portion of the stock of Indian Corn. In the operation I did not cut thro' the nasal process, but to have removed the whole of the spongy growth, and bone now diseased by this affection would probably have required the removal of the whole of the nose, and the ossa male of the face. This I did not think prudent to do. The operation was attended by considerable hemorrhage, & the diseased portion in its fleshy integuments, were considerably vascular but there was no artery that required to be taken up, the hemorrhage being commanded by the application of Alum water & the sponge.

This operation for a month or two seemed to have given some relief, and partially to have removed the affection, but in a the [*sic*] cource of a few months this again began to develope itself in a new growth on the nose, Other physicians were called, one of whom pronounced it cancer & as is usual with this class of Empirics,[17] gave the patient high prospects of cure, at the same time denouncing all others who had treated his case as ignorant & unprincipaled. but this "cure all" of a "cancer cognomen christener" acquired for himself but a cobweb standing for emin[en]ce & skill in this case, for as might have been expected his escharotics only added *torment* (torture) to suffering—And under this treatment in a few weeks Mr. B. was releived of all suffering by the kind hand of death. no doubt much assisted in his official acquisition by the servises of his friend *Mr. Cancer Doctor.*

Amputation of Finger, Threatening Lock Jaw, followed by Gangrene & Mortification. Amputation Dec. 18th. 1831

This young man whose name I have forgotten was a laboring man on the farm of a Mr. W. Woods, an Englishman residing about 11 miles

16. Sarcoma and exostosis were classified as two distinct types of tumors. While a sarcomatous tumor was a fleshy growth, exostosis was a bony tumor. Neither classification is used today, because tumors are classified by their cell type.

17. To nineteenth-century physicians, empirics were doctors who lacked formal training, practiced with no medical theory, obtained their cures by a hit-or-miss system, and proclaimed their abilities in newspapers (Joseph E. Kett, *The Formation of the American Medical Profession: The Role of Institutions, 1780–1860* [1968; reprint, Westport, Conn.: Greenwood Press, 1980], 97).

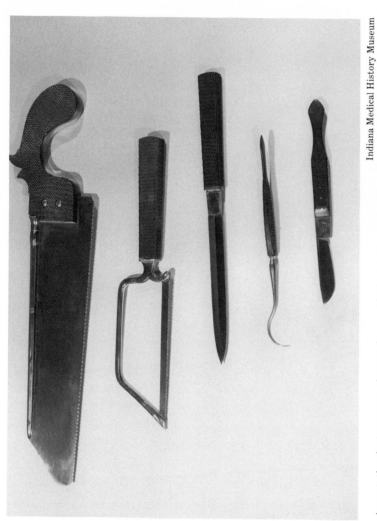

Amputation instruments, circa early-to-mid-nineteenth century (from top to bottom): large bone saw, small bone saw, double-sided flesh knife, tenaculum, and scalpel

Indiana Medical History Museum

s. west of this place. When intoxicated he got into an affray with another man who in the rencounter bit one of his fingers. Some days after the injury the finger having swelled and inflamed, being attended by rigours and a high toned nervous & spasmodic Exacerbations My friend Dr. [W. J.] Matchet was called, of the vilage of Abington, what was the treatment of Dr. A. [*sic*] have now forgotten. The symptoms however continuing so violent it was thought the finger would have to be amputated, and it now about this time had put on a gangrenous appearence in & around the part. Having been called in this state of the case, it was concluded that an application of Lytta Emplas [emplastrum lyttae or blistering plaster]. should be made to the finger, which was now enormously enlarged, and general symptoms should be met by Dr. M. as seemed to be indicated. I had hoped that on the principle of counter irritation and its reputed properties of arresting grangrene [*sic*] and mortification under some circumstances that it was worthy a triel [*sic*] in this case, But in this case I was disappointed. for in two days I was again called. & the gangrene & mortification appeared to have been increased by the vesication of the Lytta. The vesicles drawn by it were now highly gangrenous, and really in the 2d. stage of mortification. I now had to take off the finger at the 3d. joint at its union with the hand. In this case the action must have been too nervous or it was too high toned, or too late applyed. If the Lytta application is ever serviseable, (& I think it had a good effect in the Case of Lucinda Dunkin,[18] besides we have the sanction of Chapman[19] at least) I think it must be in a low grade of excitement and where nature requires a stimulent to assist in seperating, between a dead & a living substence

On the removal of the Finger this young man was releived of his neuralgic & spasmodic exacerbations. And in two weeks the hand was nearly healed. And the general health nearly restored.

Richmond Ia.
Mar. 11th. 1839

---

18. Lucinda Dunkin's case probably appeared in the second volume, the Lindsay journal now missing.

19. Nathaniel Chapman (1780-1853) was a well-known Philadelphia physician. In 1816 he began teaching the Theory and Practice of Medicine at the University of Pennsylvania and in 1820 founded the *Philadelphia Journal of Medical and Physical Sciences.* He wrote *Discourses on the Elements of Therapeutics,* 2 vols. (1817-19) and *An Essay on the Canine State of Fever* (1801). In the latter book, Chapman discussed the nature of hydrophobia.

Amputation of a Finger. Son of Mr. Murray, Keeper of the Poor house of Wayne Co. Ia. Operated Oct. 15. 1835

This youth about the age of 14 or 15 years old had when I first saw him been laboring under a morbid enlargement of the finger. There had been no abrasion of surface, swelling, or inflamation, but simply a puffy enlargement, yet not edematous. The generel health with the exception of the influence of the finger was good, however this finger had occasioned a great deal of distress frequently so violent as to interrupt sleep.

The enlargement was probably more of the Elephantiasis appearence than any other affection to which I could compare it with to give any thing like a just idea of it, which extended from the nail or near it to the 3d. joint. I learned that it had been blistered, without any aparent benefit, also various embrocations and Linaments had been used all of which had been abandoned in turn. As it had been of several years standing and was considered to be rather, tho' slowly, & almost imperceptably, on the increase, I could perceive no probable cure for it by the efforts of nature, and the treatment which next to amputation seemed to promise the most had already been tried. I was clearly of the opinion that an amputation was the only means of cure.

On removing it and dissecting it, was found that the enlargement was owing to a tissue of very healthy looking fat, regularly and naturally contained within the celular membrane, having removed this tissue of adipose growth & celular membrane, so far as I could discover the finger underneath was entirely healthy and natural. This tissue just described of adipose substence was found as abundent around the first & second joints as on any other part of the fingers, and I am still of the opinion that amputation was the only means of cure.

I said that this tissue of adipoase substance was healthy & natural, In this expression I wish to be understood as being true in regard to its growth and healthful appearence, but that it should be the cause of pain, & really a disease & yet altogether *natural & healthy, adeps*[20] can only be satisfactorily explained by considering it as a foreign & extraneous substance. Thus we would admit & contend, that a good proportion of the adipose substance when properly arranged and distributed is a symptom of good health,* but when it takes place around a joint as in this case in the form of a thick cushion thus obstructing

* and is important to good and perfect symatry.

20. Adeps is lard, or the purified fat of hogs. Lindsay probably meant adipose, or fat tissue.

the free motion of the joints as it did in this, the joints being almost stiff and Anchalosed, however healthy it may be in its growth & composition, still inasmuch as it is out of place, it must be considered as a morbid & diseased state of things, and that the finger as in this case was laboring under a morbid growth of adipose substance.

Richmond Ia.

Mr. 11th. 1839

Case of Retention of the Placenta which I was called to remove 36 hours after Parturition. Jany. 17th. 1835

History of the case—

Mrs. Mabbit of Union Co. some 10 or 12 miles south of this place, Having had a dificult & somewhat protracted labor, the child still born. The Placenta after the labor was thro' was found to be retained & by all the means made use of by those in attendance could not be disengaged. Under this state of things I was sent for & found a Midwife and her Physician Dr. [R.] Tardy then of Liberty [Indiana] in attendance.

The patient I found in a state of considerable prostration, (having suffered under the weakening effects of a free Puerperal Hemorrhage.) & much mental solicitude accompanied by considerable gastric derangement.

On obtaining all the information I could of her situation from Dr. T. I proceeded to make a manuel exexamination [*sic*]. I found the uterus to have strongly contracted on the Placenta, so much so that the hand could not at all be passed into the uterus by any thing like moderate force or exertion. The *Secale* had been given to as great an extent as the stomach would bear,[21] and no bearing down had been induced. but seemed rather to have induced a stronger contraction of the uterus, such in labor as would be called the hour glass contraction, but such as in other situations would be called the Tonic contraction.

I next proceeded to gently dilate the womb & introduce the hand this was indeed a formidable undertaking, and required several hours to accomplish it, & having made use of the right hand u[n]til it was useless, owing to the great resistence & contraction made by the uterus, next introduced the left, and operated with it until it in turn was disabled, by this time the right one had so far rested & regained its use that I was enabled to operate in this way first with one & then the other until I at last had overcome the contraction so far as to be able to introduce a hand; when, I found the Placenta strongly adhering

21. Lindsay liberally employed ergot in cases of protracted labor (see Case of Mrs. Thornton, pp. 114-23 below), but apparently did not know about the drug's harmful effects. See Glossary of Medical and Pharmaceutical Terms.

by its whole surface to the womb. This In my practice I have always found a dificult & unpleasant operation under the most favorable circumstances, but in the present situation it was truly so. which was doubly perplixing owing to the great pressure of the uterus being constantly kept up. no one can properly or correctly judge of the great dificulty of an operation, & the astonishing force which the uterus strongly contracting is capable of exerting on the hand of an operator, unless he has had the experience of a case. I was fully 2 hours in dilating the uterus, and fully another hour in detaching the placenta after having dilated the uterus sufficiently to introduce the hand. The operation was attended by excruciating suffering to the patient, and I felt sometimes fearful that she would be unable to bear up under it, and I was several times compelled to desist a short time owing to the exhausted and sinking exacerbations induced by the operation.

I remained with the patient all night, and in the latter part of it she seemed to get some rest, This was the only concern or part I had in the case. however she recoverd, but she was quite an enfeebled delicate female, and her recovery was tedious. I think her health is now tolerable, and for any thing I know as good as it was previous to this accouchment.

Castrotomy, Case of Mr. H. Hoover of the viscinity of Indianapolis. Operation July 1838

History of the case, When I first saw him, he was reduced quite low, had been 6 or 8 weeks confined to his room & the greater part of the time in bed. And at the time I saw him had sinking spells, which were preceded by much restlesness, something like a Febrile paroxysm, accompanied by a kind of neuralgic exacerbation severe pain in the back & Kidneys, in the Right Testis, being the one affected, shooting up the spermatic cord, sometimes extending to the head, & sometimes attended by a tremulous quivering agitation of the whole body,

On my enquiries concerning what was the primary injury, I could not learn any thing satisfactorily, the patient spoke something of having strained himself at heavy lifting, and I think I learned also that the Testis had received some direct injury, but have now forgotten the particulars of the case. He had been seen by severel Physicians and the prevailing opinion was that it was Hydrocele Some supposed that it was sazrcocele [sarcocele]. On my first examination it was my opinion that it was a case of Schirrous Testicle. I also gave it as my opinion that an operation was imperatively necessary to a recovery. tho' I really feared that it was now too late, I operated, being assisted by Dr. Wilson, who was now the attending Physician.—nothing occurred particularly worthy of notice during the operation, The Testis was found highly diseased, and on cutting into it was found to contain some supurative matter, also some fluid of a serous appearence.

But the operation was delayed too long; tho' for some days, subsequently, strong hopes were entertained of his recovery the hope turned out to be fallacious, in the course of 6 or 7 days he sunk in the arms of death.

As an operator & surgeon I gained nothing by this case, at least such is my opinion, had I been successfull. the result would no doubt have been diferent.

But on reflection I dont think I have any thing to accuse myself for on the score of recommending an operation. As I could not foresee that it would terminate as it did posatively, and that he could never have recovered without an operation nothing is more certain so it is, we frequently get applause from the world where there is but little of merit. while again our best efforts & real skill go neglected and unrewarded.

Richmond Ia.

Mr. 11. 1839

N.B. The Testicle when detached I should suppose would have weighed about 8 oz.

Case of Emphysema Patient W. King senr. In winter of '38 & '39 produced from injury & supposed fracture of the Ribs.

Jany 10th. 1839 was called to see the above individual, and learned the following by way of history of his case, some days previous he had been spreeing and geting into a rough kind of spoart between play & earnest, or probably more correctly <of?> the Melodrama character. It so turned out that he was considerably injured. *Apparent injury,* was a large extent of surface extending from the spine & small of the back forward to the anterior extrematies of the Short Ribs,[22] and immediately above the Illium [ilium] occupying the whole extent of the loin. but this was too low to satisfactorily account for the Emphysema which had so extensively thrown the air into the celular tissue. This surface was so bloated, that it was truly a sight to behold him, even his Eyelids were puffed to the degree that his Eyes were enclosed, and excluded from the sight.

The breathing was sterterous and labored, at this time I think he complained of considerable pain under the right shoulder, also besides

---

22. The short ribs refer to the front, or anterior, portion of the lower five ribs which are not directly attached to the sternum.

the general distress in the Thorax and its dependencies, think the patient complained considerably of pain in the upper part of the sternum, and along the course of the left clavicle, however, there was no apparent bruise on the surface beside the one first mentioned.

The suffusion had not began to make its appearence at least was not noticed until between 36 & 48 hours after the injury. and when I first saw him the suffusion had then been in progress and extending itself for about the same period of time,

On being called myself I proposed that several others, Physicians of the Town should be called in to consult concerning the case. and was met by Drs. [James W.] Salter & [John T.] Plummer & Smith[23] the result of which was that it would be expedient to make a few incisions into the celular tissue with a view of giving exit to the air suffused. consequently I made a puncture about the centre of the sternum, & one or two over the spine, by this means we succeeded in pressing out a portion of the suffused air, and of the punctures made it was found that the one on the sternum admitted the exit of the suffused air much more readily than those over the spine. There being some cough present, an expectorant was prescribed, and for the present the bowels were kept gently open by means of oil. and some days after this when from an increased action of the pulse and of pain in the Throrascic [thoracic] cavity, & that there was rather an indication of inflamation taking place in the Lungs, depletion was resorted to, and for a short time the patient was put on Tinct[ure] Digitalis & Antimonials. About this period the right Lung which must have been, in a state of collapse, had now began again to inflate as was supposed, & the suffused air had been to a considerable extent absorbed. The inflamation which had been feared was threatened, was counteracted in a few hours, and in a night had subsided, with the exception of the vol[atile] Linamant as an application to the breast & side to the surface where bruised, but little medicine was now administered. ocasionly, giving a little oil to keep the bowels soluable.

At the termination of about three weeks when the suffusion had almost entirely subsided and when I had almost remited my attentions, I was almost discouraged on having my attention called to the upper point of the sternum, & along the course of the clavicle extending to the margin of the axilla, to find that this whole extent of surface red, highly inflamed, tumefyed, & in a high degree painful. And besides this, a point just a little below the right shoulder blade, and two or thre[e] inches foward from the spine, extending over two of the

23. Lindsay was probably referring to Dr. William B. Smith. See Glossary of Personal and Place Names.

ribs; where there was an evident swelling, which was quite prominent when compared with its surrounding connexions. added to this, his appetite which had been pretty good now failed again, all these things taken together were calculate to somewhat alarm me. In a day or two after this state of things, the upper part of the sternum was the seat of a collection of supperative matter which was evident from fluctuation &c. In a day or two longer I lanced it, & found the matter to be within the celular membrane. The discharge was abundant, which required Emoluent soothing poultices, to keep up the discharge. About the time that this was done discharging, a second tumefaction was becoming prominent near the margin of the axilla, being a concentration of the inflamation in this region as first described. in a few days more this was also opened and gave outled to a free discharge of matter, which was treated with Poultices first, & next simple cerate, in the same manner as the other. This tumour in a day or two from the period of lancing it, from its discharge gave much relief to the system. To the swelled & tumefied surface under the shoulder blade, was apt-plyed freely the vol. Lin[imen]t. apparently with much advantage. This was now about the end of 4 weeks from the time I was called in. now at the time I make this record two months & more has elapsed. and for the last month he has been slowly on the recovery. To day I called to see him. found him much improved in general health & in every respect. The tumefactions are done discharging, & are completely sicatrised. The tumefyed or swolen point under the shoulder, is quite gone down, and the pain which was here felt deep within, & as was supposed from the fracture of two of the Ribs, has subsided.

The patient has not yet been beyond the dooryard. but says he expects soon will be able to sally out.

As just intimated it seems quite probable that these two Ribs were fractured, yet there was no bruise or ecchymoses perceptable, and admitting these Ribs to have been fractured; then the next conjecture is that these fractured Ribs accounts for the rupture of the right Lobe of the Lungs, & the consequent Emphysema—

I will make a remark or two in reference to the Emphysema. In the first place would just say that it is the only case I have any recollection of ever seeing.

The appearence was indeed novel. The patient is about 63 years of age. I think, his face much wrinkled & furrowed with age. While the suffusion was at its highest from the loins up to the Eyebrows the suffusion and distention, particularly over the Thorax, in the neck, & face, it was *great* the skin on these parts, & the arms, also, highly distended, no wrinkles now, his wrinkled face was now a perfect

bloat.* puffing like a man out of breath. Articulation too was changed, his voice seemed to be like a cracked bell, squeaking. as if he were practising on lessons of ventriloquism and he seemed to be respiring through the noses [sic] & mouth at the same time.
Richmond Ia.
Mr. 11th 1839.

* his breast highly distended, his neck like a sausage, 3 times its natural size. and the chin and face all in character.

[EDITORIAL NOTE]

The following journal entry is a departure from Lindsay's surgical case histories. The case, written in third person, is more a description of Lindsay's adventures in Arkansas, than a discussion of smallpox. See Introduction.

Case of varioloid,[24] In an individual who attended Capt. Gunter, a mixed Cherokee Indian, in the Small Pox. on board the Tecumseh

History of the case. This Cherokee, was part owner of the Tecumseh, Capt. G. & his wife had taken passage on board this boat at *Webbers falls.* which is a place of some notoriety on the Arks. River, 25 or 30 miles above Fort Smith, & the same distence, by the way of the River, west of the boundary, seperating the U.S. & Arks. from the Cherokee nation of Indians.[25] The Tecumseh, which was commanded on her downward trip by Capt. Stephens, sailed from Webber's Falls to Vicksburgh [Mississippi], which was her place of destination, while at this plac[e] Capt. Gunter was taken sick; & by the time the boat reached Little Rock on its return. it was ascertained that Capt. G. was laboring under small pox. or at least it was a matter of suspicion here, that his disease was small pox, and shortly after the boat left Little Rock, the matter was reduced to a certainty that it was small Pox, as

24. Varioloid: a modified form of smallpox occurring in a person who had already been vaccinated or who has had the disease. Unlike smallpox infection, vaccination with either *vaccinia* or cowpox does not create lifelong immunity to the disease. Thus, a person who had been vaccinated could still contract smallpox infection, or varioloid. Moreover, varioloid could be contagious if it were modified smallpox infection. The contagious nature of varioloid was understood by leading nineteenth-century physicians, but evidently not by Lindsay (John D. Fisher, *Description of the Distinct, Confluent, and Inoculated Small Pox, Varioloid Disease, Cow Pox, and Chicken Pox* [Boston: Wells and Lilly, 1829], 45).

25. When Arkansas became a state in 1836, the Cherokees and Choctaws were located west of the Arkansas border (Dale, "Arkansas and the Cherokees," 97).

the eruption now began to develope itself on the skin. Incidentally it is mentioned that, Capt. McCullough took charge of the boat when she left Little Rock on her return to Webber's Falls.—At Little Rock a Physician shiped on board the Tecumseh a lot of Freight. and himself took passage in charge of it. and was called to take charge of Capt. G. also, professionally. The River being now low & still on the fall. the boat was 2 or 3 days & nights in making a distence of about 75 miles by the River, & not more than 40 by land. At this point the boat was compelled to stop, and await a rise of the River. while at this point Capt. G. died with small Pox, being about 5 days after leaving Little Rock, & on the 9th. of the disease; On the 31st. of Dec. 1837. The disease was of the confluent Character.[26]

The Physician who attended the case had been vaccinated only, and that some 33 years previously. Having attended to Mr. G. in the capacity of nurse, as well as Physician, was much exposed to the contagion, having been up half the night at least during each night. The Tecumseh remained at this point of the River some 7 or 8 days longer, waiting a rise, when she put out her Freight on shore, or rather into a Large Keel Boat,[27] which was cabled to the shore and returned back to Little Rock with the officers & crew.

The Physician remained with his freight waiting a rise of the River, and for the arrival of a Steamer from below. During his stay here of 6 days, he was attacked by variolid. Previous to the death of Capt. G. On retiring one night to his Birth [berth] to rest, he felt a peculiar tingling pricking sensation, which passed over the whole body, but was more sensibly felt in the bottoms of the feet, and next all over the head, throughout the scalp.

On the day the Steamer Tecumseh returned for Little Rock he was taken with a severe chilliness, which lasted about 48 hours, alternated with flashes of febrile excitement. attended by thirst. The first night after the accession of these Chills and rigours, he spent it quite restless. The next day, he was still more miserable, and spent the greater part of it sitting in the chimney Corner,[28] burning his shins drawn up

---

26. According to early nineteenth-century nosology, there were two different types of smallpox, each distinguished by their clinical presentation. Confluent smallpox, the more dangerous form, was characterized by violent pain in the back and extremities and numerous depressed and irregularly-shaped pustules which left pockmarks on the skin. In contrast, the distinct variety of smallpox was characterized by well marked, elevated, circular pustules, which left no scars on the skin (John Eberle, *A Treatise on the Practice of Medicine*, 4th ed., 2 vols. [Philadelphia: Grigg and Elliott, 1838], 1:438-46).

27. Keelboats: flat-bottomed, river boats.

28. Chimney corner: a corner of a boat which has an open fireplace and usually a seat for the elderly.

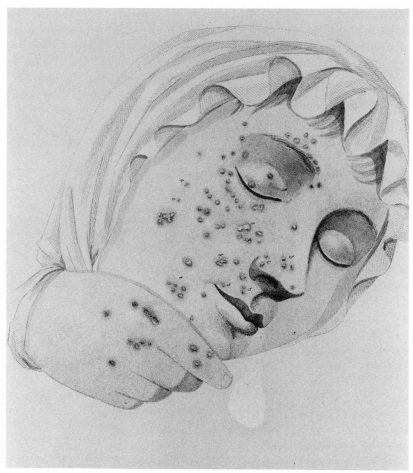

Indiana Historical Society
The early stages of smallpox (John D. Fisher, Description of the . . . Small Pox,
Varioloid Disease, Cow Pox, and Chicken Pox *[Boston: Wells and Lilly, 1829])*

close to the fire, while his kind hostess, as if she wished to keep his
misery company, sat nearly the whole of the day in the opposite chimney corner smoking her pipe, and nursing a dear ragged & dirty young
one, But she was very kind, and seemed disposed to render her indisposed & transient guest as comfortable as she knew how, and Cooked
plenty of strong fare, with *Coffee,* which for the want of the usual
Machine for Pulverising it, she broke it down in a Tin cup with the end
of the rolling Pin, or mush stick,[29] the Dr. has forggotten which. But it

29. Mushstick: a special stick used to stir mush, or porridge.

was a matter of indiference, (only for the sake of precision,) for this Arks. adventurer, had lost his appetite, being only able to taste a little of the more substantials, while he sipped a little of the Coffee, on account of his thirst. It was in the month of Jany. but it will be recollected that the weather even in the latitude of the N.W. was unusually fine. There, in the Latitude 31° or 32° the weather must have been delightful to those who were well and able to enjoy it. as an evidence of the pleasantness of this part of the Rackensack[30] as the state is sometimes familiarly called in that country. The houses or dwellings are generly Log, the interstices without any chinking,[31] all open, no windows, generly, or where found, seldom have sash or glass. This Rackensack Farmer, with whom our variolid sojourner now sojourned, was in moderately good circumstances, was the reputed owner of a fine tract of Arks. bottom land, had been there some 20 years, Kept a wood yard from which he sold abundence of fine ash & cottonwood from $2[.]50 to $3. per cord to the steam boats on the River, was one of your good natured accommodating Kind of men, without any slaves,[32] raising anually, probably, 10 acres of corn, and this abundantly more than he could use for bread & other purposes. for his cattle, Hogs, & horses, had any quantity cainbreak[33] to luxuriate in, winter & summer, what food is found here for hogs among the cane, & out of it, the writer is not informed. but that hogs here are generly killed right out of the woods, and good eating at that, he had sufficient evidence, But when our Landlord wished to change for something in the wild meat department, he could at pleasure repair to the cane or the wood, & select from the numerous herds of Deer, the venison, or the vagrant flocks of Turkey that were alwa[y]s near at hand in any quantity, or quality, at will.

But our farmer, as well off as the generality of his neighbors, seemed to be well contented with his Log Dwelling, for he had lived in it some 16 or 20 years without a loft or any intervening story between his loose puncheon floor[34] and the roof;—the cracks had some-

---

30. Rackensack: an early, uncomplimentary nickname for Arkansas. The term, which referred to the savagery of its frontier population, has survived to the present.

31. Chinking: the filling between logs, usually consisting of either mud or clay, or pieces of wood or stone.

32. Since Arkansas was south of the 36°30' line, the Missouri Compromise allowed slavery in the state. In 1820, the slave population of Arkansas was 1,617; 1840, 20,000; and 1860, 111,115. It should be noted, however, that Arkansas never had the large plantations, number of slaves, nor wealthy planters as did other slave states (Ashmore, *Arkansas*, 51-59).

33. Canebrake: land overgrown with cane.

34. Puncheon floor: a floor consisting of large pieces of timber with one hewn surface.

time or other been carelessly chincked, but now a second edition
seemed to be called for, the corners of the building had never been
sawed off, <&?> its stubling cut down, & probably to remedy the
neglect, or want of a window, the doors were hung with wooden
hinges, arranged to swing open & shut on the outside. and a matter
which our ill grained patient seemed rather to be displeased with, in
his chilling & shivering situation, the doors which were swung open
during the day—for the double purpose of light & ventilation—were
still kept swung back until bed time. And then bed time & the beds,
will long be remembered by our *testy variolid of the lancet*[35] for our
landlord like most others of the country, had no apartments or cham-
bers, kitchen and 3 kind of things called beds were all in the same
room, and during this 2d. night of his sojourning, the landlady, Land
Lord and seven or eight children, the eldest now a young woman, for
the sake of accom[m]odating their sick Pillpedlar and a brother in law
from the viscinity of Vicksburg that night there on a visit, all lodged
in two of the beds. and liberally as our invalid was accom[mo]dated,
he was so unwell & wrestless that he could not sleep. The Traveller of
the N. Western country,[36] where the country is improved, who can
almost at any farmhouse be accommodated with a clean neat bed &
fresh sheets and a seperate room, will the more readily be able to
appreciate, the feelings of our patient, who himself was from the N.W.
and had not yet been initiated or become accustomed to the usages of
the Rackensack

The 2d. night over, our guest having breakfasted, paid his bill,
moderate enough, & now feeling something better, took boarding in a
little cabin near the beach, where the Keelboat which contained his
produce and freight was cabled. & cabin as it was, it was new clean &
neat, & our patient had clean neat bed to himself. The tenant of the
cabin was a virginian, and had within a year or 15 months emigrated
from Ohio, where he had resided several years. It was here for the
first time since the chilling Exacerbations of our patient had been
induced he had an opportunity of looking at an itching kind of stye
which he had felt coming on the left lower eyelid for some days previous. And his feelings were startld as he now for the first time was
awakened to his true situation, he now felt satisfyed that his 2 previous days of indisposition, and the supposed stye was noth[ing] less
than the varioloid, however he felt thankful that this was the only

35. "Of the lancet" refers to the medical profession. The lancet was the instrument used to perform bloodletting and was a standard tool of most physicians during
the early nineteenth century. In fact, one of the most prestigious British medical
journals, founded in 1823, is named *The Lancet*.

36. On the Northwest Territory, see Glossary of Personal and Place Names.

Pages from Lindsay's Journal No. 3

Pock produced, and that, as he hoped, the worst stage of the disease had passed off so lightly. and now as there had a fine rise taken place in the River was encouraged by the expectation of a boat shortly arriving which would afford an opportunity of geting up the River to van buren & fort clark, the poarts he had shiped for when he went on board the Tecumseh 4 days after this, which was about the 15th. Jany. The Steamboat Fox came along with Capt. M'Culley, of the Tecumseh on board. The Fox was commanded by Capt. Buckner with whom arrangements were made to ship all the freight which the Tecumseh had put out at this point. The whole night was consumed in geting the freight on board. This Boat was employed by government in taking the Cherokee & Chickasaw[37] Indians from Memphis Tenn. to Webbers falls and Fort Gibson in the section of Country given these Indians, in exchange for their lands south of the Mississippi.[38] The Fox had not more than got under weigh with our varioloid subject & his freight, when it was whispered thro' the boat, that he had been Physician to Capt. Gunter, & that he now was laboring under the Small Pox. The news passed from one to another like electricity. but great as was the panic among the whites, it was still ten fold worse among the Indians.[39] Of the Indians there were 200 & upwards, and so soon as the Fox could reach the shore they commenced landing & putting out into the woods. and there was no other alternative our patient had to be put on the oposite shore. Such was the excitement that Capt. Buckner

37. The Chickasaw Indians were part of the Muskhogean language group and lived in northern Mississippi and near Chickasaw Bluffs outside Memphis, Tennessee. They were known as an independent and warlike tribe of Indians (Hodge, *Handbook of American Indians*, 1:260).

38. The removal of the Cherokee Indians from their lands east of the Mississippi began in 1837 and ended in the winter of 1838-39. Under the Treaty of New Echota (signed into law on May 23, 1836, by President Andrew Jackson), the highly cultured and educated Cherokee Indians ceded all of their land in North Carolina, Tennessee, Georgia, and Alabama in exchange for western lands. Only a minority of Cherokee Indians, however, negotiated the treaty. The majority of Cherokee so resented the agreement that most refused to move west. Those who did emigrate westward from 1837 to the spring of 1838 (including those traveling on the steamboat *Fox*) did so reluctantly. Because the majority of Cherokee remained in the East, the government removed them forcibly in 1838-39. Few Cherokee had adequate clothing to make the journey, and sickness and death were prevalent during their westward trek. For this reason, the Cherokees' westward journey became known as the "Trail of Tears" (Kenneth Penn Davis, "The Cherokee Removal, 1835-1838," *Tennessee Historical Quarterly* 32 [1973]: 311-31; Grace Steele Woodward, *The Cherokees* [Norman: University of Oklahoma Press, 1963], 192-218).

39. Indians on board the *Fox* were justifiably alarmed upon hearing of Lindsay's contact with a smallpox patient. Smallpox is a highly contagious disease and can be transmitted through contact with an infected person or through the victim's bedding, clothing, or other personal items. The disease is infectious from the first appearance of symptoms until several weeks after recovery. Smallpox had decimated many non-immune Indian groups since the seventeenth century, and in July 1837 a smallpox epidemic occurred among the Indian tribes in the upper West. By 1838 the death toll was over ten thousand (Shryock, *Medicine and Society*, 83-84; Clyde D. Dollar, "The High Plains Smallpox Epidemic of 1837-38," *Western Historical Quarterly* 8 [January 1977]: 15-38).

was apprehensive that our unfortunate patient (invalid) was endangered in regard to his personal safety, the Capt. ordered the mate to take him in the yall,[40] into which the Capt. jumped himself, and all three crossed over to the opposite side of the River, when our hero was set on the shore to get up the River as best he might, or could. This our unfortunate patient, was yet quite feeble & debilitated, altho' much better than he was some 5 or 6 days previous. However he set forward, determinded [sic] by traveling as he could stand it, to get up the River as fast as the nature of things would admit. a distance of 100 Miles or upwards. The first day he traveled about 12 miles, having been set on shore about 5 miles below Lewisburg the county seat of Conway Co. Arks. so named after Gov. [James] Conway now the Gov. of the State. The 2d. day he traveled upward of 20 miles. The last 8 or 10 miles he was much fatigued, and his feet having blistered the first day He now suffered very much from his feet, and soreness of the feet & Legs, without stopping to dine, or take any refreshments, he traveled on through a heavy shower of Rain; & just before Sundown, arrived at the 5 mile house,[41] after passing through a wilderness of this extent. But his disappointment may be better imagined than described when he arrived at the door, and asked for the hospitalities of the house, behold a passenger had just arrived from the *Fox*, who recognised our pedestrian as being the same individual who had been set a shore from the steam boat only the day before on a charge of having Small Pox. He was indignantly forbid having any refreshments or accomodations there, & ordered to leave the premises immediately, & if he had carried with him Pandora's Box, or the volatile deleterious properties of the upas Tree[42] double distilled, he could not have produced more terror than was depicted on the countenances of Major . . . . & his family. Our unfortunate pedestrian was under the necessity of continuing his line of march being looked on as a moving pestilence. at this time his philosophy had well nigh forsaken him. and he left the house dejected, fatigued, and weary. It would have been useless and bad polacy to have remonstrated with the Major or to have attempted to reason him out of his fears. so our slandered patient set out & pursued his way, under a hope of making, or arriving at some other house or hovel, of more humanity than the Major's and at least where he would not be met by any one to slander him, or accuse him of small pox. Our Itinerant had already traveled 5 miles too far, and was under the necessity of resting himself by the road side at about

40. Yawl: a small boat aboard a ship.
41. Five-mile house: an inn or tavern.
42. Upas tree: a mythical tree of Java, which was believed so deadly as to destroy all animal and vegetable life within fifteen miles.

the end of every mile. And on leaving the residence from which he had
just been forbid entering its threshold he felt as if he would have to
give over, and so thirsty that he would have been glad to have drank
of the rain which had this afternoon wet him to the skin, having two
or three times sat himself on a log by the road side, more dead than
alive, for at each time it seemed as if he could not proceed any farther,
no opening improvement could be seen in any direction on geting out
of sight of the one he had just left. It should not be thought strange
that he was now almost in dispair. and that the fond endearing recol-
lections of friends & of home more than 1000 miles distant by the route
he had come shou[l]d involuntar[il]y crowd themselves on his mind,
and the near approach of nightfall and the gloomy prospect of being
compelled to spend the night in the forest, without any refreshments,
cold & chilled as he was from his being drenched an hour two previously in the rain, without any means of striking or kindling himself a
fire; & if property should be worthy of consideration when death was
staring such an individual, in the face, he had some $1500. at prime
cost of freight & produce on board the boat he had been the day before
so unserimoniously & precipitately expelled. without even the evidence of a *receit* for it from the capt. or Clerk. and to have spent such
a chilling night in the situation he was now in. debilitated by his previous indisposition, I say to have spent such a night of the month of
Jany. in the wood, the atmosphere rendered highly chilly by the after-
noons rain, would undoubtedly have terminated his existence. Having
traveled as he afterwards learned about three miles, for the distence
to him seemed much greater, a little after dark he arrived at a little
Cottage by the road side where our traveler was received, and permited to remain for the night.

The Major who had treated our invaled traveler so indignantly, was
reputed wealthy, having a pretty extensive farm & a number of slaves.
Here where our traveler was permited to lodge. The owner, had just
put it up as a kind of makeshift, it was a Cottage with the ground for
a floor, and just large enough to be clear of the door, (which as a
substitute had a blanket hung before it inside) for a bed to stand, which
contained his sick wife, her husband a clever kind of good for nothing
fellow had been cheering himself with whiskey, while she was mourning the death of a child which they had lost a few days previous. But
says our travelor "I was made as comfortable as it was posable in the
situation of their family to make me. I was enabled to dry my cloathes
by a comfortable Fire, while the girl prepared by an out of door fire, a
kind of hotch potch dish of a kind of souse[43] & Backbones which had

---

43. Souse: the pickled feet, ears, and other parts of a pig or other animals.

apparently once before been put under contribution. & which, as a kind of beverage to wash all down with, was accompanied by a dish which the girl called Coffee. Our traveler was familiarly accosted by the good man of the Cottage, who observed "you appear quite old to be traveling on foot." which being the first time he had passed for an old man, who in truth was only a little turned of Forty, concluded he must look bad, as well as feel bad. and that light as his varioloid had been, it had increased the wrinkles in his face.

But to give another quotation in his own words "Our good man of the <hut?> had a log house in the front of their little dwelling just raised and covered in. inside which I was accompanied to bed by a young Irishman who seemed to be a boarder, and no doubt furnished our old man with whiskey in return, as I learned on retiring for the night that he was keeping a Dogary[44] at the next town or vilage about a half mile distant," (a county seat, I think of Pope, or perhaps Johnson,) called the Dardanelle being at the junction of a stream called the Dardanelle where it empties itself into the Arks.[45]

Our traveler when he reflected how narrowly he had escaped lodging in the forest among the Panthers, wolves, & Bear, which were plenty enough in that region of country to say nothing of the inclemency of the weather that night. he felt truly thankful, and his nights fare, & entertainment poor as it might have been esteemed under other circumstances, now was quite acceptable. He set out the next morning before breakfast, much refreshed by his nights rest. however, before he took his leave of his kind host & hostess, to whom he really felt very grateful, he disclosed to them his troubles, which he had encountered on the two previous days. On arriving at the vilage of the Dardanelle, where he designed taking breakfast, whom did he recognise at the Tavern door do you suppose? Why no other than the same individual, who had persecuted him the eveni[n]g before, and who again like an evil genius seemed to haunt his path. He was met some 10 or 15 yards from the Inn by the Land lord, who accused him of Small Pox, and the matter of the Steam Boat Fox.

says our pedestrain to give his own words, "I protested my innocense of the crime of having Small Pox. and after I pulled out of my pocket a certificate of character from Governor [Noah] Noble, with the official seal of the state countersigned by W J. Brown Secty. of State of Indiana. The Landlord looked more gracious, and requested me to keep a respectful distence from the house until my evil genius should have taken breakfast which was already on the Table. saying

44. Doggery: a cheap saloon.
45. The Dardanelle Stream empties into the Arkansas near the town of Dardanelle in present-day Yell County, Arkansas.

that "he would send his servant to put him across the Arks. River" (on which this Town is built,) "and that then some breakfast should be set for me out on the Piazza."["][46]

However, after his accuser had left, the Land Lord had our Pedestrian set a smoking fine Breakfast of Pork, fresh venison, served up with excellent warm Coffee, in the setting Room. and the LandLady, who, as well as her husband, had once had Small Pox, waited on our traveler herself. Here he spent the day and night—and during the day a Gentleman, Col. Martin, a Lawyer, who was a passenger on board the Tecumseh when Capt. Gunter died with Small Pox put up at the same house, who was much pleased with meeting our Traveler. and took a lively interest in his welfare, proposing to serve him in anyway he could in forwarding him in his business & journey up the River.

This days rest was very refreshing, and agreeable to our traveling invalid, The LandLord & his Lady had been a few years from the East & Philadelphia, were quite inteligent & affable, and spared no pains to make our friend comfortable, & to sooth him under his misfortunes. Our Land Lord had been a merchant; but on coming to this country (Arks). he invested in Lands which he purchased the greater part at government price,—kept a wood yard,[47] also the only Ferry here across the River. Magazine Mountain which forms the opposite Bank of the River, belonged to him which in its view, gives a fine romantic prospect from the Dardanelle, coming up bold some several hundred feet high. and is valuable on account of its timber; besides, with the LandLords possessions on its opposite side, secures to him an excellent Ferry.

But to return to our patient. This evevening [sic] at the Dardanelle when night came on, & he could no longer amuse himself by moving round, the Town, he found himself almost stifened & unable to move; his legs quite painful and an intense acheing of the bones generally, as well as of the Legs and thighs and after he retired to bed it was still so troublesome that he could scarcely sleep. This, as he supposed, was the effects [of] the great fatigue of the previous day. which was the more severe from his being so weak, and unaccustomed to walking. The next morning he was considerably refreshed, and after Breakfast, set forward on his journey. This day he only traveled about 12 miles, the last six of which found himself very tired. at Illinois Biou [Bayou], a stre[a]m so called which he crossed in a Ferry boat. (a few miles up the stream, is the old Dwight mision ground, now removed some 25 or 30 miles up the Arks. above Fort Smith, and within the cherrokee

46. Piazza: veranda or porch.
47. Woodyard: an establishment where wood is chopped, sawed, and stored.

Map of Arkansas illustrating

Lindsay's route through the state

Arkansas History Commission

country), he was overtaken by an adventurer from the state of Ohio, by the name of Huston, who had also been the previous night at the Dardanelle vilage. This young man had put up at another house. During their conversation by the way, for they traveled the same road as far as St. Martinsville where our friend spent the night. Mr. H. remarked that he was informed, at the public house where, as just mentioned, he lo[d]ged the previous night, that at the other house, meaning the one at which our friend had spent the previous day, was a Physician said to be laboring under Small Pox. some time afterwards, our invalid let him know that the individual whom he had reference to, was no other than himself. Huston, it was evident was considerably alarmed, and seemed dificult to satisfy that there was not some danger at least he had quite a suspicious appearence, as much as to say, he was fearful the accused Physician in whose company he had inadvertantly got into, might be laboring under the disease his explanations, & protestations to the contrary notwithstanding. On reaching the vilage of St' Martinsville our friend met with a Yankee Gentleman & Lady who had been on Board the Tecumseh as passengers when Capt. Gunter Decd. and as the repoart of our Pedestrian and his Steam Boat expulsion had reached the Town in advance of him, his arrival attracted much attention. and the scab on his eyelid created here as in other places rather a suspision that all was not right. This scab, solatory as it was, had been the cause of much trouble & suffering.

The next day which was about the 21st. Jany. he traveled 12 or 13 miles from St. Martinsville up the River, or rather a few miles out from the River. and when almost his days travel was over, he for want of a Log, or foot bridge was reduced to the n[e]cesity of wading the stream called the Cadron, which was very cold, and quite an unpleasant matter to our traveler, The intense coldness of the stream seemed to chill him to the very heart. This night our friend put up with a Mr. Ward by the by a clever man, and considerably the largest man he had seen in the Arks. his weight was about 320. The next night, which must have been the 22d. he reached about 16 miles. here he as usual called for a foot bath, after making use of it, he opened his toes, for all were dreadfully blistered, the serous discharge driped on the hearth, making a little puddle of the fluid his host remarked that "he had seen many cases of blistered feet, but had never seen such an aggravavated [*sic*] one as this before." He was now within 7 miles of the vilage of Ozark which by the way of the River is about 40 or 45 miles [east] of vanburen. The vilage of Ozark will in all probability some day be a place of some importence particularly should the state, as is contemplated, make a Turnpike road from this point to Fayettville, distant

about 55 miles.—This morning being sunday, while traveling over a
ridge of mountain, on his way to the vilage of Ozark, the scab fell off
from his *Eye*. which he was very willing to part with. This vesicle,
owing to the circumstance of our friend picking it before he suspected
its character, and previous to having access to a miror where he could
examine it, & while he supposed it was nothing more than a *stie* by
this means he let out the serous collection at an early period, consequently it never filled well. but the scab was well formed & full. This
day he traveled 19 miles. and was pleasantly entertained with a family
who had emigrated from northern Misouri. On Monday he dined with
Dr. [D. D.] Williams at Mulberry where the county court, of vanburen
county, was then organising. Dr. Williams is by birth a Welshman, is
said to have been some years an enlisted soldier of the regulars sta-
tioned some part of the time at Natatosh or Nachogdoches,[48] and also
some time at Fort Gibson, his wife is said to have washed for the
armey or the soldiers in garrison, and the Dr. is said to have obtained
what knowledge he has of medicine by nursing and assisting the surgeon & the surgeons mate.—Be this as it may, he stands unrivaled in
the confidence of the people in the bounds of his ride which embraces
a circuit of many miles. The Dr. has one of the finest Farms he saw in
Arks. & has it cultivated by slaves, tho' the Dr. himself is quite industrious. On Tuesday night our friend reached van buren, on Wednesday
night he visited Fort Smith & remained all night with Capt. W. Duvall,
merchant. and trader. He informed our friend that he was personally
acquainted with the celebrated *Indian, Guess*,[49] who, from the circumstance of his forming (having formed) an alphabet to the Cherokee
Language, is entitled to the respect and honours of *Cadmus*,[50] and
should be styled the Indian Cadmus.

The produce trade in which our friend had embarked in made it
necessary that he should visit Fayettville, which is, next to Little
Rock the seat of government, the best Town he saw in the Arks. Here
our friend spent some weeks, and until he had fully regained his
health. about the time he commenced his pedestrian excursion, the
lips become sore, and a scably ulceration, formed on the lower lip,
which formed quite a large incrustation. and it was some two weeks

48. Lindsay probably referred to Natchitoches, Louisiana, near Fort Jessup on
the Red River. Nacogdoches was then part of the newly independent Republic of
Texas. See Glossary of Personal and Place Names.

49. Guess, also known as Sequoyah or George Gist (1770-1843), was the inventor
of the Cherokee alphabet. He traveled widely to teach reading and writing to the
Cherokee. As a result of his work, literacy among the Cherokee spread rapidly (WPA,
Arkansas, 249-50).

50. Cadmus: the prince of Phoenicia who according to Greek legend helped found
the city of Thebes in Boetia and invented the Greek alphabet.

after the varioloid scab desquamet (desquamated); before this scab of the lower lip fell off, and his ulcerated lips well. and I learned subsequently, that some of the inmates of the house of *Major Burnside* at whose House he put up were rather suspicious that there was some risk in associating with our traveler, from the ulcerated situation of his lips. when it was understood that he had been accused of having Small Pox on the river. However he left in that place many good friends, the recollection of whom, on account of the civilities & kind offices received, will ever be cherished with feelings of much respect & esteem by our unfortunate adventurer.

Before we close this article, it should be recorded that two ind[i]viduals, officers on board the Tecumseh, viz, Mr. Galloway the Clerk, and Mr. Wyatt Pilot, on returning to little Rock took the Small Pox and died. Several others took the disease belonging to the boat, I mean of the crue, after the boat returned, all of whom, it is beleived recoverd. Of the passengers it is beleived all escaped the Small Pox. However, there were but few passengers, and it is beleived they were all vaccinated. The few that were on board were very careful not to expose themselves where it was thought they would be endangered to the contagion

one of the passengers who had freight on board it was said had a slight attack of varioloid.

It was before stated that our adventurer was vaccinated; this was done when he was about 10 years old, it had been some 32 or 33 years previous, and not done by a Physician.[51] But he had confidence in the genuineness of the process. having once before some years previous been exposed to the contagion of Small Pox, having attended to an accouchment where there were 4 or 5 down with the disease, children or step children of the Female on whom he was in waiting. A young woman of the number While he was at the house had been brot into the same room for his examination, who at the time, the Pustles were white shining and full of matter. and the Infant, to which was then given birth, died in about two weeks subsequently with Small Pox.

This was the test, and ordeal of exposure, which gave him confidence in the genuineness and validity of his early vaccination. and was this test, which encouraged him to hazard the consequence of taking the responsibility of Physician & nurse to Capt. Gunter of the Steamboat Tecumseh Having finished the narative of the foregoing case so far as our friend is particularly the subject of it, or so far as his case of

51. During the early nineteenth century (the period in which Lindsay was vaccinated), vaccination was not always reliable nor were its mechanisms entirely understood. Occasionally, doctors used impure vaccine matter, and persons thus vaccinated were not protected from the disease (Rothstein, *American Physicians*, 32).

varioloid required any investigation, It would probably be as well to avow the fact to the reader that this adventurer and hero of the foregoing narative, was no other than the writer himself. The reasons which induced the writer to speak of himself in the third person was to avoid egotism, and if occasion require that he might be releived from that delicate restraint which the writer must feel should he ever wish to read it himself, for the amusement of a friend.[52]

Perhaps it would not be out of place to remark here that it was reluctently that the officers on board the Tecumseh were forced to admit that his case was Small Pox. This was no doubt a matter of polacy to save the reputation of the boat, & for the sake of keeping up business. even when gunter died it was a matter of doubt apparently with some of them. The Clerk Mr. Galloway professed not to beleive the case Small Pox. but it so turned out that he was the next to fall a victim to the disease, during the sickness of gunter a day or two before his death Mrs. Gunter admitted to the writer of this article that among some Indians who had been some time encamped at Webbers Falls, (where it was before observed was the residence and trading House of Mr. G). the Small Pox was found to exist, had been attended by some cases of fatality, and that Mr. Gunter had been exposed to the contagion a short time previous to the Boat leaving for vixburg. So this accounts sufficiently so far as necessary to be known, for the manner in which the Small Pox was induced in Capt. G's case. The writer does not recollect posatively whether vaccination had been ever attemp[t]ed on him or not. But it seems to be his impression that Gunter informed him or perhaps his wife, that he once had what passed for vaccination.

The writer of this article has called his own case varioloid, perhaps it was what is denominated the nursing Pox.[53] or a modification of variola or Small Pox still more modifyed and milder than varioloid. And if it be admitted that varioloid is contagious, this view of his own case would appear the more plausable, when the fact is known that there was no case produced from his, so far as he has any knowledge. During 6 or 7 days stay at the residence of the famalies, on the Arks. River where the detention, as already detailed, was owing to the Teumseh putting back to L. Rock, & the want of sufficient depth of water to get up the River, there would have been a favorable time to have

52. Lindsay not only may have been making a powerful statement about the importance of vaccination, but also might have been defending his actions regarding his rift with Stipp. See Introduction, above, pp. xxiv-xxvii.

53. A reference to nursing pox could not be found in the medical literature of the period. Lindsay, however, may be referring to smallpox contracted by a nursing child from its mother.

communicated the disease if contagious. Many of the neighborhood called on him. some for trade & the purchase of Flour & other produce, and there were children in both Families who had not been vaccinated.
Mr. 15. 1839
Richmond Ia.   *W. Lindsay*

Hydrocele, Frederick Daniels patient came in from west of Jacksonburg [Indiana] to be operated on.

History of the case. about 3 weeks ago Mr. D. called on me to consult me on his case supposing it be rupture. The scrotum was much distended On examination I at once pronounced his case to be hydrocele. notwithstanding, the semitransparent appearence generly seen on darkening the room and examining with the candle was scarcely perciptible.

On June 4th. 1839 the above patient came in and submited to an operation. before operating on measurement found the circumference to be about 19 Inches. and length (of the scrotem) to be about 20 In. quantity of turbid fluid drawn off about 3 pints. nothing very peculiar, with the exception of the *Tunica Vaginalis* Testes on making the excision and examination appeared somewhat hydatid. The disease had been of between 3 and 4 years standing had not been attended by any peculiar pain. the size and weight made the organ very inconvenient.

In the operation I was kindly assisted by my friend Dr. J. W. Salter. Operated by making an incision commencing pretty high up on the side affected (right side) near the insertion of the spermatic cord, and carrying it down about two thirds of the tumour towards its lower apex.

Dressing, having inserted a tent of old muslin charged with simple cerate partially brought the incised wound together by means of 3 stiches and at the uper angle one strip of adhesive, and over all applyed a suspensary bag. put patient to bed & enjoined quietude and light diet. during the operation patient lost not to exceed 4 or 5 oz. of blood. had expected greater owing to the varicose state of the scrotem. patient stood the operation well

June 10th. patient appears to be geting along tolerably well—on the 3d. day after the operation opened his bowels with salts[54] reaction having brot up some fever & restlessness thirst &c. was releived by the operation of the aperient—tho every afternoon and evening some degree of Fever and an increase of restlessness & thirst. On yesterday

---

54. Lindsay was probably referring to epsom salts. See Glossary of Medical and Pharmaceutical Terms, s.v. "Salts, epsom."

again administered a small dose of salts. moved the bowels two or three times. tho' very sore & stiff was able to get up to the pot without assistence, To day the scrotem is at least 2/3 as large as when operated on—about 1 ince [*sic*] of the upper part of the incision united by the first intention all above the upper ligature wound below contains the seaton [seton]—and is discharging a fluid about of the same character <&?> appearence to that evacuated in the operation. dressing to day only lint in the wound moistened by Whiskey. appetite tolerably good—Tongue moist and clean—The spermatic cord but little swolen, has since the evening of the day of operation been attented by occasional shooting pains up the cord towards the kidney. Urinates without much pain—urine higher colored than natural

June 11th. Not much difference since yesterday. Still discharging a similar fluid to that found in the scrotem on operating, and rather fearful inflamation is not coming up sufficiently. in dressing to day made use of Whiskey for injecting the scrotem, with a view of exciting more inflamation. appetite, Pulse, general strength, &c. about as yesterday.

June 12th. general symptoms about as yesterday. and treatment the same. onlly [*sic*] in addition made an external application of to [*sic*] the lower part of the scrotem of the Mur[iate of] Am[m]onia in the form of a cerate. last night administered E[psom] Salts which produced two Defecations.

June 13th. Last night the part became quite painful, attended by an increase of heat in the organ. some thirst and feevervish [*sic*] excitement. loss of appetite. fearing that inflamation might run too high, removed the Seaton, & dressed the incision with a pledget of simple cerate.

This morning found that the pain had much subsided, Am in hopes too that the inflamation has ran sufficiently high to induce adhesion & destruction of the vaginal coat and sack containing the secreted fluid constituting the Hydrocele. This morning on dressing, found that the watery fluid had ceased discharging during the night. shall soon expect soon to see supurative matter in its stead. Dressing this morning the same as last night.

June 14th. patient somewhat restless last night, but less so than night before—sleep much disturbed every night—last night bled some at the nose, which has occurred every day or two since the operation. only dressing simple cerate on lint applyed to the incision.

June 17. Today my patient has considerably improved is gaining strength is able to get up and dress himself & sat up some time, the s[c]rotem is much less, continues still to run pretty freely. for the last two or three days have dressed him twice a day. last night his nose again bled a little, and his sleep is still much interrupted, says he sleeps some in the latter part of the night.

June 25th. To day my patient has so far recovered the operation that he has returned home, has for several days been able to walk out and about Town by way of Amusement & recreation. The volume of the scrotem and swelling have considerably gone down. is not much painful, the incision has much contracted in its length and would soon be healed were it not for the supuration which still keeps up from the interior parts. bowels have become regular, sleeps well at night. appetite & strength returning.

nov. 17th. at this lapse of time would remark in regard to the foregoing case that about 4 weeks ago I visited my patient at his residence. and on examination found him completely cured of *Hydrocele*. It should be mentioned that the testicle appears rather larger than the other, but am inclined to think that the membranes or sack containing the secreted fluid, which will be recollected was voluminous, however much contracted, in the cure, now are so inveloped around the organ so as to give it the appearence of being a little enlarged. He is, and has been for a considerable time actively engaged in promiscuous work and labor on his Father in law's Farm. And when I saw him expressed himself highly pleased with the result of the operation. That he is permanently cured, and the sack completely destroyed, I have not a remaining doubt.

W. Lindsay

Celular infiltration of the external organs of Generation.[55]

On the evening of the 24th. June 1839 was called to see Mrs M___k about 1 m. s. of Town. And as a history of her case learned that a few days previous, without much previous indisposition quite suddenly the whole of the soft and external organ of generation began to [be] infiltrated and soon became enormously distended with water in the celular membrane.

Dr. Parmer having been called punctured the parts and gave exit to something between a Pint & qt. of water, of a clear limpid fluid, which gave as instantaneous relief to the patient. This collection of fluid continued to drip off perhaps some 12 hours before it entirely ceased. but in something like 48 hours it had again collected. and as my friend Dr P. was from home I was called in. On my arrival I found the patient

---

55. External organs of generation: the labia pudenda. See Glossary of Medical and Pharmaceutical Terms, s.v. "Labia pudenda."

in excruciating suffering. And the celular infiltration of the Labia Pudenda and the whole of the external soft parts as greatly disten[d]ed,
apparently, as nature would admit, the whole presenting a transparent
glossy and shining appearence. in short the infiltration was now as
great as it had been at the time Dr. P. visited her first and operated on
her. And the punctures which I made with a Thumb Lancet, through
the course of the night carried off about the same quantity of fluid and
as promptly relieved her now as before. This to myself was a novel
case having never witnessed any thing like it before, such was the
enlargement of the parts and distension that the patient was compelled
to lie on the back with her thighs thrown as widely open as could be
admited. She was now about the 6th. or 7th. month of her first gestation, and as is not infrequent there was some swelling of the lower
extremities. but not more so nor indeed so much as I had often witnessed in other cases of pregnancy. What could have induced this
infi[l]tration of the celular membrane of this organ seems to be a
matter of uncertainty or difficult to be accounteded [*sic*] for. some few
days previous to its taking place she had on account of some indisposition taken a cathartic of some kind of pill, which operated rather
harshly, producing considerable griping and bearing down distress.
What these pills were composed of, Dr. P. nor myself has not any
knowledge, having been prescribed by some other physician.

having punctured the parts in several points with a Thum Lancet, I
applyed a dressing of simple cerate over the whole of the soft parts.
Dr. P. had previously prescribed as an apperient & Hydrogogue [hy-
dragogue] Cre[a]m Tart. & Nit. Potash [potassium nitrate] with which
I made no change.

June 27th. on yesterday & the day before she was visited by Dr. P.
who informs me that she still continues quite releived, without any
appearence of return of infiltration. On yesterday She was said to be
much releived in every respect, the Edematous state of the Legs having much gone down, Dr. P. had on the day before yesterday prescribed
a pill composed in part of calomel & Squill. from the time of the operation by Dr. P. of puncturing and the administration of the Crem Tart.
& Nit. Potas[h]. She had been much troubled with vomiting & gastric
derangement, but on the Subsidence of the infiltration, & the discon-
tinuence of the Crem Tart. & Nitre & the exhibition of the Pills this
derangement of the stomach ceased, and on yesterday the 26th. was
much improved generally.

nov. 17. In relation to the foregoing case at this lapse of time I have
only to add that she was still attended by Dr. P. whether there was
any return of the *Labial* infiltration or of any other part. am not
informed. In due time she was attended in her accouchment by Dr. P.

which I think was unaccompanied by any untoward symptom. And my understanding is that her health is again tolerably well established

---

[EDITORIAL NOTE]

The remaining entries in this journal contain cases of "diseased breasts," or what most nineteenth-century physicians referred to as mammary abscesses. The physician's first goal in treating this disease was to reduce inflammation through therapies such as bloodletting, light diet, purging, and bread and milk poultices. If inflammation continued, then the surgeon blistered the affected area and opened the abscesses with a lancet (Gibson, Institutes and Practice of Surgery, 1:204-7).

Mrs. Crocker's case of diseased breast.

was called on 24th. June 1839 to wife of Mr. P. Crocker, found the left mamma much diseased, some 2 or 3 months previous had been confined with her 1st. child. in consequence of taking a severe cold, as, was supposed, the Breast began to be painful, followed by swelling & inflamation and in the course of a week or two had supurated & was Lanced, or broke of itself have forgotten which, as I was called some weeks after this period and have now forgotten this particular in the history of her case as She gave it me on my being called in. the Breast was discharging from a ragged irregular opening about midway between the nipple and the axilla. at the same time there was some knotty tumefaction in the axilla which was quite tender and painful on pressure, and the whole substance of the mamma was an irregular knotty mass of Tumefaction. in a few days after I was called, a point of supuration had taken place a few inches above the nipple, on lancing it discharged a considerable quantity of an unhealthy supurative matter, mixed now & then with something like curd, and in part a purely Lacteal secretion. On examination of the breast with the probe at this opening, found it about one & a half inches deep—which operation was unattended by much pain, while the introduction of the probe in the first described opening was quite painful and followed by some hemorrhage. The 2d. opening on the upper part of the breast was not surrounded by any unnatural appearence, while the 1st. opening towards the axilla was of a blue or purplish appearence, which seemed to shoot up rather in the character of an unhealthy, irregular granulation around the margin of the sinus. while in the direction of the axilla for the distance of an inch or two the surface had the like ruguous [rugose] purplish & Bluish aspect. Some 3 or 4 weeks after I was called in, the other axilla became diseased, and shortly afterwards tumefac-

Indiana University School of Medicine Library

Drawing of a woman suffering from a mammary abscess. The breast measured twenty-three inches in circumference when the patient sought medical assistance. (George H. Barlow and James P. Babington, eds., Guy's Hospital Reports, *vol. 6, no. 12 [1841])*

tion & supuration ensued. And in a week or two more at a point about 2 inches distant from the nipple, and on the right side of the body of the breast, matter began to point, & in a few days more I lanced the part, which gave exit to supurative matter mixed as before with some secretion of milk. in a few days after opening this sinus by the introduction of the probe followed the sinus about 2 & 3/4 inches deep and upwards in the body of the breast. about this time the 1st. sinus was nearly healed, and the pain in the axilla and glandular swelling had nearly disappeared. Shortly after this period a 4th. sinus, or point of supuration took place about 1 & 1/2 half [sic] inch distance below the nipple, which on opening gave discharge to a quantity of matter much in character with the 2d. & 3d. sinuses above aluded to, at this time the 1st. described opening had healed up completely, in a few days more the 3d. described opening was also closed. and probably in about a week or 10 days the 4th. sinus was healed. during all this time the 2d. sinus on the upper part of the mamma continued open and discharged supurative matter, more or less healthy in character, tho' sometimes then at other times cheesy or curdly, and every day a considerably [sic] quantity of a Lacteal character as pure to all appearence as that which continued to be discharged by the nipple. so it was evident that all the sinuses communicated with, and ran into the Lacteal glands at this time the general complexion of the breast was much improved, and in about 1 week longer the 2d. and last sinus had healed.

I have yet said but little in regard to the treatment. Poultising with various preperations had been used previous to my being called in. by way of poult[i]ce I made use of the oak bark oose thickened with light bread first. which I discontinued in about 3 weeks for the Flaxseed & it, in a few weeks more for the light bread & sweet milk—once a day I generally made an application of the Nit. of silver [nitrate of silver or lunar caustic] to the edges of the diferent sinuses—and for a short time applyed a tent within the 2d. sinus. when all the sinuses were healed the breast still was knotty, (that it was Schirous am at a loss in deciding) but gradually these softened and became more natural, & occasionly on enquiry after her health am informed that the breast is well.

In receiving the early history of the foregoing case am deficient in recollection what I was informed in regard to the early swelling & inflamation. But at the time I took charge of her case & during my attentions of about 7 or 8 weeks it was at no period much if any larger than the sound breast from which She suckled her infant. During the time that supuration was in progress at the 3 several points described, I was surprised to find matter pointing towards the surface unaccompanied by so little swelling and inflamation. For some days previous to my suspicions, and any evidence that I could see of the fact, the patient would perhaps complain of some shooting pain in the part. which in a few days would be followed by a slight discoloration of the surface, and now a slight softness on pressure which became more and more developed, tho' without any increased heat, and but very slight swelling or tumefaction. perhaps the patient would sometimes speak of something like a burning sensation within in connection with the throbing shooting pains. during the progress of these points supurating, which would probably produce some restlessness during night. and all were surprised to see the quantity of matter that would be discharged on lancing one of these points, altho it was small compared with the quantity that is discharged from the breast in common cases of supuration.

was called to see Mrs. C.[56] in April last (1839) who some 12 or 13 months after her first acouchment took cold in the breast which terminated in Phlegmonous supuration. The supuration being fully developed on my first seeing the patient I lanced the breast which gave exit to something between 1 & 1/2 pints of healthy puss [sic]. patient soon recovered without further attentions.

was called to see Mrs. of [New] Paris O. whose name I have not. patient of Dr. J. Knox in Sept. 1839. On examination found the breast had supurated, On Lancing by the Dr. a large quantity, perhaps a Quart or more was discharged during a few hours, I have no particular knowledge of the termination, but was informed that she was doing well.

In spring of 1827 at Germantown O. I treated a case of diseased breast. patient Mrs. <Right?>, whose case was in many respects similar to that of Mrs. C. [Crocker] found at Page 108 [p. 102]. The inflamation finally setled down, and produced a schirrous knotty State of the Breast. I think it was only lanced in 2 places. it was 3 or 4 months in a slugish, ulcerated state sinuses dificult to heal, Finally succeed in healing it up by making use of arcenical injections which brought away a deep slough—soon after which a healthy sanative supuration was induced, and the sinuses sicatrised in a short time.

nov. 27. 1839   W. Lindsay

56. Lindsay identifies this patient in his table of contents as a Mrs. Cheesman.

Journal 4

July 19. 1834 was called to see Edward Webster, Mill right, who had cut off the Anterior Tibeal Artery, or a branch of it, with the Foot Adze.[1] I got to see him a few hours after the accident, distant from Town about 6 miles. The Hemorrhage had been considerable but not as great as might have anticipated. applications of cloths, by the aid of coagula had put a great check to it. which had been profuse at first and attended by syncope.

On examination of the cut and the removel of the cloths and coagula I found the artery cut off deep anteriorly just where the artery made its exit between the Tibea & Fibula a few inches below the knee. The stroke of the Adze must have been made with the angle, judging from its depth, as the muscle Tibealis Anticus [anterior tibial muscle] was cut through and entirely off. The stroke extended as deep as the Interoseous Ligament. and the artery was cut off so short anteriorly where it emerged thro' this Ligamentous membrane that I could not pass a Ligature neatly around it. And in order to take up the artery was under the necesity of passing the kneedle thro' the surrounding integuments, thus enclosing the integuments and artery all together.

This mode of operation succeeded well. was not attended by any secondary hemorrhage—The wound healed up in about three weeks. Inflamation did not run very high having no doubt been prevented by the strict regimen and antiphlogistic mode of treatment enjoined in the case. The lameness consequent on the cuting off of the muscle was never fully removed. The foot droped down much at first, and after the patient recovered from the wound, the foot in raising and stepping forward of the Leg ever continued to be attended by a slight halting & dropping of the Toe. however after a period of some months my patient was enabled to get along tolerably well without the use of his cane. And in due time was able to resume his ocupation.

1. Adze: a cutting tool with an arched, sharp blade used in the nineteenth century for hewing logs; a foot adze is larger than a regular adze and can be used with the foot.

This young man, now, while I make this record of his case, *is no more*. his death was somewhat mysterious, but had nothing to do with the injury here recorded. Some 2 or 3 years after the accident which I have just described, on returning late from Town he was thrown, as is supposed, from his horse, being found dead the next day by the road side. So far as I had any knowledge of him, he was a young man of steady habits; was quite honorably connected, and his untimely loss much regreted.

Richmond Ia.

Nov. 27th. 1839 W. L.

Case of James Whiteman wen of the Hip. removed by operation on the 28th. Sept. 1839—As a history of the case I learned that this wen had been coming 10 years. That the patient is of the opinion that it originated from a small itchy lump. perhaps not much larger than a pin head when he first discovered it. And if I understood him correctly thinks it was produced by scratching the part with his nail.

In this case I was called by my friend Dr. James Knox, had never seen the case until the day I operated. at this time the wen was probably about 6 inches long including the pedicle or stem by which it was connected to the *hip*. at the pedicle or base it was from an inch & half to 2 Inches diamater—at the fundis was between 4 & 5 and by compression could probably have been put within a Pint Tin Cup. And weighed after it was removed just 1 lb. Avoirdupois.

This operation was simple, and consi[s]ted in excision near its attachment to the hip. by a circular incision, but little hemorrhage attended the operation. two small arteries had to be taken up. one of which by the assistence of Dr. [James] Knox was taken up when the wen was about 1/3 removed, and the other after the wen was removed. This operation was rather painful, but the patient (by occupation a Blacksmith) stood it well, he was just recovering from an attack of fever. was just able to walk about. said he would have it over with and be done with it all at the same time. meaning the operation & the fever.

On removel of the wen. I closed the wound by drawing & approximating the edges so as to form a right line—and with little force was enabled by means of 3 stiches & Adhesive Strips intervening to make a snug dressing of it. without much distention of the skin and integuments.

In a few days after the operation I saw Dr. Knox, in whose charge the patient was left, by whom I was informed he was doing very well. & reported that the wound was healing finely by the first intention.

That this patient is radically cured have not even a doubt. This wen in its formation was simply Adapose. being composed of pure fatty substance.

This Tumor had been continually, according to the representations of the patient, on the increase. had not been of much inconvenience to him—only from its size & weight and being in the way. his general health had been good.

[EDITORIAL NOTE]

In the case of fracture described below, Lindsay was forced to improvise because he was ignorant of the recommended treatment for a fractured humerus. During this period fractures were first immobilized, and then the broken fragments were repositioned by means of extension and counterextension, or pushing and pulling the limb until the ends were realigned. Next, the doctor applied compresses followed by splints of wood, pasteboard, or tin, and secured the dressing with muslin bandages.

Specific treatment for a fractured humerus in the early nineteenth century consisted of wrapping the upper arm with bandages and then applying three splints to the posterior, anterior, and outer parts of the arm. Finally, the physician placed a pad between the arm and the chest and secured the limb to the chest with bandages. Unaware of this procedure, Lindsay applied four splints to the upper arm, but did not secure the arm to the chest. He found his procedure inadequate and developed a "stay case" of splints, consisting of two pieces of unbleached cotton cloth cut to fit around the arm from the shoulder to the elbow. He stitched the two pieces of cloth together at one and one-half inch intervals. He then placed corset splints inside each opening and held the apparatus in place with a bandage and linen tape. Lindsay was so pleased with the effectiveness of his new "device," he used it for both compound and simple fractures (Gibson, Institutes and Practice of Surgery, 1:369-73, 407-14; Dorsey, Elements of Surgery, 1:109, 143-45).

Jacob Shaw's case of fractured arm, broke in three places. Sept. 29th. 1839

This young man while driving a Hack in passing a 4 horse mail stage was precipitated from the seat and the coach ran over his left arm. In the course of an hour or two he was brot to Town and I was called to see him. At the time I set the Arm I was of the opinion that it was broke only in 2 places a little above the Elbow and again a little below the shoulder, This arm proved to be very troublesome, swelled very much, attended by much pain & suffering. in a few days after the accident a high degree of inflamation took place at the Elbow Joint and the lower arm became enormously distended.

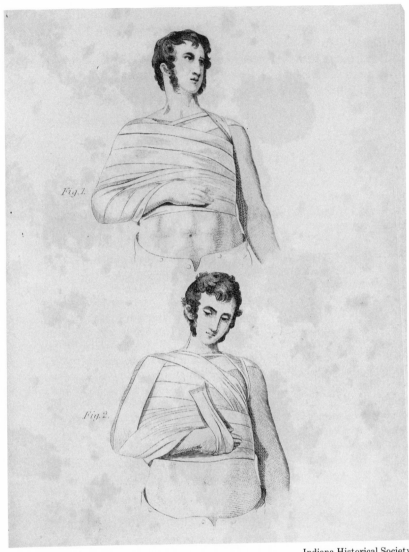

Drawings illustrating the proper procedures for setting a fractured clavicle (Gibson,
The Institutes and Practice of Surgery, *vol. 1)*

At about the end of the 1st. week I concluded to throw off the
dressing of 4 splints which I had used and substituted a *stay case* of
splints. I was induced to this change from the circumstance of some
displacement in the fractured bone being now discovered, which required a reseting, With the effects of this stay case dressing I was

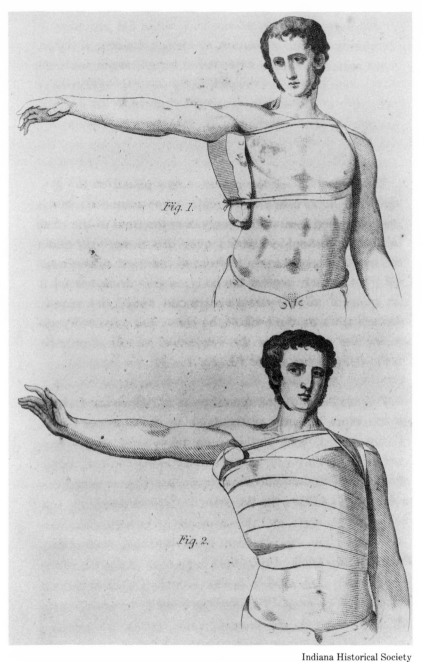

Fig. 1.

Fig. 2.

Drawings illustrating the proper procedures for setting a fractured clavicle (Gibson,
The Institutes and Practice of Surgery, *vol. 1)*

much pleased, which consisted of 2 pieces of factory[2] being first cut out of the proper length to extend from below the shoulder to the Elecranon [olecranon], & run together lengthwise at intervals of about 1 & 1/2 inches and adapted so when filled with splints to fit neatly around the arm. which I applyed over the many tailed bandage tieing on with 4 pairs of Tape Strings attached to the 2 edges of the stay case. the tapes in applying the case of splints were interlocked by crossing & tieing on the oposite side of the arm. over this the bandage was applyed in the usual way, as inflamation ran high and the arm became a little chafed in places I diped the many tailed bandage into melted Beeswax softened with a little Tallow.

This was a protracted case, the patient not being able to leave his bed until nearly 6 weeks. and at the end of 7 weeks was just able to walk about the house with the arm in sling.

about this time he left town in a carriage on a visit to his mother, where he expects to remain until he is intirely recovered. This has necessarily been a tedious case, and it will yet require a considerable time to get the use of the arm. and from the high degree of inflamation in the elbow at an early period, I had some fears that he would have an Anchalosed or stiff Elbow. but beleive now this will not be the case Nov. 28. 1839

Richmond   W. Lindsay

2. Factory: unbleached cotton cloth, produced domestically, rather than being imported.

[EDITORIAL NOTE]

The cases presented below, as well as one other case in this journal, represent Lindsay's experience with one type of difficult birth: shoulder presentation. In these cases, the shoulder rather than the head presented, and the child's arm protruded through the vagina. As Lindsay noted, this type of presentation was extremely rare. Of 15,654 children delivered by one nineteenth-century French midwife, for example, there were only 68 cases of shoulder presentation. In 1855 the Indiana State Medical Society's Committee on Obstetrics reported no arm presentations among 250 obstetrical cases.

During this period, successful delivery depended upon detecting the presentation prior to evacuation of the amniotic fluid. A well-trained physician could determine the unborn child's position by examining the presenting part. If the shoulder presented, the physician waited until the mouth of the uterus had dilated sufficiently and then introduced his hand into the uterus, located the child's feet, and positioned the child so as to effect a foot delivery.

In cases where the amniotic fluid already had escaped, the strong uterine contractions made the delivery even more difficult. As a result, the outlook

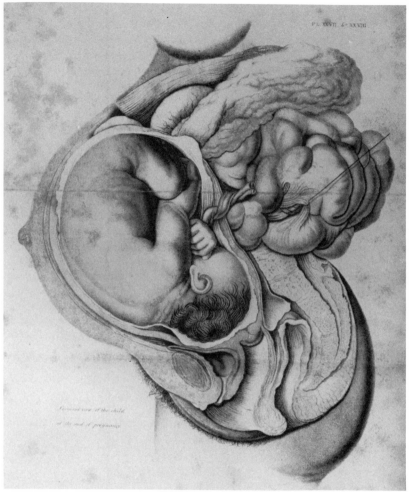

Illustration showing the position of the unborn child in normal labor (J. P. Maygrier,
Midwifery Illustrated, *trans. A. Sidney Doane [Philadelphia: Carey & Hart, 1833])*

for the child was poor. The physician first relaxed the mother by administering drugs such as opium. If the delivery were extremely tedious and
protracted, the physician gave a small quantity of wine to the patient. After
examining the presenting parts to determine the child's position, the physician held the presenting arm with one hand and introduced the other hand
into the uterus. When the uterus contracted, English midwife Thomas Denman suggested that the operator lay his hand flat against the body of the
child and continue into the uterus only after the cessation of the contraction.
The operator's goals were to grasp the feet, reposition the child, and effect
a foot delivery. By using these procedures, English midwife John Burns

claimed a child could be delivered in almost every instance. If turning proved fruitless, then the physician performed a Caesarian section. The Caesarian, however, was undertaken only as a last resort since secondary infection was common. The eighteenth-century English midwife Thomas Denman noted: "In almost every case in which the Cesarian operation has been performed in this country [England], the patients have died." Doctors avoided the Caesarian section if there was no doubt the child was dead. In these cases, they recommended the destruction of the fetus.

Nineteenth-century physicians agreed, however, that the surgeon should not amputate the presenting arm. Prior to the nineteenth century, the dismemberment of the fetus was common. In cases where the child's arm presented and protruded through the vagina, for example, the doctor often amputated the arm to facilitate turning. In the nineteenth century, however, doctors agreed that removal of the arm not only made traction difficult should it become necessary to perform an embryotomy, but also resulted in "the most distressing consequences." English midwife Francis H. Ramsbotham (1800-1868) cited an example of a physician who thought the child was dead, amputated the arm, and then was much dismayed to discover the child was alive. In fact, the disfigured child grew to manhood! It is apparent, though, from the cases which follow that neither Lindsay nor his colleaugues were aware of the recommended procedures for arm presentation. Instead, Lindsay strongly advocated the one treatment which orthodox authority scorned, i.e., the removal of the child's arm (Cazeaux, Treatise on Midwifery, 445; Thomas Denman, An Introduction to the Practice of Midwifery [Brattleborough, Vermont: William Fessenden, 1807], 285-93, 296-315; "Report on Obstetrics and Puerperal Fever," Proceedings of the Sixth Annual Meeting of the Indiana State Medical Society, Held in the City of Indianapolis, May, 1855 [Indianapolis: Indiana Journal Company, 1855], 29; Burns, Principles of Midwifery, 313-20; Francis H. Ramsbotham, The Principles and Practice of Obstetric Medicine and Surgery, in Reference to the Process of Parturition [Philadelphia: Henry C. Lea, 1865], 345-53, 362-63).

Was called to see Mrs. Thornton on the night of the 14th. Nov. 1839 distant from this place (Richmond) 12 miles. being sent for by the request of my friend Dr. Joel Bugg with instructions to bring along with me the Forceps & other instruments belonging to the case of the Acouchier.[3] On arriving at Friend Thornton's[4] I learned that Dr. Bugg

3. Instruments belonging to an accoucheur, or formally trained midwife, would have included obstetrical forceps and those tools necessary for performing an embryotomy: a perforator, crotchet, and blunt hook. The perforator was a long pair of scissors with a large point on one end for piercing and emptying the skull, while the crotchet was a sharp hook used for grasping the fetal head before and after a craniotomy. The crotchet was then used to tear apart the plates of the skull. The blunt hook enabled the physician to grasp the dead child within the uterus (Donegan, *Women and Men Midwives*, 42).

4. Friend Thornton: a reference to Thornton's religion, i.e., Thornton was a Quaker.

had been in attendance some 36 or 40 hours. And previous to my being sent for the membranes had been broken and a large quantity of water Discharged, if the women present were not mistaken in their report, something like a gallon and one half, & according to some nearly two gallons. after which it was ascertained by the Dr. that it was an arm presentation, which by any skill or effort could not be altered to that of any other. at least such proved to be the fact. had the presentation been suspected in time or previous to the evacuation of the waters it was barely probable that the presentation might have been changed immediately. on the rupture of the membranes, and before the Liquor Amni had all passed off. However, Dr. Bugg seems to be of the opinion that even with this knowledge he could not have succeeded, owing to the want of sufficient dilatation of the uterus. At all events after the removal of the Arm at the shoulder I was unsucessful in turning or geting holt of a foot. to effect which I made several attempts during a period of 3 hours. On consultation it was agreed that the exhibition of the Ergot should be tried. which was given in the form of a decoction. nothing could have succeeded better, by giving it in divided doses every 15 or 20 minutes the pains which had been quite inefficient became stronger and stronger every dose of the medicine given; and in about 2 hours from the time this medicine was commenced, she was delivered of the child.

The Placenta produced some trouble and detention of about half an hour longer, owing to some adhesion and retention at the fundus uteri. a circumstance attending this case requires particular mention. The child was born dead; and from the symptoms of putrescency should judge it had been dead several days. It was rather smaller than the average size of newborn infants, but should think she had carried about the full period. This was the 6th. I think that had been "*still born*" had generally been hard labors some of them preternatural, but none previous to this had been an arm presentation, the one previous to this had been a breech, & was also still born, as was the child in the case above described, all, or nearly all the still born were in some respect or other deformed, this above which I attended was deformed in the feet & Legs. This woman is 40 or upwards years of age—has only 2 or 3 living children. This was the only case which has ever occured in my practice in which a delivery was effected with this presentation, where turning was not effected. This indeed is the 3d. case of this presentation that I have witnessed during a period of 17 or 18 years practice. The 1st. case I witnessed was a colored woman slave of a Mr. Whitaker of Ky. which occurred during my practice at Laurenceburg this state some 15 years ago. A Female Midwife had first been called and I think had been in labor 48 hours or upwards. having spent some hours in fruitless attempts in endeovoring to turn the child, I had my friend Dr. Jabez Percival called, who was old in the practice. I well recollect with what self confidence he took his seat by the patient. but having spent 2 or 3 hours in extraordinary effort was as unsuccessful as I had been; and was very reluctently compelled to desist, for the present at least;—but the event proved that it was the last. We concluded to put her in bed and enjoin rest, in hopes that nature would in a few hours produce some favorable change of position. So we left her to repose, and returned home distant about 5 miles, proposing to return in the afternoon (this being in the morning) when as a dernier resort it was our intention to perform the "caesarian" operation,[5] in case matters still remained as we left, but before we returned a messenger informed us that this poor woman's sufferings had terminated, in which she was releived by the hand of death. In this case the arm was not taken off. what might have been gained by this operation, I cannot say, of course it would have been justifyable & should have been performed. But I was then inexperienced & young in practice, and I do not recollect that it was proposed by Dr. Percival. who indeed justly stood high as a surgeon and practitioner. he is, or was quite lately still living, and must be nearly 80 years old. and I understand that he continues still in the practice. when I located at Laurenceburg this state some 18 years ago he was then said to be upwards of 60 years of age (about 63 I think) and he then held the honorable station of President of the District Medical Society of which I had the honor of becoming a member

But I have made a little digression & must return to my Subject.

The 2d. case of arm presentation, I was called to see about 11 years ago. In this, as the preceding one, a female Accouchier had been first called. and should judge, from circumstances which it would be unnecessary to particularise, that it was her (the midwife's) first case, of the kind. I think she had been about 36 hours in labour, and the arm had been presenting some hours previous to my being called in. Having spent some hours in fruitless attempts in endeavoring to alter the position. I had my friend Dr. Jesse Par[a]more then of Eaton Ohio called. (I then practised at West Alexandria East of Eaton 6 miles.) My friend Dr. P. was a physician of considerable reputation and experience even at that period and he still sustains himself well in the profession (& continues to be a neighboring competitor.)

Dr. P. also, after some time spent in endeavoring to turn the child, gave up the attempt in despair. I now proceeded to take off the arm at the shoulder, which, with some difficulty I succeeded in performing by means of the Probe pointed Bistoury. After which and after making

5. See Editorial Note preceding this case for a discussion of Caesarian operations.

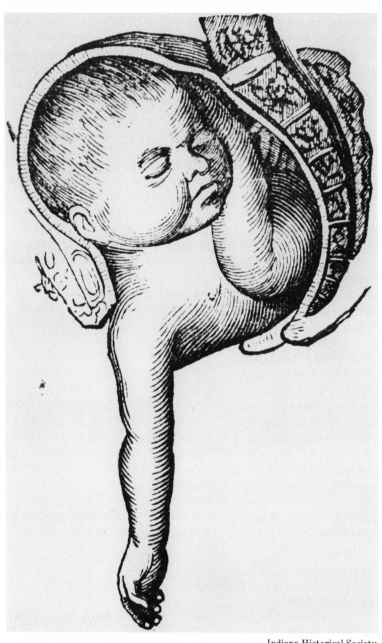

*A drawing illustrating the unborn child's position when presenting an arm
(Paulin Cazeaux,* A Theoretical and Practical Treatise on Midwifery, Including the Diseases of Pregnancy . . . , *ed. and trans. William R. Bullock [Phil-
adelphia: Lindsay & Blakeston, 1863])*

some considerable exertion I succeeded in bringing down a foot. & without much difficulty succeeded in delivering. A few hours after this we left our patient, and any thing I was able to discover tolerably comfortable. But the event disappointed our hopes, for she died I think in about 24 hours afterwards. I do not conclude that such cases must necessarily be fatal. but owing to the delay and the protraction that generly attends this presentation, particularly in country practice, it too often happens that a degree of prostration and inflamation follows which carries off the patient in the end.

It is fortunate for humanity that this presentation is rare.[6] what proportion they in their occurrence bear to natural labors, or to other preternatural cases, I do not recollect the report of Authors on the subject, but among a large circle of my professional acquaintences for many years, I recollect very few (indeed not any one),* who has had a single case of arm presentation. However, I would incidentally remark that only a few weeks ago, an unfortunate case of arm presentation occurred 6 or 7 miles South East of this place. in which the unfortunate female died without being delivered, I was not called in this case, but feel confident that I have correct information on the subject, She was first attended by an experienced female midwife, and first & last by 3 or 4 Physicians who, of the number, had a good Set of accouchery Instruments. Yet amidst all this array of skill and general experience she was not saved. Two of those in attendance are Graduates of the Philadelphia School, (if I mistake not, of the old school)[7] one of whom has the advantage of age and much experience in general practice, & both are quite respectable in the profession.—I do not wish to be understood as pointing to this case as one of "professional approbrium [opprobrium]" but refer to it as being a case in point. & only too conclusively proves the position I have assumed above to be founded in truth and experience.** In this case just refered to the arm was taken off at the shoulder as I am informed by Dr. [James W.] Salter one of the Physicians in attendance. but with all the advantage this gave, a foot could not be reached or the presentationed [sic] altered.

* Leaving out of the account the cases here described under this head.

** That cases of Arm presentation are generally fatal.

6. See Editorial Note preceding this case for statistics on the frequency of cases of arm presentation.

7. Lindsay probably refers to the Medical College of Philadelphia, founded in 1765. After the Revolutionary War the college's charter was revoked, but with the help of Benjamin Franklin, the school's charter was restored and the original faculty returned to their teaching positions. In 1791 this school merged with the medical department of the University of the State of Pennsylvania to form the University of Pennsylvania School of Medicine (William Frederick Norwood, *Medical Education in the United States before the Civil War* [1944; reprint, New York: Arno Press, 1971], 63-108).

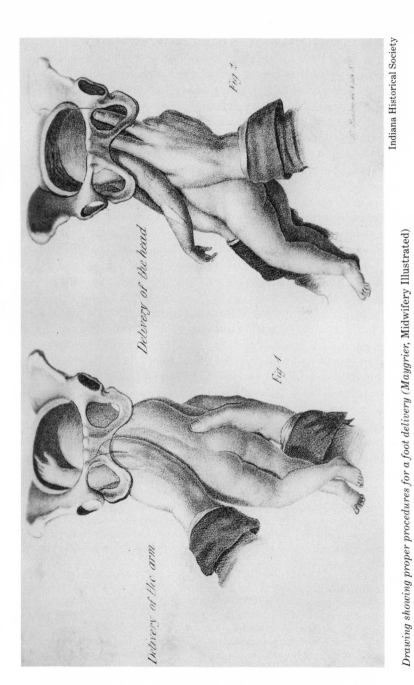

Drawing showing proper procedures for a foot delivery (Maygrier, Midwifery Illustrated)

Indiana Historical Society

My success in Mrs Thornton's case has not made me sanguine, or inspired me with much confidence that I should again succeed.—had the child been large I doubt much that it would have been a successful case: for to turn the child or alter its position seemed to be out of the question and altogether impracticable, And as labor pains were represented at any period of her labor; not to have been strong, and as her strength seemed not much exhausted, we concluded that in case the Ergot acted well, it was posable the child might be born in the position then so pertinaciously presenting. or, (as *Denman*[8] or *Burns*,[9] one of the other have forgotten which, hold out the encouraging idea,) that nature might produce the change which we were unable to control by manipulation, or effort of the hand.—So far as my recollection of Authority goes we had little to build on, or found a hope from; that we should succeed in its then presentation. However, the arm being removed the *breast* was fairly presented, and the child *doubled on itself* and was delivered by the natural effort of labor pains, resussitated & strengthened by the exhibition of the Ergot.[10] and I have nothing to the contrary, that she is doing well. and recovering as usual after former accouchments.

In conclusion I would remark that the result of my little experience would point out to me hereafter the necessity of guarding against the usual delay in such cases. The arm should be removed promptly on failing by a proper and well directed effort to return it. To remove the arm safely & successfully of course will require a pretty free dilatation of the os uteri. This is the only delay that should prevent a prompt removal of the arm, when once satisfyed that to return it is impraticable.

In cases where the child in this presentation is evidently large, where after removal of the arm, by a proper effort we fail in altering the position, or fail in bringing down a foot, would not the caesarian

8. Thomas Denman (1733-1815), a successful English midwife whose writings were popular in early nineteenth-century America, advocated the use of the Caesarian operation only in cases of absolute necessity and use of the forceps only when difficulty arose in delivery (Donegan, *Women and Men Midwives*, 46). He also described the procedure by which arm presentation could be altered. See Editorial Note preceding this case.

9. John Burns (1774-1850) was an English midwife and author of several midwifery texts including *Principles of Midwifery* (1809) and *Popular Directions for the Diseases of Women and Children* (1811). He believed that if proper procedures were followed, a physician could alter an arm presentation and successfully deliver the child in almost all cases. See Editorial Note preceding this case.

10. From Lindsay's writing, it is unclear whether he believed ergot caused the child to move, or caused the uterus to contract. Ergot causes uterine contractions and does not affect the child's movement. See Glossary of Medical and Pharmaceutical Terms.

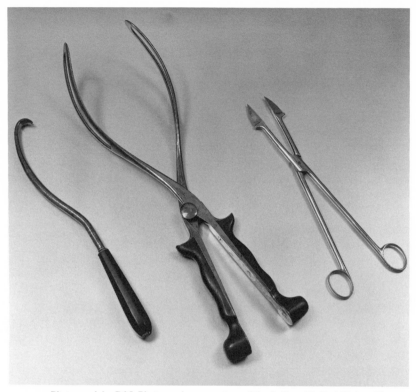

Photograph by B&L Photographers, courtesy of the Indiana Medical History Museum
Mid-nineteenth-century obstetrical instruments (from left to right): crotchet, forceps, and perforator scissors

operation be justifiable? To turn, seems generally to result in failure;
& so far as my experience goes, to succeed by dissection & removal of
the child by piecemeal is, in my opinion, equally doubtful. hence it
would seem that in many cases the caesarian section would be a justifiable practice before the removal of the arm, as it would seem to
promise as much, if not more, to save the life of the mother, than the
usual practice attended by the usual delay in these cases. and it would
promise abundantly more, so far as the life of the child is concerned.

I must not take my leave of this case without paying a small tribute
of respect to my friend Dr. [Joel] Bugg. with whom, I am proud to
acknowledge, I have been on terms of intamacy for several years. he
has the advantage of many years experience in the profession; having
had the advantage of attending Lectures at Philada. has practised
many years in Tenn. and for the last six years been engaged in a
respectable practice in this state (Ia.) and as a Gentleman of high noble

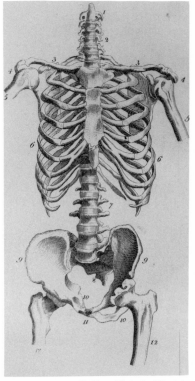

Drawing showing the pelvic girdle composed of the coccyx (8), the ilia (9), the ischium (10), and the pubic arch (11). The inferior strait of the pelvis is located at the lower end of the pelvic girdle, and the superior strait is located at the upper end of the pelvic girdle. (*Cheselden*, The Anatomy of the Human Body)

& honorable feelings, I know of no one, among my professional acquaintences, in possession of superior claims.

The position of the child in the foregoing case in detail I have neglected to mention. The arm removed & which presented was the left one. The head as doubled back, with the uterus very strongly contracting on it against the back (I mean the of [*sic*] the child,) the face laterally in the right side, and in this position passed thro' the superior strait, which in descending the inferior changd. with the face in front, and the belly facing the sacrum of the mother. This position necessarily gave the back of the head & portion of the posteriour Fontanelle a very flat shape as it was pressed with great force against the back & spine of the child's own body. The face & forehead was also moulded very flat. In this position the anterior Fontanelle was the most projecting part of the head, This situation gave such a peculiar moald, that all the portion posteriour to the Anteriour Fontanelle was in the relation of a side or base to a right angle. The top of the os frontis forming

Conner Prairie
*Drawing of a woman suffering from a dislocation of the lower
jaw (R. U. Piper,* Operative Surgery Illustrated . . . *[Boston:
Ticknor, Reed, and Fields, 1852])*

a side or leg. Had this order of things been reversed the labor would
have been much easior.
Richmond Ia.
Nov. 30th. 1839   *W. Lindsay*

Was called Sept. 10th. 1839 to Daughter of Nathanil Lewis (Friend)[11]
in case of Luxation of the *Lower Jaw.*

This Female a married woman had visited at her Father's being
fatigued and otherwise indisposed had taken a dose of salts[12] as I

11. Lindsay probably refers to the Society of Friends or Quakers.
12. Lindsay might have employed any number of salts with emetic properties.
Tartar emetic, however, was the most commonly employed salt of this type. See
Glossary of Medical and Pharmaceutical Terms, s.v. "Tartar emetic."

learned on enquiry by way of history of her case. Owing to the nausea induced the salts vomited her and produced a Luxation of the Maxilla Inferiora my friend Dr. Bugg hapening to be at my house from Newport [Indiana] I prevailed with the Dr. to accompany me. This to me was a noval case never before having seen this dislocation But my success was quite satisfactory; having placed the Female on the edge of the Trunnel [trundle] Bed (on which she had been reclining) in a siting position with her forehead leaning forward against the breast of her husband who sat facing the bed on a low seat. and placing myself behind him, (according to the instructions of *Lisfranc by coster)*[13] having armed my Thumbs with a Hndkf. in the usual way placed a thumb far back on the molar teeth of each jaw, pressing downwards, while with the hand & fingers placed under the jaw at the same time pressed the chin upwards, and thus succeeded in reducing the Luxation almost instantaneously.

Altho' this is indeed a simple operation, I must acknowledge that I somewhat dreaded it. being as above stated my first case. But simple as this operation is, I beleive physicians have sometimes been a little puzled. A Physician of my acquaintance informed me that in a case which was dificult, & in which he was unsucessfull in his attempts in the usual way at first, succeeded by intoxicating his patient (a male) and thus overcoming the spasmodic contraction.[14]

Richmond Ia.

Dec. 1st. 1839   *W. Lindsay*

Case of Miss Wright. Febry. 10th. 1840. was called after Dark to see this young woman, who early on the previous morning, had, in the act of splitting some kindling wood for the fire, by an awkard stroke of the axe struck it in the upper part of the foot. & woun[d]ed an *artery*. am not now certain what one but must have been either a branch of the Anteriour Tibeal or an Inosculating branch of the *Plantaris Externa* given off from the *Fibular Artery*[15] During the day much

13. Jacques Coster, *Manual of Surgical Operations; Containing the New Methods of Operating Devised by Lisfranc*, trans. John D. Goodman (Philadelphia: H. C. Carey and I. Lea, 1825). Coster (1795-1868) and Jacques Lisfranc (1790-1847) were French surgeons.

14. Alcohol (especially wine) was often recommended for calming a patient, as well as treating cases of debility, typhoid fever, and tetanus (Wood and Bache, *Dispensatory*, 675-76). Despite alcohol's known therapeutic value, Lindsay consistently avoided prescribing it. This may have been because Lindsay was a member of the Methodist Episcopal church, which at that time strongly opposed the use of alcohol.

15. An inosculating artery connects one artery to another. In this case, Lindsay refers to an anomalous artery which connects the external plantar artery to the peroneal artery. The external plantar artery passes outward and forward from the

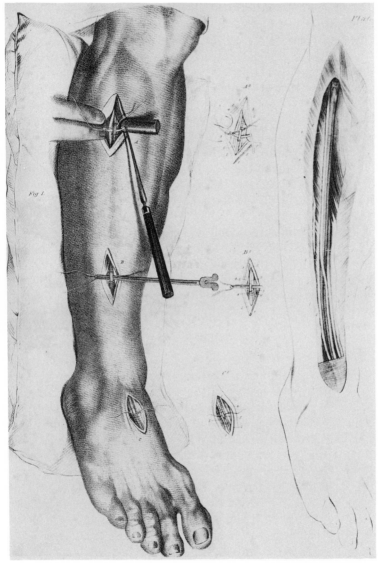

Illustration of the procedures for ligating the anterior tibial artery (Pancoast, A Treatise on Operative Surgery)

top of the foot to the fifth metatarsal bone. The peroneal artery passes outward to the fibula, or smaller bone of the leg, and descends along the inner border of that bone to the foot.

blood had been lost at intervals. which had been treated by various applications & wet cloths. It seems that she & her friends were not aware of the fact that an artery was cut but from the profuse hemorage & frequent recurrence of it were induced at last to send for me; and it was only on my anouncement of the bleeding being from an artery that she & her friends were awakend to the danger of her case.

This was the 2d. time only agreeably to my present recollection that I had been called to take up an artery of the foot.[16] I think the wound was between the flexer Tendons of the great Toe, & the one next it, on the Tarsal portion of the foot. The wound had extended quite thro' the integuments to the bone. and owing to the retraction of the artery or the depth of it by the aid of candle light found it a difficult operation to take up. and only succeeded by passing the kneedle deep into the cut & inclosing the surrounding integuments with the end of the artery. however the operation was successfull, & without any untoward occurrence the ligature came away in 12 or 14 days & the wound healed in due time. It was some 6 or 7 weeks before she was able to walk on it; but by degrees acquired strength & complete normal action of the foot.

July 8th. 1840

Was called on Apl. 24th. 1840 to see Shady Henderson in consultation with his attending Physician and my old friend Dr. Swain of Centreville this county. The history of the case was that 10 or 12 days previous Mr. H. had had his hand caught between two saw Logs at the mill. the flesh not much torn. and the injury was not thought to be very serious at the time. had until the day previous got along without much suffering, was not confined to his bed & for the most part was able to walk about the house. Dr. Swain had in consequence of the little pain & apparently good geting along of the patient only visited him 3 or 4 times during the period, who, I beleive, had been called on the same day of the injury. It had been only for the last day or two, say 24 or 30 hours that there had been any distrust that the patient was not doing well. Day before my seeing him had had some rigors. & the previous night had been quite restless. I saw him about 11 oclk A.M. on opening & removing the dressings found the Thumb black shriveled & in complete State of Phacelous [sphacelus]. almost seperated from the hand. which had spread to the whole hand to a considerable de-

---

16. See the case of Edward Webster, the first case in this journal, pp. 107-8.

gree. There had been some swelling & Inflamation of the hand & arm
but now the swelling had subsided & the whole hand & greater portion
of the arm at least to the Elbow was flabby & relaxed. & from the
back of the hand particularly discharging a very foetid dirty sanious
fluid. The pain in the arm & hand was intense. and the whole body
was covered with a dripping cold clammy sweat. much like that of the
worst cases of *Cholera*. The countenance sunken & cadaverous. pulse
still perceptable at the wrist, tho' very weak & could scarcely be
counted it was so frequent. The teeth were clenched & a Tea Spoonful
of brandy & water in the effort made to swallow it was well nigh
strangling the suffering patient tho' he could scarcely articulate a word
so as to be understood. Yet he seemed to be anxious to swallow when
water & brandy was offered him in the spoon (tho' he could not) and
apparently was still in the enjoyment of his reason & consciousness.
What do you think of an operation? was the interrogatory propounded
by the Dr. in (attendance on) consultation as well as by some of his
friends on returning again into the room. *Too late*, was my reply. And
so the sequel proved. I left him 12 oclock & he died at 2. only two
hours afterwards.

This case if worth recording at all will go to show how insideously
Lock Jaw. and I may say Gangrene & mortification sometimes steal
on. The Physician & friends had all been deceived in this case. his age
perhaps had something to do. & was evidently against him. he was
about 70 years old. tho' his constitution was good, & had been one of
the earliest Pioneers of the Country. had been one of that class who
had been subject to all the hardships privations & toil of clearing up
the rugged western forest.

However, advanced age, as we have abundant experience, has not
much to do in seting limits to, or in determining who are most subject
to this dreadful disease. In this case this result must be looked on only
as the result, and the effect, of gangrene & mortification, as Locked
Jaw did not assail until Gangrene & mortification had been fully established. The nervous temperament, would seem to me, to be more likely
to favor this termination viz. Lock Jaw. tho' from my little acquaintence with this patient I have no evidence that such was his
temperament.

An early operation would in my opinion have saved the life of this
patient. And the patient might probably have been saved by a judicious treatment without an operation. Warm bathing of the hand &
fore arm, with emoluent & soothing poultises would have been my
treatment. I think the treatment by Dr. S. had been Lint & cerate, &
perhaps Linament applyed to the hand.

This I beleive is the second (3d.)* case only of Trismus or Lock Jaw
that it falls my lot to have seen. Danl. Rue's son was the first (2d.)
which has been detailed in the lst. or 2d. No. of this series.[17]
Richmond Ia
July 7th. 1840   W. Lindsay

June 30. 1840. was called to see Mrs. Meyrs. in the Neighborhood of
[New] Paris O.

This was a case of Twins and my friend Dr. [David] Cox was in
attendence previous to my being sent for Dr. C. had delivered her of
the first child, which was living & healthy, this was a foot presentation.
but was not attended by any difficulty. On waiting some little time the
other child presented an arm.[18] and his efforts to return the hand was
unsuccessfull. On arriving there the arm was still presenting to the
very shoulder. And forming my judgment or Prognosis by my former
experience I had but little expectation of succeeding better than my
friend Dr. C. in reducing the arm. however much to my Satisfaction &
that of all present, in about an hour I succeeded in returning the hand
and bringing down a foot & in a few minutes more in finishing the
delivery. This is the 4th. Arm presentation that I have seen all of which
have been detailed in the previous Nos. of this series. The bad success
in these 3 previous cases had given me but little confidence of changing
the presentation as above s[t]ated. And my success in this case was
owing much in my opinion to the dilatation of the uterus & vagina
attendant on the delivery of the first Twin child. This 2d. child was
dead born and must from the swolen state of the presenting hand and
arm & absense of all motion, been dead sometime previous to my
arrival. from the little force that I had occasion to use. I feel confident
the means made use of could not have occasioned the death of the
child. On the 4 Inst.[19] I saw Dr. Cox from whom I learned that Mrs.
Meyers was doing well, & had every prospect of soon being up.
Richmond Ia
July 7th. 1840   W. Lindsay

---

* Andrew Clemmer's son being the lst. of *Traumatic Tetanus*, or Lock Jaw detailed in this volume.

17. The case of Daniel Rue's son was not recorded in the first or third volumes of
Lindsay's journals. Lindsay may have recorded it in the second, missing, volume of
his journals. He refers to Rue's case again in this journal (see p. 150).

18. This presentation of twins was extremely rare. In only one case out of 329
pregnancies recorded by the French midwife Paulin Cazeaux (1808-1862) did one twin
present a foot and the other an arm (Cazeaux, *Treatise on Midwifery*, 630).

19. Fourth instant: the fourth day of the present month (July).

was called on yesterday (July 6th. 1840) to see Mr. Mathew Cochrane laboring under a dislocated shoulder the Dislocation was downwards & forwards. having made 2 unsuccessfull attempts, on the 3d. one succeeded in reducing the Luxation. In this last attempt succeeded by confining him to a poast with a sheet his back to the post. placing one man to study [steady] him & make counter extension while 2 strong men made extension at the Elbow & forearm, while with a ball of yarn in the axilla I directed the head of the humerus within the socket.

This I beleive Constitutes the 3d. case of this dislocation I have seen, the first while I was a student. The first in my own practice was Smith the Carriagemaker some 4 or 5 years ago whose case is probably recorded in a previous no. of this series.[20]

As it regards placing the patient, I am now much in favor of securing the patient, with his back to a poast. as it favors the distention with more certainty than trusting to counter extension in the usual way by placing an individual at the back merely.
July 7th. 1840

June 21st. 1840 was called to see Joseph Cochrane laboring under compound comminuted fracture of the Tibea & Fibula about midway between the ancle & knee. It is said by those present at the time that the Leg (right one) broken at the fracture formed about a right angle laterally outwards being occasioned by a horse falling with C. on his back & precipitating his leg under the fore legs of the horse in some way. The part of the leg *torn* is the inside of the Leg. at the first dressing it was evident that there were some fractured & entirely detached spicula of bone within the fractured part & integuments. & since, within the leg of his Pants; also which was removed on a subsequent dressing, a piece of bone found within the Leg. In this case I dressed as I usually do with the stay case of corset splints. with a large piece of pasteboard on either side extending from the knee to the bottom of the heel & foot. all neatly confined with bandage and the Leg thus dressed placed within the box.

1st. dressing after seting on the 22d. blood still discharging out of the ruptured integuments—

24. The leg has not been much painful. Salts taken a few days ago operated well. appetite good—I forgot to mention that on my first visit next day I bled about 16 oz.[21]

20. If recorded, this case was probably in the second, missing, volume of the journals.

21. Bloodletting was a common, early nineteenth-century therapy often employed in diseases which were accompanied by inflammation. In these cases, most doctors advocated removal of between twelve and twenty-four ounces of blood. Benjamin

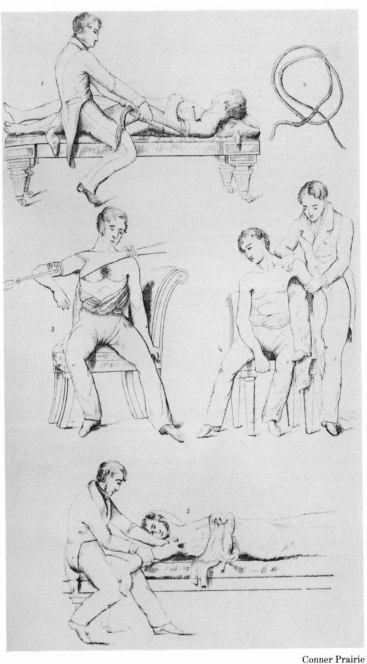

Illustration showing the use of extension and counterextension to treat a dislocated humerus (Piper, Operative Surgery Illustrated)

27. The Leg looks favorable tho' rather with the flesh & integuments a little distended with a collection of a bloody serous fluid but no fever, and the appetite good.

July 1st. a considerable quantity of dark bloody & dirty fluid discharge from the wound on removing the dressings & some slight symptoms of Gangrene to day applyed a poultice of bread & milk. appetite good.

July 5th. The black dirty discharge nearly ceased the wound looks better bowels regular & appetite good.

A few days after the 5th. July young Cochrane was removed to his Father's in the western part of the county. and did not require any more special professional attentions. I have seen him twice since, and it affords me pleasure to say that his leg has done well, will have one without any deformity. And it has not been much protracted in its cure beyond the usual time of simple fracture.

Oct. 21st. 1840   *W. Lindsay*

Rush, the prominent Philadelphia physician of the previous generation, advocated the removal of four-fifths of the body's blood (Pickard and Buley, *Midwest Pioneer*, 109; Shryock, *Medicine and Society*, 70).

[EDITORIAL NOTE]

In the following case, Lindsay discusses the death of his first wife, Rhoda Allison Smith. Throughout her life, Mrs. Lindsay had suffered uterine hemorrhages, but was never given a vaginal or pelvic examination. During the nineteenth century, these examinations were viewed as a violation of a woman's modesty and thus were performed only when diseases such as uterine cancer were suspected (Donegan, Women and Men Midwives, 153-55). From the symptoms described in this case, it is very likely that Lindsay's wife died of a septic or infected abortion. She was probably ten weeks pregnant when she had an incomplete abortion which in turn resulted in a massive infection. She then showed symptoms of confusion, renal failure, hemorrhaging, headache, low backache, chills, and fever. The goose-egg size discharge to which Lindsay referred could have been the aborted fetus. Even had he correctly diagnosed his wife's ailment, he could not have saved her life in this age before antibiotics.

Case of R. A. Lindsay.

It now falls to the fortune of the surviving husband to record the Death and last illness of his dear Decd. wife & consort.

On Saturday night Sept. 26th. 1840, my companion was taken in the night after retiring to bed with a severe chill, which lasted a consider-

Drawing showing the treatment for a fractured leg and foot (Gibson, The Institutes and Practice of Surgery, *vol. 1*)

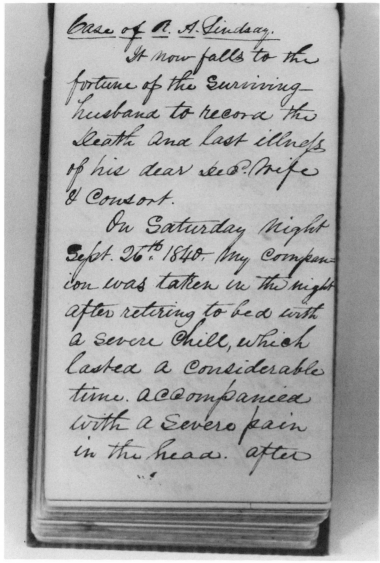

Case of R. A. Lindsay.
It now falls to the fortune of the Surviving husband to record the death and last illness of his dear dec?. Wife & Consort.
On Saturday Night Sept. 26th 1840, My companion was taken in the night after retiring to bed with a severe Chill, which lasted a Considerable time. accompanied with a severe pain in the head. after

Page from Lindsay's Journal No. 4

able time. accompanied with a severe pain in the head. after the chill passed off the pain in the head continuing excruciating, I took about 12 oz of blood from the arm. this did not much abate the pain in the head. & some hours subsequently placed the ligature on the arm and drew a few oz. more blood from the same orifice. bathed the feet in

warm water. and having drank some warm Penyroyal Tea she broke
out into a general moisture, & the pain in the head became less violent
and seemed to be considerably relieved generally. during a period of
about 2 hours previous to bathing the feet. during which time her
misery was so very severe, she was at times quite wandering and
incoherent in her mind & conversation. The state of the pulse not now
recollected. but the countenance was deathly pale, deeply anxious, and
indeed her sufferings seemed to be beyond description until after she
became moist, from bathing her feet, & drinking the warm tea. This
was early on Sunday morning. On breaking out into the moisture and
her head becoming somewhat releived, she began to complain of pain
in the small of the back. during the day she lay tolerably quiet and
seemed to be the greater part of the time between a sleep & a kind of
stupor. Sundy night she rested tolerably well.

On Monday after the operation of cathartic medicine, she seemed to
be much better than on the day previous. And on Tuesday night after
taking a Dover's Powder at bed time rested well. And for the most
part seemed to be gradually recovering during the balance of the
week. On Friday and Saturday she had so far recovered that she was
able to sit up a little & walked without assistence into the front room
and at another time into the Kitchen. On Saturday night, (she having
taken an anodyne (Pulv. Dov.) [Dover's Powder] on the 3 previous
nights in consequence of rather a nervous restlessness & continuing to
be somewhat griped from the operation of the cathartic, & as I thought
in part from the effects of 2 or 3 doses of the Elixer vitriol which she
had taken in pursuence of her own prescription,) I thought proper to
omit the anodyne, and she spent rather a restless night of it. however,
on Sunday morning appeared to be still on the mend. And her appetite
seemed to be coming up. But in the act of drinking a warm cup of coffe
at breakfast, which our Daughter Mary Jane waited on her mother
with, at the bed side, she was suddenly taken with uterine Hemorrhage. which in her then debilitated situation prostrated her & seemed
to threaten almost instant dissolution. In this situation I administered
a dose of the Acetate of Lead with Dover's powder and although it was
soon rejected by the stomach it seemed to have acted promptly in
checking the flooding. as it soon subsided, but again recurring in the
afternoon I gave her a portion of the Secale Cornutum (the Ergot) in
the form of a decoction. This as well as every thing else I think was
soon rejected by emesis. but the hemorrhage almost instantaneously
ceased, During the whole of this day after the attack of hemorrhage
she remained in a very debilitated & prostrated situation, scarcely able
to whisper, or move a finger, during her frequent attacks of hemorrhage which she had had during a period of many years She had never

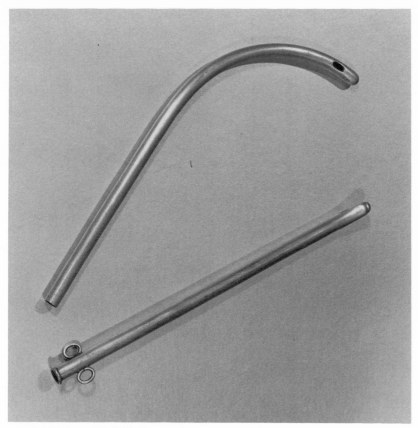

Photograph by B&L Photographers, courtesy of the Indiana Medical History Museum
Catheters, circa mid-nineteenth century

been so completely prostrated, and so continued to be during a period of 40 hours, And during this time her feet & legs were cold to the Knees, notwithstanding every exertion to keep them warm, On Monday night reaction came on in the form of a high paroxysm of fever, & lasted nearly all night. Attended by great thirst. and general restlessness. however during the period of her previous sinking she was quite restless & although she was so very week as not be able to help herself or scarcely raise a hand, she continued to throw her feet about.* During this period of extreme prostration her pulse was small & frequent. But when the reaction & Fever came on the pulse became full strong and bounding, and still more increased in frequency. As the paroxysm

* and almost continually drawing up her legs in much restless anxiety. and if interogated would not locate her misery.

of Fever subsided, on Tuesday she appeared better, and evidently had gained strength so as to help herself a little. was again able to converse a little. The Stomach which had been so very irritable during Sunday & Sunday night, and during the greater part of Monday, by Tuesday noon had become so much restored to its natural functions as to receive a little nourishment. And at times she was quite cheerful; and so continued, as we fondly hoped, to be rather better up to Wednesday night, when after a period of 40 hours or a little upward a second paroxysm of Fever came on which if posable was more violent than the former one. The thirst was very great indeed. The pulse as before, or during the previous paroxysm, & the whole surface so hot that it was quite unpleasent to touch her with the hand. The next morning (Wednesday) the fever had nearly subsided, tho' the surface still continued rather hot, thirst also rather more than natural. And a restlessness which not very considerable, was such as to create some uneasiness that she was not so well as on the previous morning (,Tuesday) Such had been her prostration since Sunday morning that I had not ventured to move her bowels with Cathartic medicine but had moved them entirely by means of *enemata.* and another symptom or attendent I would here mention, since Sunday she had been unable to *urinate,* excepting once, & I had releived her as often as it appeared to be necessary by means of the catheter. On this morning she seemed more anxious than she had before been to have her bowels moved by the syringe. And immediately after Breakfast I sent for Mrs. Siddall, with whose assistence I laid her out on a low Trunnel bed, for the purpose of having her bed made up. & while here administered the Syringe. in a few minutes she appeared to be in a quiet sweet sleep still remaining on her side, this was probably about 9 oclock in the morning & as she had passed the previous night without sleep & so very restless. I felt glad that she now seemed to rest so easy, however I had been revolving the matter some time in my mind whether she was not sleeping too long, but I did not make up my mind to awake her, so she remained for a period of between two & three hours when suddenly she awoke very sick at the stomach, her mouth filled with fluid which she must have raised in consequence of the nausua, but was unable to vomit or spit it out. On being asked by me what sickened her, replyed that it was the Dover's powder she had taken that morning. The fact was she had asked for a Dov. Pulv. in the latter part of the night but I had not thought it proper to give her one & she was incorrect in her then impression of having taken one. These were the last words she spoke From this time on she gradually sunk into an apparent stupor, by degrees the breathing became sterterous, and more & more dificult until she expired at about a quarter of an hour of

Photograph by B&L Photographers, courtesy of the Indiana Medical History Museum
Late-eighteenth-century scarificator and cupping glasses

2 oclock the next morning, (Friday.). Shortly after she sunk into this stupor, from which she never could be roused, I called in my friend Dr. [Joel] Vaile. By his advice mustard applications were made to the fore arms and 5 or 6 oz. of blood were drawn by the cupping glass from the Temples. but all with out any apparent advantage. Her days were numbered, her time had come, nature had failed, The silver cord was loosed. and she paid the debt of nature. She departed this life on the 9th. of October 1840. and had she lived to the 27th. of this month she would have been 49 [39] years of age, being born on the 27th. Oct. 1801.

I would here remark that my wife was the mother of 9 living children at her death, and a son which died in child birth makes 10. This was her first born, & lies entombed at the burial ground of Dayton Ohio. I do not recollect the precise number, but from the best of my recollection she had during the 21 years of our living together as many abortions as she had of living children, all of which were, as is usually the case, attended by considerable uterine Hemorrhage. These misfortunes, had often brot her to the brink of the grave. and she had had 3 or 4 attacks of uterine Hemorrhage when not in a state of *gestation*, it had only been 6 or 7 weeks previous to her death that she had had an attack of Hemorrhage, & from the debility consequent thereon she had not yet recovered. A week or 10 days previous to her last ilness she had her monthly visitations, which I understood her to say in her last ilness had been too sparing—& had not come on until something like 6 weeks from the previous period. as the period just passed, according to her account of it, had been too sparing, when she was taken in her last ilness with such excruciating pain in the head, and, after being bled, pain also in the small of the back, I was of the impression that she was laboring under suppression. And as it was not before mentioned, would here remark that during the first week of her ilness in which she appeared to be recovering as before stated, she had a slight shew, of what I supposed to be of a *catamenial* character, which she was of the opinion was quite too sparing. When in her last ilness she informed me that she had been suspicious that she was in a state of gestation (family way) when she had gone beyond the usual period as above stated. And another symptom she mentioned in her last ilness for the first time to me. about a week or 10 days previous to her last ilness. one night when I was absent,* she had a sudden discharge, as she supposed, from the uterus, amounting in quantity to nearly half a chamber[pot] full. And as she expressed to me supposed, as she had rather a bloated appearence, that it was some thing of the nature of Dropsy of the uterus. I am at a loss to make up a clear opinion of her case, It is among the posable things that there was an *adventitious* membrane formed containing this fluid. and another matter which still throws mystery around her case with me was the discharge of a substance, in her *dying hour*, in size & form about that of a goose egg. Mrs. Siddall gave me this information since her Decease. I knew nothing of it at the time and the women in attendance did not know of it until in the act of laying her out. On reviewing her case I have been unable to satisfy myself. whether if it were posable to meet with just such another, I could pursue a more judicious treatment. In the first

---

* on professional business. at Williamsburg to see Mr. Boid & Dr. Otwell.

instance, as already expressed, I treated her case as one of suppression, & after the uterine Hemorrhage took place, then treated it as a case of Hemorrhage. I should be better satisfyed with myself if I had made an examination of the uterus during her ilness. but taking the view of her case which I did, such examination did not to me then seem necessary. As it is a matter quite uncertain what was the character of the substance which passed *off per vaginum* all I can offer is conjecture. I have no means now of ascertaining whether it was an organised morbid, or pathological substance, or that it was merely coagula.

I would here mention another symptom, attendant on her case, but I am at a loss to give it any specific origin or cause. it was this, during the monday afternoon, Night, & once next morning, she had something like a spasm, or fit, the first was a slight sinking or twitching of the arm & oposite Leg, and attended by a slight distortion of the countenance. the last spasm was on Tuesday morning and was most severe of any that she had had.

The Injection which was administered on the morning on which she sunk into the stupor produced several involuntarily [*sic*] dejections,* I feared at the time the runing off existed that it was too drastic. It was composed of about 8 oz water 2 Teaspoonsfull Muriate [of] Soda (Table Salt) & about 2 Teaspoonsfull of Lard. The bowels I am inclined to think had become coliquative, as the discharge was considerably putrescent in its character. and had her strength been able to bear up under it, from the morbid character of the evacuations, perhaps the catharsis might have been of an advantage, but being watery in their character, I feel sorry that such was the result. Knowing that her bowels were generally very soluble & quite easily acted on by medicine, & had often sunk down considerably under an active catharsis in former cases of indisposition, I had, during her present ilness, been very careful not to excite or move her bowels much, and in preparing injections had in every instance, until this morning, made use of the starch emulsion, tho' on the previous day had added a little, Lard & salt. perhaps about 1/2 or 2/3 the quantity as this morning. & the result had been merely a single motion. On this morning I had concluded on the propriety of using the tepid water instead of the starch emulsion. making it more stimulating than formerly, beleiving the severe paroxysm of fever under which she had suffered so much the night previous, might have been in part induced by the morbid secretions accumulated in the alimentary canal.

---

* not until something like 2 1/2 hours after its exhibition did her bowels commence runing off.

By way of previous history of her life I would here remark she had been, from early habit and inclination, quite an industrious & hard working woman. and our misfortunes at Indianapolis,[22] and large family, made it necessary that she should labor hard, and as her health had become rather delicate, I feel concerned that she frequently labored beyond her strength. and in the business of washing for the family altho' she sent every week a part of it to a washerwoman, yet I feel fearful she fatigued herself with what she chose to do herself too much. and on the Saturday previous (day preceding her attack at night), I think it was, she had done a washing, when her health, or a due regard for it, should have prevented her doing it. And a matter which added to the fatigue of this day, we had received a small hog or shoat. & instead of overseeing our son LaFayette in attending to it, as I had requested, she chose to do the principal work herself of cutting it up & salting it away.[23] This she mentioned to me the next day during her first week of ilness. & remarked that salting away the pork had chilled her very much, and that she refered her chill with which she was attacked, and accompanying cold, on the same night to this cause. and it is my opinion that her fatigue & exposure just referd to was the immediate or proximate cause[24] of her last ilness.

As it is not unlikely, this manuscript, & record of the last ilness of my dear companion may be kept as a memorial in the family, & perhaps be preserved & handed down to our posterity, her surviving husband and partner in life would here take the liberty to add something by way of *chronology*, & such reflections as may occur to him after making the record. And I can assure my children & those who may chance to read this record that his mind while he makes it is laboring under a heavy load of sorrow; and expects long to mourn, if his life should be spared, this seperation & bereavment by the hand of Death. For to him she has truly ever been an affectionate & dutiful wife & helpmate. never was a woman more sincerely devoted to the comfort & well being of her family.

And although her husmand [*sic*] expects long & deeply to mourn his afflictive bereavement, he is happy in the reflection that he does not mourn as those who have no hope or comfort. In the midst of his mourning he is happy in the reflection & well grounded hope, that she

22. On Lindsay's partnership with Dr. George Stipp of Indianapolis, see Introduction, pp. xxiv-xxviii.

23. Salting away pork: a widely used method of curing and preserving pork at this time.

24. As in a previous case, Lindsay misused the term proximate cause. See Journal 1, p. 50, n. 53. In this case, fatigue and exposure would have been the exciting, or external causes, of his wife's disease, rather than the proximate cause.

is gone to a more blissful clime. It cannot be otherwise, that one possessing so much virtue, piety, & sterling merit, has gone to join the society of those who are truly happy. & where she will forever be associated with those kindred spirits who make up that glorious retinue continually in attendence & surrounding the throne of heaven, engaged in devotions & adorations to her saviour, who redeemed her, & executed a plan of redemption for a lost & ruined world.

Rhoda Alison [sic] Lindsay was the Daughter of the Rev. Peter & Catharine Smith. her parents were natives of N. Jersey. And her Father was regularly Educated for the ministry in Princeton College of his native State. Shortly after marriage & the Revolution he resided a short time in virginia, & some years in Wilkes Co. Georgia. In the year '95 he with his family removed to the then North Western Territory and setled in that year for a short time at Columbia 5 miles above Cincinnati on the Ohio River, Shortly after he setled on Duck Creek* a few miles N.E. of Cincinnati Hamilton Co. O. but in a few years afterwards removed to Donaldses Creek [Donnel's Creek], now Clark Co. O. Her Father spent a long & useful life as an industrious farmer & as baptist Divine. also had in Georgia & in the Western Country spent some time in surveying government lands. and was highly respected by all classes of society.[25]

It was only a year or two previous to his death that I became acquainted with his family. and with his Daughter, who afterward, & subsequent to her Father's decease, associated with him who makes this record in the holy band of matrimony. His first acquaintence with her was in the fall of 1815 at which time she was about 14 years of age, Her husband was united with her in marriage on the 6th. of March 1819 in her 18th. year. and at her death, as before stated, which took place on the 9th. of Oct. 1840, her husband had been united with her 21 years & upward as before stated

Her Mother Decd. in the summer or fall of 1830. having survived her Husband something like 13 years. and was a woman much respected for her inteligence, piety. & devotion to the interests & welfare of her Family & children. at the age of 16 or 17 their Daughter & subsequently my wife united herself with the Baptist church of which her parents had been long members. and as a member she was much

---

* It was on Duck Creek that the Decd. was born. She being the youngest Daughter & child of her parents.

25. Lindsay never mentions that his father-in-law was also an Indian doctor (see Introduction and Glossary of Personal and Place Names). He may have feared that his relationship to Peter Smith implied agreement with, or even frequent use of, Indian doctors' remedies. Most nineteenth-century physicians considered Indian doctors quacks.

respected, and of unexceptionable character. Her husband when he married her was engaged in Teaching in the Dayton Academy, and at the same time was a student of medicine. Here we remained until after the birth of a son* Decd. and our Eldest Daughter Catharine. In the summer of 1821 we removed to this county. & spent a Term of Teaching at *Salisbury* formerly the County Seat, and spent the ensuing winter teaching at Centreville. In the spring of 1822 we went to Lawrencburg on the Ohio River 22 miles below Cincinnati Dearborn Co. (Ia.) here we remained 4 years where I was engaged in the practice of my profession, part of the time in connexion with Dr. Ezra Ferris of that place, who had when he was a young man received much of his Education from my wife's Father. during our residence here we had an accession to our family of Eliza Ann, Mary Jane, & La Fayette, In the spring of 1825 or '26 we removed to Germantown [Ohio] where we resided two years, In the spring of '27 or '28 we went to West Alexandria Preble Co.O. where our Daughter Rebecca was born. In the fall of 1829. we came to this place. where we resided until the summer of 1837. we went to Indianapolis, where In consequence of an unfortunate partnership with one Dr. G. W. Stipp lost some *Six Thousand Dollars* which had been the result of many years professional labor and the strictest economy of which my dear companion seconded my exertions. I said we exercised the strictest economy. At the same time we expended freely for the Education of our children. And at this place we had an accession of Eleanora, Dewitt Clinton, Wm. Washington Irving, & our youngest now motherless little son, who at the death of his dear Mother was lacking only one day of being 21 months old, viz. Edwin Smith Blackstone

I have been thus circumstantial, that my children & posterity hereafter may have a record of the place of my children's nativity. and that my several places of residence may be traced by those of *my* (our) posterity may have the wish or curiosity to do so.

During our residence at Laurenceburg my dear companion attached herself to the M[ethodist] E[piscopal] Church and was entitled to membership at the time of her death.

Richmond Ia.   *Wm. Lindsay*
Oct. 21st. 1840

P.S. as a medical man were I called on to report the foregoing case, of course it would be presented in a somewhat diferent dress. Something recorded, would be rejected as irrelavent &, as uninteresting to the medical community. and only interesting to her children, relatives, and particular friends.

* a sweet little babe died in childburth.

Membership at the time
of her death.
Richmond Va.
Oct. 21st 1840
Wm Lindsay

P.S. As a medical man
were I called on to report
the foregoing case, of course
it would be presented in
a somewhat different dress.
Somethings recorded would
be rejected, as uninteresting
to the medical communi-
ty. and only interesting to
her children, relatives, and

particular friends.
I endeavored to give in
detail, the circumstances
& symptoms as they occur-
red under my own eye
together with some cir-
cumstances & symptoms
given me by herself, in which
she was no doubt as correct
as her knowledge of things, &
of her situation, could furnish her with data. I have
stated that I was at a loss in
coming at a definite opinion
what was the diagnosis, & posative nature or identity of her
case & situation.

*Pages from Lindsay's Journal No. 4,
showing signature*

I endeavor to give in detail, the circumstances & symptoms as they occurred under my own eye, together with some circumstances & symptoms given me by herself, in which she was no doubt as correct as her knowledge of things, & of her situation, could furnish her with data. I have stated that I was at a loss in coming at a definite opinion what was the *diagnosis*, or posative nature or identity of her case & situation.

However, I am of the opinion that she was not in a state of *gestation*, but am inclined to think that there was what is termed in common parlance a *false conception*, or in other words that there was a morbid or pathalogical gravidity[26] of the uterus The sudden discharge of the watery fluid, as related by herself, which took place on the night I was at Williamsburg [Indiana] most naturally is accounted for by taking this view of her case, and is still strengthened by, the supposition, that, the substance discharged *per vaginum* (as related to me since her decease, by Mrs. Siddall) in her dying hour, was an organised substance. and the symptoms generally might be pretty naturally refered to this state of things, under such a view of her case. for instance the hard chill on Saturday night, the severe pain in the head, back &c. Also the Flooding, and spasms of Monday afternoon Monday night, and on Tuesday forenoon. But if it be true that this diagnosis of her case is correct, I was misled, & I think too very naturally by her report of having had something of her monthly visitations* a week or 10 days previous to this Saturday night, & attack of chill &c. and as she supposed a recurrence of the catamenia during the first week of her last ilness. And taking this view of her case, the necessity of an examination per vaginum did not occur to me. But on the supposition that the uterus had been in a situation morbidly gravid, the circumstance of the membranes being ruptured 3 weeks or upwards previous to passing off the organised contents of the uterus must be reconciled. So far as I recollect neither my reading or long practice furnish me with a similar or parallel case. In conclusion I would remark that when considered the many & numerous attacks she had had during a period of 19 or 20 years somewhat similar to this, at least so far as the Uterine Hemorrhage was concerned, and when the fact is recollected that perhaps there is no disease more debilitating in its character to which the Female is subject, & that every attack leaves the unfortunate female more & more debilitated, it is not a matter of surprise that this attack proved fatal. Yet I am of the opinion that the peculiar season of the year had its influence, and it must be recollected that during the time

* and in this I feel confident She was not mistaken
26. Pathological gravidity: unnatural heaviness.

she labored under her last ilness it was the most unhealthy season of the year.[27] And that during this period as well as some time previous, there had been a good many deaths in our vilage, & viscinity most of which had occurred with a short period of ilness.

Oct. 23d. 1840   *Wm. Lindsay*

Mr. Samuel Boid's case of Hydrocele. Operation on the 20th. of Oct. 1840

This patient residing 13 miles distant, on the above day put him under my care in this place & submited to the operation in which I was kindly assisted by my friends Drs. [Joel] Va[i]lle & [Richard] Pretlow disease on left side, nothing unusual about the case operated by incision in the distended state about 3 or 4 inches long, but when contracted about 2 inches. water clear, & in quantity about 6 oz. should suppose. I made the incision thro' the *Tunica vaginalis* not to exceed 1 inch. Patient bore the operation well did not exceed 20 seconds having finished with the 3d. stroke of the scalpel. Dressing first time used Wheat flour in the wound, & over which applyed a light compress, & pouch over all. 1st. night rested pretty well—2d. day appetite pretty good, directed patient to make generous diet, but to stop short of satiety. at night applyed a light bread poultice. passed a restless & feverish night. 22d. being the 3d. day continued the poultice. gave salts, which did not operate until following morning. appetite not quite so good, patient complains much of pain in the small of the back, poultice continued. rested rather badly.

23d. appetite tolerably good. wound looks well, Testicle & general integuments swolen nearly as large as before the operation. has had little or no fever since the 2d. night. but is considerably restless & still has considerable pain in the back. poultice still continued. and occasionally warm Whiskey has been driped on the wound & surface of the part generally for the purpose of releiving pain of the back, & always for the time being. has a soothing effect.

Friday 24th. Took salts last night at bed time, bowels moved in about an hour rested better than any night heretofore. This morning found the wound had bled a little, & shewed a little sign of supuration coming on. last night drew the wound together for the first time with adhesive plaster pain in the back very much abated, appetite continues, pretty good. and patient quite cheerful, poultice continued.

Thirsday Oct 29th. my Patient returns home to day, strength much restored, the incision healing up, and discharge from the scrotem

27. The "sickly" or unhealthy season occurred in the late summer and fall months. Many fevers and epidemic diseases were prevalent at this time (Pickard and Buley, *Midwest Pioneer*, 11).

nearly ceased. has been siting up since Sunday. he leaves in excellent spirits and says he would be willing to pay 3 times the amt. I charged him rather than have hydrocele again.

My bill in this case $40.

Peter Kepler's Little Daughter Fracture of the Humeris.

Oct 27th. found the arm fractured a little above mid way. occasioned by waggon wheel running on it. 3 days ago. a Steam Doctor[28] was first called on the day of the injury & pronounced it not fractured, I found the arm swolen inflamed & quite painful, application had been the Comfrey Poultice, I made the usual dressing by the many tailed bandage & stay case of splints. The case being about 4 miles west, or N. W. of Centreville, Dr. [John] Pritchet of Centreville will take charge of the patient.

28. Steam doctors: a nickname for the Thomsonians, a nineteenth-century medical sect that believed all diseases were a result of a loss of body heat. They therefore tried to restore the body's heat through the use of herbal remedies and "steaming." "Steaming" consisted of wrapping the patient in a blanket and having him or her stand over a tub of hot coals and water (Pickard and Buley, *Midwest Pioneer*, 170-72). See also Introduction, p. xvi.

[EDITORIAL NOTE]

This case of fistula in ano described below is the only one recorded in Lindsay's journals. In these cases, the first goal of the nineteenth-century physician was to reduce the inflammation which often accompanied this disorder. This was accomplished by applying either soothing poultices or leeches to the area around the rectum. Once inflammation had been reduced, then the surgeon opened the fistulous sinus with a bistoury, so that the rectum and fistula formed one cavity with one external outlet. To prevent the edges of the wound from reuniting, lint was placed between the wound's edges (Dorsey, Elements of Surgery, 2:160-61; Gibson, Institutes and Practice of Surgery, 2:426-32).

operation Nov. 12 1840

Case of *Fistula in anno* Patient Alanson Dunham age about 35. I think understood him to say had been laboring under the disease 10 or 12 years, is by occupation a Taylor. after being some time at his trade and having made use of aloes & oloetic [aloetic] Pills to releive constipation, was affected with Piles and the first symptom he noticed of the fistulous affection. a small protuberence from the Anus of the Hemorrhoidal character commenced discharging. sometime afterwards a sinus formed towards the nates when this discharge from the Lit<tle?> protuberence ceased. The sinus which now communicated with the bowel, had changed its course occasionally and as might be seen from the Sycatrixes [cicatrices] had had its exit at different points at different times. at the time of my operation the sinus externally opened at about 1 or 1 1/2 inches from the anus in the nates. and in the rectum just above the *Sp*[h]*inchter Muscle,* In sounding it there was some difficulty, as the sinus in passing the director on reaching the bowel, the rectum at first seemed to act as a valve over the director. though after a few attempts the director was passed into the bowel. The operation was made by passing the probe pointed bistoury on the director & having introduced the fore finger of the left hand directed the point of the instrument with the finger and cut out at once which was done with little trouble. and was attended with less pain according the declaration of the patient than was experienced in sounding, & the introduction of the finger.

The operation was attended by little hemorrhage, The dressing was finished by introducing lint into the incision & sinus.

Nov. 29. The patient continued under my special care for 1 week after the operation, at the termination of which time he returned home to Centreville. The dressings were lint introduced generally once a day and in a few days after the operation Poultices of light bread. on the third day I think it was the introduction of the lint gave much pain and was followed by a restless night. The next day the poultice had such a soothing effect the pain had much subsided & did not again recur to much extent. On yesterday I called at Centreville to see Mr Dunham & found him at work on the board[29] where he informed me he had been since Monday. I examined him & found that the sinus had become obliterated, granulations having sprung up from the bottom of it. and in short the discharge had ceased & the incision had the appearence of being nearly cicatrized.

I should have mentioned that my friend Dr. [Joel] Vaile assisted me in the operation.

Nov. 28th. 1840   *W. Lindsay*

Mr. Lewis James case of *Strangulated Hernia* operation on Tuesday night last week of Ap. 1841.

History of the case. On the previous Saturday morning I saw Mr. James who had symptoms of violent Bilious cholic.[30] And was treated

29. Lindsay probably refers to a pressboard, or an ironing board used by tailors.

30. According to nineteenth-century physicians, bilious colic was caused by either a deficiency or abundance of bile in the system. The symptoms of the disease included an irritable stomach, occasional vomiting of bilious matter, intestinal pain, abdominal cramps, and coldness of the hands and feet. After a short period, the skin became hot, the face flushed, and the complexion sallow (John Bell and William Stokes, *Lectures on the Theory and Practice of Physic*, 4th ed., 2 vols. [Philadelphia: Edward

as such. first with Anodines & secondly with cathartic medicines On Monday had so far recovered as to go to the mill, but in the afternoon was again violently attacked with vomiting & severe distress of the bowels. however Mr. James did not call on medical aid until some time in the night my friend Dr. [John] Steele of the immediate vicinity was called. who unsuspecting any strangulation of the bowels in the case gave Laudanum freely as an anodyne which gave temporary relief. during the forenoon of Tuesday Cathartics were freely administered. but did not operate. nor did the free use of enemata in conjunction with the cathartics produce any effect. Some time during the day the patient made known to Dr. Steele that he had had rupture of the bowels of some two years previous. & from the pain now attending concentrating in the right Pubo-Iliac region it was suspected that the bowel had descended. & on examination Dr. S. found this to be the true state of the case & that the case was one of Strangulated hernia The Dr. having made use of pressure with the hand & such other means as the case seemed to suggest without effect I was sent for late in the after noon. When the warm bath, & emoluent applications were <pursued?> in until midnight without any beneficial result. An *operation* was now resorted to as the only hope of relief. was performed by Dr. Steele & myself between 2 & 3 oclk in the morning. On cutting down & exposing the bowel, the strangulated portion of 6 or 8 inches long was found to be in a highly congested state. The whole portion below the ring of a very dark colour & indeed quite black. The incision was made at first about 4 inches long. but in order to relieve the stricture, & return the bowel had to be continued up from one & a half to two inches higher. & such was the stricture at the ring, that the point of the finger could not be forced into it along side the bowel without very considerable exertion & the bowel could not yet be reduced, nothwithstanding Dr. S. & myself made repeated efforts to effect this object, until the ring was freely enlargd. by means of the probe pointed bistoury.

The bowel reduced the incision was closed by means of 3 sutures or stiches, carefully including in the needle the peritoneum, thus bringing the lips of the incision in juxta position, over which was applyed a dressing of lint spread with Basilacon cerate, & over this the compress & bandage. The stiches were left in until the 6th. or 7th. day when a considerable portion of the incision found to have untied [united] by the first intension. however a considerable discharge of supurative matter continued during the first 2 or 3 weeks, & up to this date on

---

and George D. Haswell, 1848], 1:312). Today, bilious colic refers to symptoms of abdominal pain accompanied by greenish evacuations. The term itself, however, is no longer used.

which this record is made, the 5th. week since the operation the incision is not yet completely cicatrised.

I trust the patient will recover his health, for some time he has been able to walk about the house on the farm. & about the end of the 4th. week rode out about 2 miles from home but he is yet far from being restored to good health. & has had two or three attacks of severe distress in the bowels, & twice has been accompanied by vomiting. The bowels have not yet been restored to a healthy tone. And the patient has been under the necessity of procuring their daily Alvine motion by means of some laxative or cathartic medicine. The patient at times has had a good appetite. and contrary to his instructions admits that he has indulged too freely at the table. & is willing to refer all the unpleasant symptoms enumerated to this cause. And it is to be hoped that he is correct; tho' I have my fears that he is laboring under partial stricture of the bowels, probably at the point contained immediately within the ring during the period of strangulation. Perhaps it would be in place here to remark that the patient states that the bowel had at times been within the scrotem. & that the rupture had been induced by over straining while engaded [engaged] in clearing up some grounds in the act of rolling logs. And that he had had occasional distress from the discent of the bowel but had always previous to the attack which was followed by the operation succeeded himself in returning the bowel. In this case it must be mentioned that it was the province of Dr. Steele to use the knife. As I was called in the sequel only in consultation. And in justice to the Dr. must say that he acquitted himself well but in the spirit of candour would just remark that if the incision at first had been made sufficiently extensive, so as at once to have exposed the ring of the stricture, the operation would have occupied much less time, & would have saved the patient much suffering.

Here I would remark that during my long peri[o]d of practice this was the first operation of the kind that has occurred. And it is fortunate for humanity that this operation is in the fewest number of strangulated cases necessary. & owing to the success which had attended me hitherto I was slow in consenting to the operation, hoping the stricture would finally yield to the usual treatment, but on cutting down & finding the situation of the bowel I was well satisfyed that the operation had not been gone into prematurely. but as is frequently the case no doubt in unsuccessful operations had been delayed almost too long.

Saturday May 29th.

Clark Co. Ohio

1841.   W. Lindsay

The case on next page of *Traumatic Tetanus.*[31] is the 4th. of this character that I now recollect having met with in my practice.

Clemmer's son on the Eaton & Dayton Pike, Toms Run, Montgomery County 1829, being the 1st. and Mr. Rue's son 3 miles south of Richmond Ia. being the 2d. case & Shady Henderson 3d. The 1st. from running a heated wheel spindle thro' the hand in preparing sugar spiles of the Box Elder—. The 2d. from jumping off a high fence & alighting barefooted on a dry Elder snag penetrating the Instep of the foot & a portion remaining in the foot. See cases as on record in manuscript.

Wm. Young during the first week of March run with his foot against a splinter in the night which penetrated through his shoe & wounded slightly the foot penetrating near the flexor Tendons of the two little or least toes & near the articulation of their Metatrarsal [*sic*] with their corrisponding Tarsal bones. I was called in April about 4 weeks after the injury to see Mr. Y. and learned that his sufferings had been great having had for several days occasional severe spasms apparently approaching nearly to lock jaw. On examination of the foot. found it but little swolen and unaccompanied by any external inflamation. the fisure or sinus made by the snag on the upper part & rather inside of the foot was still open which could readily be traced by the introduction of the probe but not attended by any supurative discharge. Being at a loss to determine whether the pain & the unfavorable symptoms were to be refered to a portion of foreign or extraneous substance a portion of the splinter broken off, or to Tendenous inflamation, I introdu[c]ed the director & freely laid the Sinus open with the *Bistourie.* and as a soothing remedial application, directed him to frequently bathe the foot in weak lye as hot as could be bourne, & to make use of the light bread poultice. & until suppuration could be induced at each dressing, to apply a few drops of hot spirits Turpentine. With the exception of an injury sustained some two weeks subsequently after laying the wound open by falling off his feet which hurt the foot considerably, he had but barely one attack of the spasms which he had previously suffered so much from & which as before remarked seemed to threaten *Tetanus* However he has had a very bad foot of it, & two months & upwards have elapsed since the injury, he is yet unable to walk without his crutches or cain, & could not a week ago bear more than one half his weight upon the foot.

31. In the nineteenth century, traumatic tetanus was also called symptomatic tetanus. Physicians believed traumatic tetanus was either a result or an indication of some other disease (William P. Dewees, *A Practice of Physic, Comprising Most of the Diseases not Treated in "Diseases of Females," and "Diseases of Children,"* 2nd ed. [Philadelphia: Carey, Lea, and Blanchard, 1833], 290-91). Today, the term refers to tetanus following wound poisoning.

This case I have concluded to regard as a case of wounded Tendon believing the slow & insiduous & deep situated inflamation, attending at the same time taking the extreme sufferings of the patient into the account, warrent me in forming this diagnosis of the case. Those who have had cases of inflamed Tendon will recollect that the inflamation not only comes on slowly, but that it takes place seldom at the point of injury, but higher up at the point of its origin. So in this case the most pain was deeply seated under the fascia, & as described by the patient in the ancle among the ancle bones, & when the integuments had swolen by means of the warm bathing & poulticing, (or I would say distended) supurative matter was thrown up from some point an inch & half below the depth of the incision which I made in dilating the wound.
May 29th. 1841

W. Lindsay

Case of suppurated breast. Mrs. Cox of Enon [Ohio].

When called to her learned that she had had an accouchment about 2 1/2 months previous had taken cold & setled in the left *mamma*. had suffered severely for the last 2 or 3 weeks producing as is usual considerable fever. I found the breast unusualy large even for an inflamed breast. I first made an unsuccessful attempt to open it about an inch & half below the nipple. but succeeded in giving exit probably to 3 half pints of matter from an incision on the upper side. however this did not give exit to near all the matter & in 3 days subsequently opened freely on the under side near the nipple & near the first incis[i]on made unsuccessfully. This last opening gave exit to probably as great a quantity of supurative matter as at the previous opening, and continued to run unceasingly for a peri[o]d of several days.

My instructions to the patient was a moderately generous diet, the bowels to be kept soluble by gentle apperients. and the light bread poultice as long as matter continued to discharge I have not since seen my patient but am informed that she is fast recovering.
May 29. '41

W. Lindsay

Remarkable case of *Gun shot wound* Young man Snyder then of the neighborhood of Enon, on Mad river, Clark Co. O, 1845.

History of the case, Having occasion to shoot something on the farm took down the Rifle under the impression that it was not *charged*, but in order to be certain in regard to the matter, placed his *toe* on the *cock*, at the same time placing his mouth over the muzzle for the purpose of blowing his breath through the tuchhole.[32] when the gun which happened to be already loaded was discharged.

The *ball* displacing the two central (Incisors) teeth of the superior maxilla; traversd., the cavity of the right (incisor) tooth coursing up under the nares, angling near the inner angle of the left Eye, manifested by the bloodshoten appearance of the organ; entering the cavity of the crannium to the left of the Ethmoid bone; and having spent its force, the ball was lodged within the crannial structure. Its locality was suspected from a slight bulging of the skin, about an inch & 1/4 or 1/2 above the orbital arch, and about a half inch of the mesial or central line of the forehead, on the right side, and on cutting down was enabled to *extract* the *Rifle Ball* without much difficulty.

The treatment of the case during a period of some three weeks, which resulted in considerable Febrile action as was expected from the character of the lesion, was such as to meet the indications from day to day, but to undertake a detail of the treatment, or to note all the symptoms & changes developed during its progress through the period of treatment would afford but little of interest to the casual reader. Suffice it to say that in the course of a few weeks the young man had so far recovered that I discontinued my attentions on his case, I might have noted in the detail of the above case that the *patching* around the *ball* was, a portion of it at least, carried up to where the ball was found embeded, and which was removed at the same time with the ball. during the treatment portions of spicula of bone, were removed as manifested & attached [detached?] by the supurative process. and some few weeks after I had discontinued my visits & treatment the young man came in company with his father to have still another spicula of bone removed from the floor of the left nare, that had become detached.

This was the last of the detached spicula, and so far as I know, any other attentions needed in the case

It might have been noted that at my first visit, and during the greater progress of the treatment of this case, the breathing was attended by some peculiariti[e]s. at first some portion of his breath, or the atmospheric air, passed out at the opening made in the extraction of the *ball*, and if I am not mistaken in my recollection his breathing for some months to come was marked by a peculiar nasal derangement. However his general health was good, & so far as I could judge was completely restored.

This patient might have been 17 or 18 years old at the time he met with the injury. And a few years subsequently, with his fathers family,

---

32. Touchhole: the small tubular hole, or vent, on the breech of a gun, through which the charge is ignited.

emigrated to Ioway, Consequently for some years past I have now lost the run of him.

Remarkable as this case is. and great as the recovery of the young man was. It must be regarded as another evidence of those hair breath escapes we occasionly meet with in which some individuals escape instantaneous death as if by a special providence & miraculous inter- posostion [sic]. We have a case repo[r]ted in several Medical Journals, and authenticated by the Eastern Press generally, if posable more remarkable than this detailed above.

In substance as we now recollect the case as reported, and have it in the Columbus, O. and a N. Y. Med. Journal. as one of the hands employed on some public work in one of the Eastern states while boaring & blowing rock an Iron rod of some 18 inches or more in length was by the accidental detonation of Gunpowder, blown through a por- tion of the side of the head. entering the side of the face and coming out near the top of the head through the *parietal bone* if which, incre- dulous as it may appear; it seems that the patient after a few months duration of severe suffering recovered.[33]

1855   *W. Lindsay*

Strangulated Hernia

In the summer of 1841. while at Dayton, was called with the late Dr. Henry Van Tuyl to see a German Female laboring under Hernia, which on full investigation of her case proved to be *irreducable* and as the length of time in which the bowel had been impacted within the sac indicated the danger of further delay, we proceeded to operate, making cautiously the usual incision. found the contained bowel very firmly impacted within the Inguinal sack, Inflamation having ran high adhesions to some considerable extent had taken place, and gangrene seemed to be threatened.

To remove the ahesions, & Enlarge the stricture of the Inguinal Ring sufficiently to permit the return of the bowel required dissection, cautiously & carefully performed,

33. The case to which Lindsay refers appeared in the January 1849 issue of *The Ohio Medical and Surgical Journal*. The accident itself occurred in Cortlandville, New York, on September 13, 1848. Phineas P. Gage, a foreman on the Rutland and Burlington Railroad, was preparing a charge for blasting when the charge acciden- tally exploded and the tamping rod (a rod used to fill up the blasting charge) passed through Gage's head. The rod measured three feet, seven inches in length, and an inch and one quarter in diameter, and weighed thirteen and one-fourth pounds. By late November 1848 Gage had recovered from the accident. He was still alive in November 1860. Physicians claimed his intellectual faculties were not impaired (J.M. Harlow, "Passage of an Iron Rod Through the Head," *The Ohio Medical and Surgical Journal* 1 [1849]: 243-49; "The Man Through Whose Head an Iron Rod Passed Still Living," ibid. 13 [1860]: 174).

Having succeeded in returning the bowel within the Abdomen, closed the wound by *stiches* & *adhesive* straps. placed the patient in bed, giving the necessary instructions to her attendants, left her to repose & quiet. I think I did not see her more than once after the operation. my friend Dr. Van Tuyl having subsequently the charge of her case. I learned that our patient recovered rapidly. and subsequently attended to her houshold matters as usual

The patient was probably aged about 40 years.[34] had been ruptured several years previou[s]ly. being poor, and dependant on hard toil & labor for her living & the support of her family did not receive any compensation for my attentions in the case.

This record is made some <13?> years subsequently to the operation.

1855.   *W. Lindsay*

Hezekiah Kesslering's case of *Hernia*.

In the year 1850 was called in consultation with Drs. [F. J.] Stratten, Davey, [Nelson] Donnellan, and [R. P.] Nisbet, and found the young man suffering intensely under hernia of the strangulated character, the bowel firmly impacted within the scrotum. which during the whole night, and til 9 or 10 oclock A.M. remained persistantly, & obstinately down

Removing the bowels, by cooling injections, warm bath, subsequently cold applications, nauseating antimonials.[35] Tobacco smoke,[36] & Decoction all carried as far as seemed prudent thrown up the bowels freely alike seemed to be unavailing.

How long the bowel had been strangulated or impacted within the scrotem dont now definitely recollect. but such was the great sufferings & obstinate persisistance [*sic*] of the bowels in remaining firmly within the scrotem. that an operation was seriously contemplated, when all of sudden by means of manipulation the bowel per Taxes was returned through the ring within the Abdomen.

A year or 18 months subsequently Dr. Nisbet & myself were called to this young man, and found him severely suffering much as in his former attack. having now as before taken cold the bowel down be-

---

34. Inguinal hernia is uncommon in females, especially in older women.

35. Lindsay could be referring to a wide variety of compounds, including tartrate of antimony (tartar emetic), prepared sulfuret of antimony, antimonial wine, precipitated sulfuret of antimony, and antimonial powder, all of which had emetic properties, although prepared sulfuret probably caused the most extreme vomiting (Wood and Bache, *Dispensatory*, 749-63).

36. On tobacco smoke enemas, see Glossary of Medical and Pharmaceutical Terms, s.v. "Enema, tobacco smoke."

Pages from Lindsay's Journal No. 4

came painful and not being able to return the bowel were then called
to his case. Now as before the patiently [*sic*] suffered most intensely,
especially when efforts were mad[e] at reduction *per Taxes* and now as
before almost incessant efforts were made by aid of all the remidies

which seemed to be indicated. and it was a Night, a day & a night, & not until the 2d. day that we succeeded in a reduction,

We now again prescribed the Patterson Truss.[37] Previous to this 2d. attack he had worn this Truss by our advice and had as he supposed become so far cured that the Truss was not needed & had left it off. when the bowel again came down by violence & Exposure,

Since this 2d. attack the Truss was again worn, and our patient now having by painful experience become convinced of the necessity of taking care of himself, have learned that he now considers himself radically cured of rupture by means of the Truss.

The fact of this case being cured is a matter of some interest. But it goes to show how by means of *patient perserverance* we may sometimes succeed *in reduction* of the bowel. & avoid a painful operation, & in some degree hazardous.

37. The Patterson Truss was patented on February 5, 1847, by A. W. Patterson, M.D., of Cincinnati. It consisted of an elastic band with an egg-shaped wooden pad emanating from it. A special spring mechanism attached to the pad controlled the degree of pressure applied to the hernial protrusion. Patterson's device was claimed superior to other trusses because the special pad provided uniform and steady pressure, comfort, and a speedy, radical cure of hernia (A. W. Patterson, *The Radical Cure of Hernia: Embracing a Description of the Disease, Its Varieties, Peculiar Conditions, Causes, Symptoms, Dangers, Treatment, and Permanent Cure* . . . [Cincinnati: A. Shephard, 1849], 12-16).

Recipes From Lindsay's Journals

An old man an acquaintence (J. Charles) was cured of old ulcerated Leg as he informs me by a cerate composed of Lard in which the Large sarsaparilla was simered to which some proportional of Spts. Turp. was added before cooling. This sarspaparil[la] is said to have a root as large ones wrist. myself am unacquainted with it.

Aromatic aperient
R. senna
Magnesia
Rhei [rhubarb]
Cloves āā Ɔ j [one scruple of each]
Sugar alb. [white sugar] 1/2 lb.
Water 3 pints—Reduce to 1 Pint

"Rev. T. Sullivan"

For uterine debility

℞ Red Oak Bark, bruised,	℥ iv [four ounces]
Tansey herb	℥ jij [three ounces]
Chamamile Flos. [flowers]	℥ i [one ounce]
Rad Rhei Pulv. [powdered rhubarb root]	℥ i [one ounce]
Cinamon & Cloves ā ā	ʒ ij [two drams of each]
Aqua Font[ana] [spring water]	8 lb.

Simmer down to 4 lb. Then add Sugar alb. [white sugar] 1 lb. & 4th. proof Brandy 2 gills. Dose 2 or 3 Tablespoonfulls twice or thrice per day

"Rev. T. Sullivan"

Cologne Water

℞ [to make] Ol. Lavender	ʒ i [one dram]
" Lemon	ʒ ij [two drams]
" Cinnamon *Drops*	viij [eight]
" Burgamot	ʒ i [one dram]
" Rosemary	ʒ ij [two drams]
" Cloves	viij [eight]
R.S.V.	oj [to make the volume of one pint]

Tinct[ure] Musk small quantity

Pro *Burns Piles* & c.
R. Nine bark say 1/2 or 1 lb
1 Gal. or more water
boil the roots first nicely cleaned. having simered an hour or two
remove the roots, & add say one Teacupful Hogs Lard which simmer
down until the water is dissipated.
    The above is said to be very valuable.

                                                        Aron Smith

    This Recipe has the authority of a somewhat selebrated Empiric
by the name of McKinsey of German Town O. & was prescribed by
him for a man laboring under occasional hemorrhage perhaps
bronchial

℞ 3 oz. ol. camamile
   4 " Bals. Gilead
   2 " ol. woormwood
   2 " Ext. Liverwort
   2 " Seneca Snakeroot

Glossary of Medical and Pharmaceutical Terms

Terms defined in this glossary include both modern and archaic medical terms. If the term is archaic, or its definition has changed since the nineteenth century, appropriate citations for the period definitions are given. Most of the drugs listed here are no longer in use. A few have limited modern usage and this is indicated after the former usage. Information regarding modern usage was obtained from Arthur Osol and Robertson Pratt, *The United States Dispensatory*, 27th ed. (Philadelphia: J.B. Lippincott, 1973).

Abdominal ring. See Ring, abdominal.

Abortion. Miscarriage. In the nineteenth century, the term primarily referred to accidental miscarriages, rather than ones which were induced.

Abscess lancet. See Lancet, abscess.

Absorbent. In the nineteenth century, the term referred to either a medicine used for neutralizing acidity in the stomach or any substance which when applied to a hemorrhage caused coagulation (Dunglison, *Medical Lexicon*, 38). Today, the term refers to a medicine which promotes the absorption of fluids by the skin, mucous surfaces, and absorbent vessels.

Accouchement. Lying-in, or the state during and after childbirth.

Accoucheur. A formally trained midwife.

Acetate of lead (sugar of lead). A drug with strong astringent and sedative powers. During this period, the medicine was employed primarily to control hemorrhage. It was also used in cases of dysentery, diarrhea, and cholera infantum. Prolonged use of the drug, however, resulted in lead poisoning (Wood and Bache, *Dispensatory*, 489-501).

Adhesion. A fibrous band to which organs abnormally adhere.

Adhesive emplas. See Plaster, adhesive.

Adhesive inflammation. See Inflammation, adhesive.

Adhesive strips. See Plaster, adhesive.

Adipose. Fat tissue.

Adjuvant. That which assists in eliminating a disease.

Adventitious. Unnatural or accidental.

Alimentary canal. See Canal, alimentary.

Aloes. A plant, the leaves of which possess cathartic and emmenagogue properties. In the nineteenth century, it was employed frequently in the treatment of roundworms (Wood and Bache,
Dispensatory, 66-67). Today, it is occasionally used for various skin
conditions.

Aloetic pills. See Pills, aloetic.

Alterative. A nineteenth-century term used to describe a medicine
which restored health without the production of any evacuations.

Alum, powdered. A drug with astringent properties used both externally and internally to stop bleeding (Wood and Bache, *Dispensatory*, 69). Today, it is used as a local astringent to check excessive
perspiration and is also used as an astringent in leukorrhea (a disease characterized by a whitish discharge from the vagina) and infected ulcers.

Alvine motion. A bowel movement.

Amniotic. Pertaining to the amnion, the fluid-filled sac surrounding
the embryo, and to the fluid which it contains (amniotic fluid).

Analgesic. Pain-relieving.

Ankylosis. Stiffness of a joint.

Anodyne. Pain-relieving and sleep-producing.

Antacid. A medicine which neutralizes acidity.

Anterior fontanelle. See Fontanelle.

Anterior tibial artery. See Artery, tibial (anterior).

Anterior tibial muscle. See Muscle, tibial (anterior).

Antimonial. Any preparation of antimony. The most frequently employed preparation of antimony was tartrate. This drug had sedative
powers, as well as the ability to stimulate the various secretions.
Other antimonials employed in the nineteenth century included antimonial wine, precipitated sulfuret, and antimonial powder. These
drugs were primarily employed as diaphoretics (Wood and Bache,
Dispensatory, 749-63).

Antiphlogistic. A medicine opposing inflammation and fever.

Antiseptic. In the era before the germ theory, the term referred to
any medicine which opposed putrefaction or decomposition (Dungli-

son, *Medical Lexicon*, 86). Today, the term refers to a substance which inhibits the growth and development of microorganisms.

Antispasmodic. A medicine which relieves spasms.

Aperient. A gentle laxative.

Aperient diuretic. A medicine which both gently opens the bowels (aperient) and increases the flow of urine (diuretic).

Approximate. To bring close together, as the edges of a wound.

Apyrexial. Fever-free; the absence or intermission of fever.

Arachnoid. A web-like membrane encasing the brain and located between the dura mater and the pia mater.

Arch, orbital. The upper, curved portion of the orbit, or curved part of the bony cavity containing the eye. The orbital arch is covered by the eyebrows and separates the face from the forehead.

Arsenic. A drug used both externally and internally by nineteenth-century physicians for the treatment of cancer. Doctors, however, debated the benefit of the drug in this disease. It was also used as a febrifuge in cases of malaria and was purported to be effective in the treatment of rheumatism and neuralgia (Wood and Bache, *Dispensatory*, 18-20).

Artery, labial (superior). The main artery of the upper lip.

Artery, peroneal. The artery which passes on the outside and back of the ankle and over the fibula.

Artery, plantar (external). The artery which passes outward and forward from the top of the foot to the fifth metatarsal bone of the leg.

Artery, radial. The artery which runs from immediately below the bend of the elbow, along the radius, or outer bone of the forearm, to the wrist and then through the palm of the hand.

Artery, spermatic. The major artery of the spermatic cord.

Artery, temporal. The artery which passes over the temporal bone.

Artery, tibial (anterior). The artery which extends down the front of the leg to the ankle. At the lower part of the leg, it rests on the anterior ligament of the ankle.

Articulation. The union of bones at a joint which permits movement.

Ascites. Swelling of the abdomen from excess water or dropsy.

Astringent. A medicine which constricts tissue or stops discharges.

Axilla. The armpit.

Bandage, eighteen-tailed. A bandage commonly used in the nineteenth century for fractures of the leg, the thigh, or, occasionally, the forearm. It consisted of a longitudinal portion of cloth with long, transverse pieces of cloth affixed to it. These long pieces were wrapped over the injured limb (Cooper, *Dictionary of Practical Surgery*, 1:178).

Basilicon cerate. See Ointment, basilicon.

Bistoury. A long, narrow surgical knife with either a curved or a straight blade and either a blunt (probe-pointed) or sharp end.

Black oak. See Oak, black or white.

Blistering plaster. See Plaster, blistering.

Bone, ethmoid. A light, cubical spongy bone at the anterior of the cranial base. The ethmoid bone forms the upper bony nose.

Bone, frontal. The forehead.

Bone, temporal. The bone located on the sides and base of the skull.

Bones, metatarsal. The fine, long bones of the foot.

Bones, parietal. The two quadrangular bones which form the superior and lateral surfaces of the skull.

Bones, tarsal. The seven bones of the instep of the foot.

Bread and milk poultice. See Poultice, bread and milk.

Breech. In reference to labor or birth, the presentation of the fetus's buttocks.

Cachectic. Pertaining to cachexia, or showing signs of general weakness and malnutrition.

Calomel (mercurous chloride or mild chloride of mercury). A drug used as a powerful purgative, sedative, vermifuge, and sialagogue (a drug used to promote salivation). It consisted of sulfuric acid, mercury, and sodium chloride. Calomel was widely used during the early nineteenth century, especially in cases of cholera, dysentery, and yellow fever (Wood and Bache, *Dispensatory*, 869-70). Calomel was probably the most used and most abused drug during the nineteenth century. In the stomach, it broke down into its poisonous components, causing mercury poisoning characterized by excessive salivation; sore and swollen gums, tongue, and salivary glands; and finally, destruction of the gums. The effects of calomel were cumulative since the drug tended to remain in the system (Rothstein, *American Physicians*, 49-51). The drug was used extensively in the early twentieth century in the treatment of syphilis. Today, it has very limited usage because of its tendency to remain in the system.

Camphor. A plant derivative with narcotic and anodyne properties used in the nineteenth century in inflammatory diseases and nervous disorders. It was frequently prescribed in cases of typhoid fever. Externally, it was used for gout and rheumatism (Wood and Bache, *Dispensatory*, 144-48). Today, it is employed externally as a rubefacient and mild analgesic and is used in conjunction with phenol and menthol as a local anesthetic and to relieve itching.

Canal, alimentary. The canal which extends from the mouth to the anus and assists in digestion.

Carbonate of iron, precipitated. See Iron carbonate, precipitated.

Carbonate of iron, prepared. See Iron carbonate, prepared.

Carious. Affected with caries, or bone decay. A carious bone is one which has become softened, discolored, and porous.

Carpus. The wrist.

Castration. An operation to remove the testicles.

Catamenial. Pertaining to menstruation.

Cathartic. A strong purgative or laxative.

Catheter. An instrument for withdrawing urine from the bladder by introduction through the urethra. During the nineteenth century, catheters were made of silver. The first flexible metal catheter was made in 1831 by John Weiss of England. Catheters designed for female patients were not curved until after 1830 (Bennion, *Antique Medical Instruments*, 78).

Cellular membrane. See Membrane, cellular.

Cerate. Any pharmaceutical preparation consisting of oil or lard and wax or resin. Cerates were used externally, and any number of medicines could be added to them to increase their therapeutic value.

Cerate, basilicon. See Ointment, basilicon.

Cerate, simple. A medicinal preparation consisting of white wax and lard and used externally as an emollient dressing for wounds and blisters (Dunglison, *Medical Lexicon*, 188; Wood and Bache, *Dispensatory*, 790).

Cervix uteri. See Uteri, cervix.

Chalybeate. Any medicine containing iron.

Charcoal. A drug used in powder form primarily as an absorbent and antiseptic in cases of indigestion and dysentery. It was frequently employed for malaria, hemorrhage accompanied by trauma, and diarrhea. Externally, charcoal was often mixed with other ingredients and used as a poultice in cases of gangrene and ulcers. It was also applied externally to control hemorrhage and was an ingredient in tooth powders (Wood and Bache, *Dispensatory*, 164-65). Today, powdered charcoal is occasionally used as an antidote.

Cholera. An infectious disease characterized by diarrhea, vomiting, and painful cramps. The term often refers to the Asiatic cholera which is caused by the *Vibrio cholerae*. The disease first appeared in the United States in 1832, and frequent epidemics of cholera occurred from that date through 1866 (Rosenberg, *Cholera Years*, 1-5).

Cicatrize. To form scar tissue.

Clavicle. The collarbone.

Coagula. Plural of coagulum, or a clot.

Coccyx. The small bone at the end of the vertebral column formed from the fusion of four vertebrae; the "tailbone."

Colliquative. Characterized by an excessive fluid evacuation which noticeably decreases the strength of the body.

Comfrey. A plant, the root of which was used for its demulcent, or soothing, effects. It was commonly used as an ingredient in cough remedies. The root was also used in poultices (Wood and Bache, *Dispensatory*, 1104).

Comminuted fracture. See Fracture, comminuted.

Compound comminuted fracture. See Fracture, compound comminuted.

Compound fracture. See Fracture, compound.

Compression of the brain. A pathological state caused by either extravasated blood, bone, or fluid pressing against the brain and characterized by unconsciousness, dilated pupils, stertorous breathing, and a slow pulse.

Copperas. See Iron sulfate.

Cord, spermatic. A cord which extends from the inguinal abdominal ring to the back of the testis. It contains veins, arteries, and excretory ducts.

Counterextension. The procedure of holding firmly the upper part of a limb while extension is practiced on the lower part of the limb in cases of fractures and dislocations.

Counterirritation. The principle that inducing irritation in one part of the body relieves irritation in another part (Dunglison, *Medical Lexicon*, 246).

Cranium. The skull.

Cream of tartar (potassium bitartrate). A white powder frequently used by early nineteenth-century physicians as a cathartic, diuretic, and refrigerant, and in small doses, as an aperient. In large doses, it was employed as a hydragogue cathartic, producing copious, watery discharges. Often it was prescribed in cases of dropsy because of its ability to stimulate urination (Wood and Bache, *Dispensatory*, 521). Today, it is occasionally used as a saline cathartic, but large doses of the drug can cause kidney damage. It is also used as a dusting powder for surgical gloves.

Crepitus. The cracking noise made by joints when defective in fluid production.

Cribriform plate. See Plate, cribriform.

Crus penis. That part of the penis attached to the pubic arch (or the posterior or root of the penis).

Cupping. A common, nineteenth-century medical procedure which entailed lacerating the skin by use of a lancet, or scarificator, and then applying a glass cup to the lacerated area to remove blood or excess cellular fluid. Before applying a cup to the skin, however, the physician created a vacuum in the glass by burning an alcohol-soaked piece of paper inside the cup (Gunn, *Domestic Medicine*, 597-98).

Cuticle. The epidermis, or the outermost nonvascular layer of skin.

Decoction. A medicine made by boiling various ingredients.

Dejection. Fecal discharge or stool.

Deltoid muscle. See Muscle, deltoid.

Demulcent. In the nineteenth century, the term referred to mucilaginous and saccharine medicines which corrected acrid conditions of the body fluids (Dunglison, *Medical Lexicon*, 276). Today, the term refers to a medicine which is soothing, mucilaginous, or oily.

Depressed skull fracture. See Fracture, skull.

Derangement. Insanity. Also, the term meant disturbance of a function of an organ. For example, nervous derangement referred to a disturbance of the nervous system.

Desquamate. To scale.

Diaphoretic. A drug which promotes perspiration.

Diathesis. Any state or condition of the body. For example, febrile diathesis is a state of the body characterized by fever.

Digitalis (foxglove). A drug prescribed in the nineteenth century as a narcotic and sedative. It was primarily used to control palpitations of the heart. Because of its diuretic properties, it was also employed extensively in cases of dropsy. Doctors during this period also recognized digitalis's strengthening effect upon the heart (Wood and Bache, *Dispensatory*, 271-74). Today, it is used in congestive heart failure.

Dilatation. The condition of being dilated; dilation.

Diluted sulfuric acid. See Elixir vitriol.

Director. A grooved instrument used for guiding a surgical knife.

Disarticulation. Amputation or separation at a joint.

Diuretic. A medicine promoting the secretion of urine.

Dogwood. A plant possessing tonic and astringent powers. The drug was given in powder, decoction, or extract (Wood and Bache, *Dispensatory*, 256-57).

Dover's powder (powder of ipecac and opium). This medicinal preparation was made by mixing powdered ipecac with opium and potassium sulfate. It was used both as an anodyne to soothe pain and a diaphoretic to induce copious perspiration. It was considered a useful remedy in diseases such as dysentery, diarrhea, and uterine hemorrhage (Wood and Bache, *Dispensatory*, 959).

Dressing curved forceps. See Forceps, dressing curved.

Dropsy. The accumulation of serous fluid in the cellular tissue or a body cavity.

Dura mater. The thickest, most fibrous, and outermost of the three membranes covering the brain and spinal cord.

Ecchymosis. A black and blue swelling from a bruise.

Edematous (or oedematous). Swollen because of an excess of fluid in the tissue's interstices.

Eighteen-tailed bandage. See Bandage, eighteen-tailed.

Elephantiasis. A disease in which the extremities swell and the skin becomes rough and scaly as a result of an obstruction of the lymphatic channels.

Elixir vitriol (diluted or aromatic sulfuric acid). A drug prescribed as a tonic and astringent. Frequently, it was employed in night sweats, loss of appetite, and convalescence from fever (Wood and Bache, *Dispensatory*, 720-21).

Elm, slippery. The bark of the slippery elm was employed in the nineteenth century as an emollient in cases of external inflammation. The bark was also used internally to soothe the digestive system and prescribed particularly in cases of dysentery, diarrhea, and diseases of the urinary tract (Wood and Bache, *Dispensatory*, 660-61).

Embrocation. A liniment.

Emetic. A medicine or drug which produces vomiting.

Emmenagogue. A medicine producing a discharge of blood from the uterus.

Emollient. A substance used to soothe the system.

Emphysema. In the nineteenth century, emphysema referred to any tumor that resulted from the introduction of air into the interstices of the tissue. More commonly, emphysema meant the suffusion of air into the tissue of the lungs (Dunglison, *Medical Lexicon*, 864). Today, the term refers to swelling caused by the presence of air although it is used most commonly in reference to pulmonary emphysema, a condition in which the air spaces farthest from the terminal bronchioles of the lungs increase beyond normal size.

Emplastrum lyttae. See Plaster, blistering.

Emulsion. A pharmaceutical preparation composed of oil suspended in water by mucilage, or a gelatinous substance (Dunglison, *Medical Lexicon*, 324).

Encysted. Tumors which consist of fluid or other matter enclosed in a sac or cyst.

Enema, tobacco smoke. The use of tobacco smoke enemas dates to the 1600s when the English used flexible pipes to introduce tobacco smoke into the bowels. Tobacco smoke enemas were especially popular in the eighteenth and nineteenth centuries in cases of constipation, strangulated hernia, and intestinal obstructions. Doctors needed a special apparatus to introduce the fumes of tobacco into the rectum. The standard apparatus consisted of a closed metallic container in which tobacco was burned and the fumes propelled into an enema tube by means of a bellows (Julius Friedenwald and Samuel Morrison, "The History of the Enema with Some Notes on Related Procedures," *Bulletin of the History of Medicine* 8 [February 1940]: 239-79).

Enemata. Plural of enema (clyster), or a liquid injected into the rectum to produce an evacuation.

Engorgement. Local congestion; the state of being completely filled.

Epispastics. Medicines which when applied externally cause inflammation and blistering.

Epithelium. The membranous, cellular tissue covering the external and internal surfaces of the body. The epithelium lines the vessels and body cavities.

Epsom salts. See Salts, epsom.

Ergot (secale cornutum or spurred rye). A drug used to cause powerful uterine contractions. It often was employed in cases of protracted labor to hasten the expulsion of the placenta. There was, however, considerable danger in using ergot in these cases because the constant and unrelenting contractions caused by the drug often resulted in the death of the child and rupture of the uterus. Thus nineteenth-century physicians were urged to use the drug only when the uterus had been sufficiently relaxed, the presentation was normal, the fetus was already dead, or when protracted labor threatened the life of the mother (Wertz and Wertz, *Lying-In*, 65-66; Wood and Bache, *Dispensatory*, 586-87). Today, doctors use a compound of ergot as an analgesic for migraine.

Eschar. A slough, or scab produced by a corrosive application.

Escharotic. A caustic or corrosive substance capable of destroying the skin's texture.

Ethmoid bone. See Bone, ethmoid.

Exacerbation. The increase in the symptoms of a disease.

Exostosis. A bony tumor.

Expectorant. A medicine which promotes mucus discharge from the lungs and trachea.

Exsanguinated. Anemic, or deprived of blood.

Extension. The pulling of a fractured or dislocated limb to restore it to its natural position; opposite of counterextension.

External plantar artery. See Artery, plantar (external).

Extract. A drug made by removing the active constituents of a vegetable or animal substance. Today, it refers to an alcoholic solution.

Extravasated. In reference to blood, that which has escaped from a vessel into the surrounding tissue.

Fascia. Connective tissue which holds together muscles and various organs of the body.

Febrifuge. A medicine or agent which reduces fever.

Febrile. Of or relating to fever.

Felon (whitlow or paronychia). A pus formation in the fingers. According to nineteenth-century nosology, there were several varieties of whitlow. One type formed below the cuticle while another had its center under the flexor tendons. The latter type was confined to the area between the periosteum and bone (Hooper, *Lexicon Medicum*, 2:156).

Femur. The thigh bone.

Ferri carbonas praecipitatus. See Iron carbonate, precipitated.

Ferri sulfas. See Iron sulfate.

Fetid. Having a bad or disagreeable smell.

Fibula. The smaller, or outside, bone of the lower leg.

Fistula. An abnormal opening or passage, usually between two internal organs or an internal organ and the body surface.

Fistula in ano. An abnormal opening or sinus near the anus.

Flax. A plant, the seeds of which were primarily used as an emollient and demulcent. The seeds, when mixed with water, were used as an emollient poultice (Wood and Bache, *Dispensatory*, 396-97).

Flexor tendons. See Tendons, flexor.

Flooding. In the nineteenth century, this term referred to uterine hemorrhage that occurred during pregnancy (Burns, *Principles of Midwifery*, 231). Today, the term refers to a copious loss of blood per vagina, especially during menstruation.

Foetid. See Fetid.

Fontanelle. A soft spot in the skull. Before birth, the bones of the skull are separated. At the places where the bones fail to meet, there are openings or anterior (towards the forehead) and posterior fontanelles. After development, these openings become soft spots.

Forceps, dressing curved. Small forceps used to remove lint and dressings from wounds.

Fracture, comminuted. A fracture in which the bone is broken into a number of pieces.

Fracture, compound. A fracture in which the bone fragments protrude through the skin.

Fracture, compound comminuted. A fracture in which both the bone is broken into a number of pieces and the bone fragments protrude through the skin.

Fracture, skull. There are two types of skull fracture: linear and depressed. In the linear fracture, the skull is cracked. In depressed skull fracture, the bone is pushed inward toward the brain and there is a likelihood of brain damage.

Frontal bone. See Bone, frontal.

Fundus. The base of an organ, or the part farthest from the mouth.

Fundus uteri. The upper, broad extremity of the body of the uterus.

Fungus cerebri. Many nineteenth-century physicians believed this was a growth of the brain. Today, the term refers to a protrusion of swollen brain tissue through a fracture site. It often has the appearance of a toadstool.

Funis umbilicalis. The umbilical cord.

Gamboge. A plant, the resin of which was used by nineteenth-century physicians to treat dropsy, obstinate constipation, and tapeworm (Wood and Bache, *Dispensatory*, 313-14). Today, it is occasionally used as a drastic hydragogue cathartic. Since it is so severe, however, it is often used in combination with other cathartics.

Glands, lactiferous. The mammary glands.

Gleet. A chronic stage of gonorrheal urethritis (or gonorrheal infection of the urethra).

Granulation. Grain-like, fleshy tissue or masses which form in wounds.

Guaiac. A tree, the juice of which was used in the nineteenth century as a stimulant and alterative. When given with opium, ipecacuahna, and warm drinks, it induced perspiration. It was also employed as a diuretic and, in large doses, as a purgative. It was deemed beneficial in the treatment of rheumatism, as well as gout, scrofula, secondary syphilis, and a variety of skin diseases (Wood and Bache, *Dispensatory*, 330-32).

Healing by first intention. Normal healing.

Hemlock. A plant, the leaves and seeds of which were used as a narcotic (Wood and Bache, *Dispensatory*, 247-48).

Hemorrhage, secondary. Hemorrhage occurring a considerable time after an injury.

Hepatic. Pertaining to the liver.

Hernia. A protrusion of any abdominal organ through an abnormal opening. This protrusion is usually covered with peritoneum.

Hernia, irreducible. A hernia in which the contents of the hernial sac cannot be returned to the abdomen by hand.

Hernia, reducible. A hernia in which the contents of the hernial sac can be returned to the abdomen by hand.

Hernia, strangulated. An irreducible hernia in which a stricture has formed over the opening where the parts have protruded through the abdomen.

Hernia, umbilical. A hernia in which part of the intestines protrude near the umbilicus, or navel. The protruding bowel is covered with skin and subcutaneous tissue.

Hernial sac. See Sac, hernial.

Hops (Humulus lupulus). A plant, the fruit of which was used in the nineteenth century as a tonic and narcotic in cases of local debility associated with nervous problems. It was used to relieve pain and procure sleep. Hops was given in substance, infusion, tincture, or extract. Externally, it was used in poultices to reduce pain and swelling (Wood and Bache, *Dispensatory*, 344-46).

Horseradish. A plant, the root of which was used by nineteenth-century physicians as a stimulant to promote appetite and improve digestion. It also increased the flow of urine and, therefore, was occasionally used in cases of dropsy (Wood and Bache, *Dispensatory*, 109-10).

Humerus. The bone of the upper arm.

Humulus lupulus. See Hops.

Hydatid. Cyst-like.

Hydragogue. A medicine used to produce watery discharges.

Hydrargyrum. See Mercury.

Hydrocele. An excess of fluid surrounding the tunica vaginalis, or serous membrane, of the testes.

Ilium. The large bone of the pelvic girdle forming the superior portion of the hip.

Indication. A sign, or symptom, which shows the cause of a disease. To treat a disease per indication is to treat each symptom as it appears, rather than treating the disease.

Indolent. In reference to tumors, indolent means painless.

Infection, secondary. Infection by a microorganism followed by infection by another type of microorganism.

Inferior strait. See Strait, inferior.

Inflammation. A disease characterized by heat, pain, redness, swelling, and fever. Inflammation can terminate in resolution, suppuration, gangrene, or scirrhus.

Inflammation, adhesive. Inflammation which terminates in healing or adhesion of the separated parts.

Inguinal ring. See Ring, abdominal.

Inguinal sac. See Sac, inguinal.

Integument. A membrane covering or enveloping an organ.

Interosseous ligaments. See Ligaments, interosseous.

Iodine. An element used medicinally in diseases of the absorbent and glandular system. It was primarily used in the cure of scrofulous diseases and, after 1820, in the treatment of goiter. Externally, it was used as a rubefacient (Wood and Bache, *Dispensatory*, 359-63). Iodine is still used for the treatment of early forms of goiter and is also used as a local irritant and germicide.

Iron carbonate, precipitated. A drug consisting of iron sulfate, carbonate of soda, and water. This reddish powder was used to restore the body to health and also induce menstruation (Wood and Bache, *Dispensatory*, 847-49).

Iron carbonate, prepared (ferric oxide or rust). This drug was employed during the early nineteenth century to restore the body to health. Because of the drug's insolubility in acid, nineteenth-century physicians often substituted the precipitated carbonate of iron for rust (Wood and Bache, *Dispensatory*, 849).

Iron sulfate (green vitriol or copperas). A bluish-green salt manufactured from iron wire, sulfuric acid, and water. Medicinally, it was used as a tonic and astringent. Commercially, copperas was used primarily in dyeing and tanning (Wood and Bache, *Dispensatory*, 852-53). Today, iron sulfate is most widely used in the treatment of iron-deficiency anemias and also is employed in the treatment of chronic conjunctivitis and leukorrhea.

Irreducible hernia. See Hernia, irreducible.

Ischium. The inferior, back part of the hipbone.

Jalap. A plant, the root of which was employed as an active cathartic to produce copious and watery stools (Wood and Bache, *Dispensatory*, 373-77).

Labia pudenda. The folds of skin located on either side of the vagina.

Labia superiora. The upper lip.

Labial artery (superior). See Artery, labial (superior).

Lacteal. Milk-like.

Lacteal glands. See Glands, lactiferous.

Lactiferous glands. See Glands, lactiferous.

Lancet. An instrument containing a small, razor-sharp knife and commonly used for bloodletting during the nineteenth century.

Lancet, abscess. A large lancet for opening abscesses.

Lancet, thumb. A lancet consisting of a small flexible razor-sharp blade with folding guards of ivory, tortoise, or mother-of-pearl. This bloodletting device was called a thumb lancet because the blade was thrust into the vein by the thumb, rather than by a spring mechanism (Bennion, *Antique Medical Instruments*, 40-41).

Lard (adeps). The prepared fat of hogs was used in the nineteenth century as an ingredient in cerates, ointments, and enemas (Wood and Bache, *Dispensatory*, 51-52).

Laudanum. A tincture of opium. As with opium, laudanum was also employed as a narcotic and anodyne (Wood and Bache, *Dispensatory*, 1009). Opium is rarely used today. Its alkaloids, however, are used for analgesic purposes.

Lesion. Any abnormal or pathological change in the function of an organ due to an injury.

Levigation. To separate (fine powder) from coarse material by suspending it in a liquid.

Ligaments, interosseous. Ligaments situated between the bones they unite. In his journals, Lindsay used the term to refer to those ligaments between the tibia and fibula.

Ligature. Thread or wire used for tying a vessel.

Liniment. A liquid or semiliquid preparation that is applied to the skin as an anodyne or a counterirritant.

Liniment, volatile. A liniment which vaporizes rapidly and is made from ammonia and an oil (such as olive oil or flaxseed oil).

Liquor amnii. Amniotic fluid.

Lockjaw. Tetanus.

Loins. Part of the back between the thorax and the pelvis.

Lunar caustic (silver nitrate). A drug used externally as an escharotic (Wood and Bache, *Dispensatory*, 774-75). Today, it is recognized as a powerful chemical germicide.

Luxation. Dislocation.

Lye. A preparation formed from leaching pearlash (wood ashes), or potassium carbonate. It was commonly used in making soap. Medicinally, potassium carbonate was employed as a diuretic, antacid, and diaphoretic. Lye also had caustic properties (Wood and Bache, *Dispensatory*, 943). Lye is a very potent escharotic and is used as an alkalizing agent.

Lyttae emplastrum. See Plaster, blistering.

Mala. The cheek bone.

Mamma. Breast.

Materia medica. The study of drugs and their uses and preparations.

Maxilla inferior. The lower jaw.

Maxilla superior. The upper jaw.

Medicatrix naturae. The healing power of nature.

Meliceris. In reference to tumors, those which have a honey-like consistency.

Membrane, cellular. The loose connective tissue of the body.

Mercury (hydrargyrum). A metallic element, used in a variety of medicinal compounds during the nineteenth century (see also entry under "Calomel"). It was commonly employed in the treatment of syphilis, digestive disorders, and febrile diseases (Wood and Bache, *Dispensatory*, 346-52). In the early twentieth century, doctors frequently used mercury for the treatment of syphilis. It was replaced by arsenical and bismuth compounds and then penicillin. At present, it is used in a compound for treating cardiac edema.

Mesial. Pertaining to the center line dividing the human body into the left and right halves.

Metastasis. A change in the seat or location of a disease.

Metatarsal bones. See Bones, metatarsal.

Morbid. Diseased.

Mortification. The death of a part. In the nineteenth century, doctors believed that the first stage of mortification was gangrene; the second stage was sphacelous, when the part was totally destroyed (Dunglison, *Medical Lexicon*, 573).

Muriate of ammonia. See Sal ammoniac.

Muriate of soda (sodium chloride or common salt). In small doses, this drug was given as a stimulant tonic and a vermifuge and in larger doses, as a purgative and emetic. It was occasionally used to stop the flow of blood. It was believed to promote digestion and used frequently for enemas (Wood and Bache, *Dispensatory*, 613-15). Sodium chloride injections are used to treat deficiencies in sodium.

Muscle, deltoid. The muscle located on the shoulder which lifts the humerus, or upper arm.

Muscle, pectoral. The broad, flat muscle at the upper part of the chest.

Muscle, temporal. A muscle of the lower jaw. The muscle radiates from the side of the head and occupies the entire temporal fossia (or depression of the skull surrounded by temporal ridges).

Muscle, tibial (anterior). The superficial muscle located in the lower leg, on the outer side of the tibia.

Muscles, sphincter. The several ring-shaped muscles closing and contracting the anus.

Mustard. A plant, the seeds of which were used in cases of indigestion to promote the appetite and improve digestion. The seeds were also used as laxatives and emetics. Because of its ability to stimulate the kidneys, small doses of bruised mustard seeds were used in cases of dropsy (Wood and Bache, *Dispensatory*, 600-602, 787). Physicians also used powdered mustard seeds in poultices. See Poultice, mustard.

Mustard application or poultice. See Poultice, mustard.

Narcotic. A drug which produces insensibility and stupor.

Nares. Nostrils.

Nasal process. See Process, nasal.

Nates. The buttocks.

Neuralgia. A group of diseases accompanied by pain extending along the course of the nerves (Dunglison, *Medical Lexicon*, 597).

Nine-bark. A plant indigenous to Ohio, and particularly plentiful along the Ohio River. Native Americans used a decoction of its root in soothing poultices (Smith, *The Indian Doctor's Dispensatory*, 27-28).

Nitrate of silver. See Lunar caustic.

Nitre. See Potassium nitrate.

Nosology. The science of classifying disease.

Oak, black or white. Plants, the bark of which was employed internally as an astringent and tonic, but was primarily employed in baths and poultices for gangrene and mortification (Wood and Bache, *Dispensatory*, 530-31).

Oil, olive (sweet oil). A substance valued for its nutritional and mildly laxative powers. Doctors claimed the oil, when applied externally, relaxed the skin. More often, however, it served as an ingredient in liniments, cerates, ointments, and plasters (Wood and Bache, *Dispensatory*, 453; Gunn, *Domestic Medicine*, 618). Today, it is recognized as a nutritious and mild laxative and is occasionally used in milder cases of constipation. It is also used as an enema and an external emollient.

Ointment, basilicon (resin cerate). A medication consisting of resin, lard, and yellow wax and generally used as a gently stimulating application to burns, scalds, blisters, and ulcers (Wood and Bache, *Dispensatory*, 791).

Ointment, simple digestive. A soft ointment.

Olecranon. The bony projection of the ulna at the elbow.

Olive oil. See Oil, olive.

Opiates. A reference to either opium or any preparation of opium such as laudanum or morphine. Opium was used as a narcotic and pain reliever during this period (Eberle, *Treatise on Materia Medica*, 317-42).

Orbital arch. See Arch, orbital.

Os femoris. See Femur.

Os frontis. See Bone, frontal.

Os humerus. See Humerus.

Os tempora. See Bone, temporal.

Os uteri. The mouth of the uterus.

Ossa malar. See Mala.

Oxalic acid. An acid present in wood sorrel. In small doses, oxalic acid was commonly used in the nineteenth century as a cooling drink in febrile diseases. If administered in large doses, oxalic acid is fatal (Wood and Bache, *Dispensatory*, 1092-93).

Palliative. In reference to treatment, one which offers relief but does not cure.

Parietal bones. See Bones, parietal.

Paroxysms. Periodical fits attended with fever.

Parturient. Relating to childbirth.

Parturition. Childbirth.

Pathological. Abnormal or diseased.

Pathology. That branch of medicine which studies the nature of disease and the structural and functional changes in tissue and organs which result from or cause disease.

Pectoral muscle. See Muscle, pectoral.

Pedicle. A stemlike part of tissue. The word now refers to the narrow strip of tissue by which a skin graft remains attached to the donor site.

Pendulous. Hanging loosely.

Pennyroyal. A gentle stimulant usually given in cases of flatulent colic and sick stomach. When administered as a warm infusion, it produced a gentle perspiration and also worked as an emmenagogue to promote menstruation (Wood and Bache, *Dispensatory*, 333-34).

Per indication. See Indication.

Per taxis. See Taxis.

Pericranium. The external connective tissue covering the skull.

Periosteum. Connective tissue covering the bones of the body.

Peritoneum. A serous membrane lining the abdominal cavity and surrounding the organs within that cavity.

Peroneal artery. See Artery, peroneal.

Peruvian bark (cinchona). A drug used internally primarily for the cure of malarial, or intermittent fevers. As a tonic, it was judged beneficial in cases of debility. The drug was also used externally. Bark baths, for example, were commonly applied to blistered surfaces (Wood and Bache, *Dispensatory*, 225-29). Cinchona contains twenty or more alkaloids the most important of which is quinine, which is still used for the treatment of malaria.

Phlebitis. The inflammation of a vein. During the early nineteenth century, this condition often resulted because of bloodletting.

Phlegmon. The inflammation of connective tissue, which is accompanied by redness and swelling and is subject to suppuration.

Phlegmonous. Of or pertaining to a phlegmon.

Pia mater. A thin, transparent membrane encasing the brain.

Piles. Hemorrhoids.

Pills, aloetic. Pills composed of aloes and soap. In the early nineteenth century, physicians prescribed these pills in cases of persistent constipation. Soap was added to the pills not only to give them a proper consistency, but also to prevent irritation to the rectum (Wood and Bache, *Dispensatory*, 926).

Plantar artery (external). See Artery, plantar (external).

Plaster, adhesive. Commonly used in wound management, the plaster consisted of powdered resin and lead plaster (a mixture of semi-vitrified lead oxide, olive oil, and water) and was spread on linen strips and applied directly to the wound to prevent gaping (Wood and Bache, *Dispensatory*, 817-19).

Plaster, blistering. This preparation consisted of powdered cantharides (Spanish flies), wax plaster, and prepared fat. In the nineteenth century, it was applied to the skin to cause blistering (Hooper, *Lexicon Medicum*, 2:328).

Plate, cribriform. The horizontal portion of the ethmoid bone perforated for the olfactory nerves.

Pledget. A small compress of lint, used in the nineteenth century as an application for wounds and ulcers.

Pleura. The serous membrane enveloping the lungs and lining the thoracic cavity.

Posterior fontanelle. See Fontanelle.

Potassium nitrate (nitre or saltpeter). A drug used to reduce fever in inflammatory diseases. This drug helped promote the secretion of urine and perspiration, lowered the body's temperature, increased the frequency of the pulse, and acted as a laxative (Wood and Bache, *Dispensatory*, 517).

Poultice, bread and milk. An external application commonly used in the nineteenth century for reducing inflammation and fever, as well as inducing suppuration (Wood and Bache, *Dispensatory*, 658).

Poultice, mustard. This application consisted of powdered mustard seeds, powdered linseed, and vinegar. When applied to the skin, this poultice acted as a rubefacient, producing a large amount of heat and blisters when left on the skin for an extended period of time (Wood and Bache, *Dispensatory*, 787).

Powdered alum. See Alum, powdered.

Powdered charcoal. See Charcoal.

Precipitated carbonate of iron. See Iron carbonate, precipitated.

Prepared carbonate of iron. See Iron carbonate, prepared.

Presentation. That part of the fetus which can be touched upon examination per vaginum.

Preternatural. In reference to childbirth, unnatural or abnormal.

Probe-pointed bistoury. See Bistoury.

Process, nasal. The nose.

Pubo-iliac region. The lower abdomen consisting of the right and left inguinal regions and the pubic region.

Puerperal. Of or relating to childbirth.

Puerperal fever. A highly contagious disease popularly referred to as childbed fever and often the result of infection by the *streptococcus* bacillus. The disease, characterized by inflammation of the abdominal cavity and blood poisoning, was common in large hospitals where sterile birthing conditions were absent. The contagious nature of the disease was first noted by American physician Oliver Wendell Holmes (1809-1894) in 1843. Ignaz Philipp Semmelweis (1818-1865), a Hungarian physician, was the first to demonstrate statistically that the disease was contagious and could be controlled through certain antiseptic procedures (Wertz and Wertz, *Lying-In*, 119-21).

Radial artery. See Artery, radial.

Radical cure. In reference to treatment, one in which the disease is completely destroyed (opposite of palliative) (Dunglison, *Medical Lexicon*, 739). Today, the term is most often used in connection with surgery.

Raspatory. An instrument used to file off the rough edges of the skull after a trephining operation.

Red precipitate (red oxide of mercury). A drug used externally by nineteenth-century physicians as an escharotic and stimulant. In powder form it was sprinkled on venereal sores and external ulcers (Wood and Bache, *Dispensatory*, 875-77).

Reducible hernia. See Hernia, reducible.

Reduction. In cases of hernia, reduction refers to returning the protruding parts to the abdominal cavity.

Refrigerant. A medicine which has a cooling effect on the body; a medicine which relieves fever and thirst.

Resection. Removal of a large part of an organ or structure.

Resolution. The termination of a disease.

Rigor. Coldness, attended by shivering; a symptom of fever. To nineteenth-century physicians, a chill was not as severe as a rigor (Dunglison, *Medical Lexicon*, 756). Today, the term is used as a synonym for a chill.

Ring, abdominal (inguinal ring). The natural circular area of the abdomen which forms the junction of the groin and the scrotum.

Rubefacient. A medicine causing redness when applied to the skin.

Rugose. Wrinkled.

Sac, hernial. The pouch consisting of peritoneum which contains the herniated abdominal organs.

Sac, inguinal. The hernial sac protruding at the groin.

Sacrum. The triangularly-shaped bone located between the two hip bones. The bone is part of the vertebral column and is formed from five fused vertebrae.

Sagittal suture. See Suture, sagittal.

Sal ammoniac (muriate of ammonia). A drug primarily employed as a refrigerant (Wood and Bache, *Dispensatory*, 74-77).

Salts, epsom. A neutral salt used as a mild cathartic, refrigerant, and diuretic. The drug was frequently used in the treatment of fevers and various forms of inflammation (Wood and Bache, *Dispensatory*, 407-8). Today, epsom salts is used as a mild cathartic, an antidote, an anti-inflammatory agent (when applied locally to sprains and bruises), and an anti-convulsant.

Sanative. That which heals or restores; curative.

Sanguineous. Bloody.

Sanious. Containing sanies, or an offensive smelling, blood-tinged discharge consisting of blood, serum, and pus.

Sarcocele. A hard and fleshy tumor of the testicle.

Sarcoma. A fleshy, malignant tumor originating in the bones or connective tissue.

Scammony. A powerful cathartic which was used infrequently because of its harsh effects (Wood and Bache, *Dispensatory*, 581-82).

Scarification. A procedure common in nineteenth-century therapeutics. Scarification was performed by using a small, square brass box containing concealed blades. This instrument, or scarificator, was placed next to the skin. When the trigger was released, the skin was lacerated by hidden blades. Small glass cups were then placed over the wound to draw blood, or remove excess cellular water.

Scarificator. A small, square brass box containing concealed blades on its underside and used for localized bloodletting. See also Scarification.

Scirrhous. Pertaining to scirrhus.

Scirrhus. A hard cancer.

Scrofula. Tuberculosis of the lymphatic glands, or a disease characterized by painless tumors of the lymphatic glands. These tumors eventually abscess, suppurate, and form ulcers.

Scrotum. The external pouch containing the testes.

Secale cornutum. See Ergot.

Secondary hemorrhage. See Hemorrhage, secondary.

Secondary infection. See Infection, secondary.

Serous. Producing or containing serum, or the watery portion of an animal fluid.

Seton. A piece of thread or silk which was placed under the skin to irritate (Hooper, *Lexicon Medicum*, 2:285).

Sheep sorrel. One of two species of plants: yellow wood sorrel (*Oxalis stricta*) or sour dock (*Rumex acetosa*). As an external application, yellow wood sorrel was used as a folk cure for cancer (Varro E. Tyler, comp., *Hoosier Home Remedies* [West Lafayette, Ind.: Purdue University Press, 1985], 35-36, 187).

Silver nitrate. See Lunar caustic.

Simple cerate. See Cerate, simple.

Simple digestive ointment. See Ointment, simple digestive.

Skull fracture. See Fracture, skull.

Skull fracture, depressed. See Fracture, skull.

Slippery elm. See Elm, slippery.

Sounding. The introduction of an instrument into the cavities of various organs to determine the conditions there (Dunglison, *Medical Lexicon*, 799).

Sour sorrel. See Sheep sorrel.

Spermatic artery. See Artery, spermatic.

Spermatic cord. See Cord, spermatic.

Sphacelus. Mortification or death of any part (Hooper, *Lexicon Medicum*, 2:299). Today, the word gangrenous is used to describe this condition.

Sphincter muscles. See Muscles, sphincter.

Spicule. A small, slender, needle-like body.

Spirits of turpentine. See Terebinth.

Squill. The root of the squill primarily was used by nineteenth-century physicians as an expectorant, diuretic, and in large doses, as an emetic and purgative. It was believed particularly effective in cases of dropsy, since the medicine stimulated the kidneys (Wood and Bache, *Dispensatory*, 583-84).

Starch. This preparation was used as an ingredient in enemas. It was also prescribed as a soothing application for an irritated rectum (Wood and Bache, *Dispensatory*, 80-83). Corn starch is a nutritive substance and is still used today in enemas and various pharmaceutical preparations.

Sternum. The breast bone.

Stertorous. Characterized by snoring or gasping.

Stimulant. A drug which induces stimulation, or increased activity of an organ.

Strait, inferior. The lower aperture of the pelvic girdle, formed on the top by the coccyx and on the sides by the ischium (Velpeau, *Elementary Treatise on Midwifery*, 25-26). Today, the inferior strait is known as the outlet of the pelvis (or the apertura pelvis inferior).

Strait, superior. The superior aperture of the pelvis (or the apertura pelvis superior). Today, this strait is referred to as the inlet or brim of the pelvis.

Strangulated hernia. See Hernia, strangulated.

Stricture. An abnormal narrowing of a body passage.

Strumous. Affected with scrofula, or tuberculosis of the lymphatic glands. These indolent, glandular tumors have slowly suppurating abcesses and fistulous passages and inflamed structures.

Stylet. A thin surgical probe.

Sub-carbonas ferri praeparatus. See Iron carbonate, prepared.

Sulfuric acid, diluted. See Elixir vitriol.

Superior labial artery. See Artery, labial (superior).

Superior maxilla. See Maxilla superior.

Superior strait. See Strait, superior.

Suppression. In the nineteenth century, this term referred to the cessation of menstruation for reasons other than pregnancy or menopause. William Dewees, a nineteenth-century midwife, felt the foremost cause of suppression was cold. Symptoms of this malady were failure of menstruation to reoccur and violent pain in the head, back, or bowels (Dewees, *Treatise on the Diseases of Females*, 117). Today, the term refers to the sudden stoppage of any secretion, excretion, or normal discharge.

Suppuration. The formation of pus.

Suspensory. A bag or bandage used to suspend the scrotum.

Suture. A stitch made to approximate the edges of a wound; an articulation of bones which are united by serrated edges (such as the bones of the skull).

Suture, sagittal. The fibrous tissue or ligaments which keep the rough and interlocking edges of the parietal bones in place. The sagittal suture extends from the middle of the frontal bone back to the superior angle of the occipital bone (or bone on the back part of the head).

Sweet oil. See Oil, olive.

Syncope. Fainting.

Syringe. An instrument primarily used for the administration of enemas and the introduction of liquids or powders into body cavities and wounds (see Journal 1, n. 16, above, p. 12).

Tables of the cranium. The two layers of compact, or hard, tissue of the skull. Between these two layers of hard tissue is a layer of cancellous, or spongy, tissue.

Tap. To draw water off by paracentesis (puncturing a cavity and drawing off water by aspiration).

Tarsal. Pertaining to the tarsus, or instep of the foot.

Tarsal bones. See Bones, tarsal.

Tartar emetic (antimony potassium tartrate). A drug used to stimulate various secretions. In the nineteenth century, doctors primarily used the drug as a powerful emetic although it was also used as an alterative, diaphoretic, diuretic, expectorant, and purgative (Wood and Bache, *Dispensatory*, 755-56). Today, physicians use tartar emetic in the treatment of parasitic infections.

Taxis. To reduce the contents of the hernial sac by hand.

Temporal artery. See Artery, temporal.

Temporal bone. See Bone, temporal.

Temporal muscle. See Muscle, temporal.

Tenaculum. An instrument with a small hook at one end used for grasping blood vessels.

Tendons, flexor. The tendons which flex a particular joint.

Tent. A roll of lint used to dilate openings (Hooper, *Lexicon Medicum*, 2:342).

Terebinth. Turpentine, or those vegetable juices consisting of oil and resin. During this period, terebinth was used internally as a stimulant, diuretic, and vermifuge. When administered in large doses, it acted as a laxative. Externally, turpentine was used as a rubefacient especially in cases of rheumatism and paralysis (Wood and Bache, *Dispensatory*, 458-60).

Tetanus. An acute infectious disease characterized by contraction of voluntary muscles, especially of the jaw, caused by bacteria which is usually introduced through a wound.

Thoracic. Pertaining to the thorax.

Thorax. The chest.

Thumb lancet. See Lancet, thumb.

Tibia. The larger, or inside, bone of the lower leg.

Tibial artery (anterior). See Artery, tibial (anterior).

Tibial muscle, anterior. See Muscle, tibial (anterior).

Tibialis anticus muscle. See Muscle, tibial (anterior).

Tincture. A solution of any substance in wine (Hooper, *Lexicon Medicum*, 2:350).

Tobacco smoke enema. See Enema, tobacco smoke.

Tonics, vegetable. Medicines used to invigorate the frequency of the pulse. The most frequently employed ingredients of vegetable tonics during this period were cinchona, Virginia snakeroot, angustura bark, colomba, gentian, quassia, simarouba, and cascarilla. Other ingredients included wild cherry, dogwood, white willow, centaury, tulip tree, and chamomile (Eberle, *Treatise on Materia Medica*, 174-221).

Torpid. Constipated; a debilitated or sluggish condition of the body.

Trepanation. Trephining, or an operation in which a circular piece of bone is removed from the skull.

Trephine. Cylindrical saw for removing a circular piece of bone from the skull.

Trismus. A spasm of the muscles of the lower jaw, causing difficulty in opening the mouth; common in tetanus (*Clostridium*) infection.

Trocar. An instrument used to evacuate fluids from the body cavities. The instrument consists of two pieces: a perforator and a cannula, or a tube. The tube fits over the perforator, and once the cavity is punctured, the perforator is withdrawn, leaving the cannula in the body cavity to provide an exit for the excess fluid.

Truss. A bandage for keeping a hernia reduced which in the nineteenth century consisted of an elastic band and either a hard or soft pad emanating from it. A special spring mechanism on the pad controlled the degree of pressure on the hernial protrusion.

Tumefied. Swollen.

Tunica vaginalis. The serous membrane surrounding the testicle.

Ulna. The inner bone of the forearm.

Umbilical hernia. See Hernia, umbilical.

Umbilicus. The umbilical cord.

Unguentum. Ointment.

Union by the first intention. Normal healing.

Uteri, cervix. The lower, narrow end of the uterus.

Varioloid. A modified form of smallpox occurring in a person who has been vaccinated or who has had the disease.

Vascular. Full of vessels.

Vegetable tonics. See Tonics, vegetable.

Venesection (venisection). The operation of opening a vein to draw blood.

Vermifuge. A medicine producing the expulsion of worms or internal parasites.

Vesication. The process of blistering.

Vesicles. Small blisters.

Vis medicatrix naturae. See Medicatrix naturae.

Viscera. Entrails, or organs in any one of the three large body cavities, but especially in the abdominal cavity.

Volatile liniment. See Liniment, volatile.

Wen. In the nineteenth century, this term was a synonym for an indolent, or painless tumor. It could also refer to an encysted tumor (Dunglison, *Medical Lexicon*, 919). Today, wen means a cyst containing a thick, semifluid substance consisting of fat and epithelial debris from cells.

White oak. See Oak, black or white.

Whitlow. See Felon.

Yeast. A drug believed effective in the treatment of typhoid fever. In large doses the drug exhibited its laxative powers. Externally, it was applied to sloughing ulcers and was usually combined with starchy substances to form poultices (Wood and Bache, *Dispensatory*, 189-90).

Glossary of Personal and Place Names

Terms defined in this glossary include persons and places mentioned by Lindsay in his journals.

Abington, Wayne County, Indiana. A town located six miles southeast of Centerville. In 1830 it contained sixty inhabitants and several tradesmen (Scott, *Indiana Gazetteer*, 29).

Arkansas River. The major river of Arkansas, 1,450 miles in length. The river begins in central Colorado and flows eastward through southern Kansas and across the northeast corner of Oklahoma. It runs diagonally through Arkansas, bisecting the state, and empties into the Mississippi River in southeastern Arkansas.

Aurora, Dearborn County, Indiana. A town located on the right bank of the Ohio River, four miles below Lawrenceburg. It was laid out in 1819 by Judge Jesse L. Holman and was incorporated in 1822. By 1840 it had six hundred inhabitants, one physician, a lawyer, and several tradesmen (Scott, *Indiana Gazetteer*, 31-32; WPA, *Indiana*, 365; *History of Dearborn, Ohio, and Switzerland Counties*, 303, 306).

Brown, William John (1805-1857). A lawyer who served as Indiana's secretary of state, 1837-41, and as a congressman, 1843-45 and 1849-51 (Shepherd, *Biographical Directory*, 1:42).

Bugg, Joel. A physician who practiced with Lindsay, 1834-36 (Richmond *Palladium*, May 17, 1834, May 7, 1836).

Butler, Thomas T. A physician who settled in Economy, Indiana, in 1826 and moved to Noblesville, Indiana, in 1837 (Young, *History of Wayne County*, 309; Noblesville [Ind.] *The Newspaper*, June 15, 1837).

Butler County, Ohio. A county located in southwestern Ohio bounded on the north by Preble and Montgomery counties, the east by Warren County, the south by Hamilton County, and the west by the state of Indiana. Established in 1803, it contains the towns of Hamilton, Fairfield, and Middleton (Jenkins, *Ohio Gazetteer*, 95-96).

Cadron Creek. This creek joins the Arkansas ten miles west of Morrillton (formerly Lewisburg) (WPA, *Arkansas*, 245).

Centerville, Wayne County, Indiana. A town located on the National Road in the center of Wayne County, approximately sixty-two miles east of Indianapolis and six miles west of Richmond. It is the oldest town in the county. In 1830, it was the county seat and had three hundred inhabitants, three physicians, and several taverns (Scott, *Indiana Gazetteer*, 46; Young, *History of Wayne County*, 166).

Cincinnati, Hamilton County, Ohio. The county seat of Hamilton County, which in the 1830s was the largest city in the Midwest and at that time the seventh largest city in the United States. The city was laid out in 1789. In 1820 its population was ten thousand, and by 1830 it had twenty-nine thousand inhabitants (Jenkins, *Ohio Gazetteer*, 110-11).

Clark County, Ohio. An Ohio county organized in 1818, with Springfield as its county seat. It is bordered on the north by Champaign County, the east by Madison County, the south by Greene County, and the west by Montgomery and Miami counties (Jenkins, *Ohio Gazetteer*, 120-21).

Cleves, Hamilton County, Ohio. A small town located on the Big Miami River, fifteen miles west of Cincinnati. In 1830 its population was approximately one hundred (Jenkins, *Ohio Gazetteer*, 127-28).

Columbia, Hamilton County, Ohio. A small town located six miles east of Cincinnati (and is now part of Cincinnati). First settled in 1789, it was the first settlement in Hamilton County and the second in the state of Ohio (Jenkins, *Ohio Gazetteer*, 133-34).

Connersville, Fayette County, Indiana. The county seat of Fayette County, located approximately sixty miles east of Indianapolis. In 1830 it contained five hundred inhabitants and four physicians, four lawyers, and several businesses. John Conner (1780-1826), a fur trader and interpreter/guide for William Henry Harrison during the War of 1812, founded the town in 1813 (Scott, *Indiana Gazetteer*, 53; WPA, *Indiana*, 460-61).

Conway, James S. (1798-1855). The first governor of Arkansas, serving from 1836 to 1840.

Conway County, Arkansas. A county located in central Arkansas, presently bounded on the north by Van Buren County, the east by Van Buren and Faulkner counties, on the south by Perry County, and the west by Pope County. Organized in 1825, it was named after

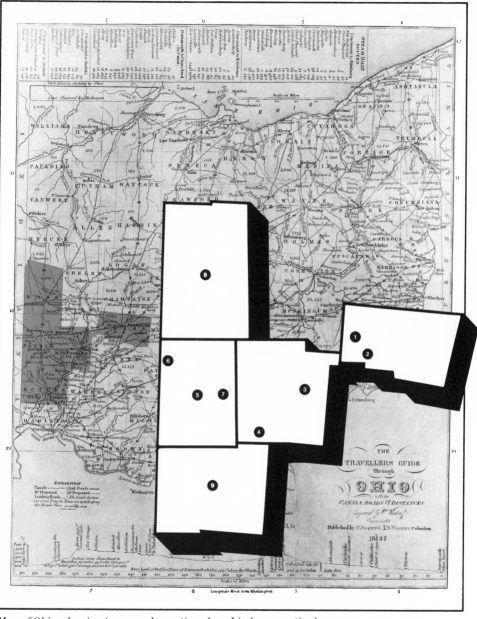

Map of Ohio, showing towns and counties where Lindsay practiced

Ohio

Clark County

1. Donnelsville

2. Enon

Montgomery County

3. Dayton

4. Germantown

Preble County

5. Eaton

6. New Paris

7. West Alexandria

8. Darke County

9. Butler County

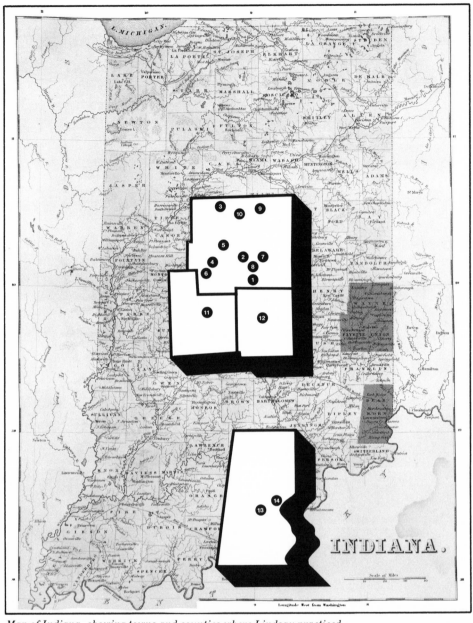

Map of Indiana, showing towns and counties where Lindsay practiced

Indiana

Wayne County
1. Abington
2. Centerville
3. Economy
4. Germantown
5. Jacksonburg
6. Milton
7. Salisbury
8. Richmond
9. Newport
10. Williamsburg

Fayette County
11. Connersville

Union County
12. Liberty

Dearborn County
13. Aurora
14. Lawrenceburg

the Conway family who was active in Arkansas politics (WPA, *Arkansas*, 245; *Historical Reminiscences and Biographical Memoirs of Conway County*, 11).

Cox, David. A physician who came to New Paris, Ohio, and later served as director of the Dayton and Western Railroad (*History of Preble County*, 270).

Crawford County, Arkansas. A county in west central Arkansas presently bounded on the north by Washington County, the east by Franklin County, the west by the state of Oklahoma, and the south by the Arkansas River. Established in 1820, it has undergone several boundary changes. In 1830 its population was 2,440 and in 1840, 4,266. Van Buren is the county seat (*Reminiscent History of the Ozark Region*, 35-36).

Dardanelle, Yell County, Arkansas. A small village in west central Arkansas. It is located on a rocky peak jutting out on the Arkansas River and was one of the first settlements in Arkansas. A Cherokee trading post was established there in 1819. The origin of the town's name is debatable, but the town was probably named after the Dardanelles, a narrow strait between the Gallipoli Peninsula in Europe and Turkey in Asia which it connects. Officially platted in 1843, the town is located approximately half way between Little Rock and Fort Smith (WPA, *Arkansas*, 284-86).

Dardanelle Stream. A small watercourse near Dardanelle Rock on the Arkansas River. The village of Dardanelle is located near Dardanelle Rock.

Darke County, Ohio. A county in western Ohio, bounded on the west by the state of Indiana, the north by Mercer County, the east by Miami and Shelby counties, and the south by Preble County. In 1830 it had a population of 6,203 (Jenkins, *Ohio Gazetteer*, 155-56).

Dayton, Montgomery County, Ohio. The county seat of Montgomery County, Ohio, located on the east bank of the Great Miami River, immediately below where it joins the Mad River. It was laid out in 1795 and first settled in 1796. The population in 1820 was 1,139; in 1830, 2,954; and in 1833, approximately 3,400. It was one of the larger cities in which Lindsay practiced medicine (Jenkins, *Ohio Gazetteer*, 157).

Dayton Academy, Dayton, Ohio. A private, secondary school incorporated in 1808. The school remained open until 1850, well after the public education system was firmly established in Dayton (Conover, *Dayton and Montgomery County*, 1:342-45).

Dearborn County, Indiana. A county located in southeastern Indiana. It is bounded on the north by Franklin County, the west by Ripley

County, the south by Switzerland County, and the east by the state of Ohio and the Ohio River. It was organized in 1802 and had 14,573 inhabitants in 1830. The county seat is Lawrenceburg (Scott, *Indiana Gazetteer*, 57-59).

Donnel's Creek, Clark County, Ohio. A small creek running through the village of Donnelsville. Both the creek and a town were named after Jonathan Donnel, one of the area's first residents (Benjamin F. Prince, ed., *A Standardized History of Springfield and Clark County, Ohio*, 2 vols. [Chicago: American Historical Society, 1922], 1:21).

Donnellon, Nelson. The second physician to practice in West Alexandria, Ohio (Lindsay was the first). After many years of practice in West Alexandria, Donnellon moved to Indianapolis (*History of Preble County*, 328).

Dorsey, Isaac V. A physician who practiced in Centerville, Ohio, and by 1832 in Richmond, Indiana (Richmond *Palladium*, February 6, 1833).

Duck Creek, Hamilton County, Ohio. A small stream near Columbia, Ohio (presently a part of Cincinnati).

Dwight Mission, Arkansas. A settlement located at the present site of Russellville, Arkansas. In 1820 the American Board of Foreign Missions in New York sent Yankee Congregationalist, Cephas Washburn, to teach the Cherokee Indians in Arkansas and found the settlement. It was named after Timothy Dwight, then president of Yale College. The missionaries built living units, a meetinghouse, and a school on the site. When the Indians moved out of Arkansas, the Dwight Mission was also relocated (Ashmore, *Arkansas*, 36-37).

Eaton, Preble County, Ohio. A town in southwestern Ohio located approximately twenty-two miles west of Dayton. It is the county seat of Preble County. Laid out in 1805-6, it was named for Captain William Eaton who in 1805 led a successful land and sea operation during the Tripolitan War. By 1830 Eaton had approximately one thousand inhabitants. The town also boasted thirty tradesmen, five lawyers, and three physicians (Jenkins, *Ohio Gazetteer*, 170-71; *History of Preble County*, 98).

Eaton and Dayton Pike, Ohio. A turnpike road running from Springfield through Eaton to Dayton.

Economy, Wayne County, Indiana. A town located approximately eleven miles northwest of Centerville, Indiana. The town was laid out by Charles Osborn, and the plat was recorded in 1825. In 1830 Economy contained two hundred inhabitants (Scott, *Indiana Gazetteer*, 63; Young, *History of Wayne County*, 312).

Enon, Clark County, Ohio. A small town on the Mad River, located approximately seven miles southwest of Springfield.

Espich, C. G. (d. 1853). An Ohio physician who came to Montgomery County in the 1820s and set up practice in German Township (*History of Montgomery County*, bk. 3, pt. 1, p. 50).

Fayette County, Indiana. A county in the eastern part of the state bounded on the north by Wayne and Henry counties, the west by Rush County, the south by Franklin County, and the east by Union and Wayne counties. It was organized in 1818 and by 1830 had a population of 9,112 (Scott, *Indiana Gazetteer*, 67-68).

Fayetteville, Washington County, Arkansas. The county seat, settled in 1828, located in northeastern Washington County.

Ferguson, Clement. The first physician in New Paris, Ohio, who began his practice there in 1814 (*History of Preble County*, 270).

Ferris, Ezra. A Lawrenceburg, Indiana, physician who at various times in the 1800s served as a state representative, secretary of the district medical society, and trustee for the school lands. He was also a Baptist minister and owner of a large drugstore (*History of Dearborn, Switzerland, and Ohio Counties*, 167-68; Lawrenceburg [Ind.] *Oracle*, November 3, 1821, January 19 and July 13, 1822, and June 28, 1823).

Fort Clark, Jackson County, Missouri. A fort founded by William Clark in 1808, east of present-day Kansas City and Independence, and originally known as Fort Osage.

Fort Gibson, Muskogee County, Oklahoma. A fort established in 1824 to protect the frontier from the Indians and to prevent war between the Cherokee and Osage tribes (Dale, "Arkansas and the Cherokees," 96).

Fort Smith, Sebastian County, Arkansas. A fort built in 1817 in western Arkansas at the junction of the Arkansas and Poteau rivers to prevent the Cherokee and Osage Indians (who were located north of Arkansas) from warring. The fort was named after Thomas A. Smith, the first general sent to the fort (Ashmore, *Arkansas*, 27).

Franklin County, Arkansas. A county in northwestern Arkansas, presently bordered on the north by Madison County, the east by Johnson County, the south by the Arkansas River, and the west by Crawford County. The county was formed on December 19, 1837 (shortly before Lindsay's trip through Arkansas), and by 1840 had a population of 2,664 (*Reminiscent History of the Ozark Region*, 35-37).

Germantown, Montgomery County, Ohio. A town located approximately fourteen miles southwest of Dayton. In 1830 the town had one thousand inhabitants and several businesses, five physicians, and twenty tradesmen (Jenkins, *Ohio Gazetteer*, 201).

Germantown, Wayne County, Indiana. A small town located seven miles west of Richmond (called Georgetown prior to 1832 and East Germantown today). George Shortridge and John Beard laid out the town in 1827. Pennsylvania Germans heavily populated the town and surrounding area (Young, *History of Wayne County*, 244).

Griffith, _____. A physician who practiced briefly in Richmond, Indiana, and then moved west (Young, *History of Wayne County*, 377).

Hamilton County, Ohio. A county in southwestern Ohio bordered on the north by Butler County, the east by Clermont County, the south by the Ohio River, and the west by the state of Indiana. In the 1830s it was the most populous Ohio county, containing Cincinnati which had a population of over ten thousand (Jenkins, *Ohio Gazetteer*, 215-16).

Hindman, A. A cancer doctor who on January 8, 1831, advertised in the Richmond *Palladium*. Like most of these doctors, Hindman was an itinerant, moving from city to city, advertising his ability to cure cancer.

Illinois Bayou. A tributary which enters the Arkansas River from the north, immediately to the west of Russellville and opposite Dardanelle.

Indianapolis, Marion County, Indiana. The state capital, located on the east fork of the west bank of the White River. Laid out in 1821, the town in 1830 had a population of sixteen hundred. By 1850 its population had grown to 8,091 (Scott, *Indiana Gazetteer*, 89-92; James H. Madison, *The Indiana Way: A State History* [Bloomington: Indiana University Press; Indianapolis: Indiana Historical Society, 1986], 96-97).

Jacksonburg, Wayne County, Indiana. A village approximately four miles northwest of Centerville with a population of one hundred in 1830 (Scott, *Indiana Gazetteer*, 95).

Johnson County, Arkansas. A county in northwestern Arkansas, presently bordered on the north by Madison and Newton counties, the east by Pope County, the south by Logan County, and the east by Franklin County. It was organized in 1833 with Clarksville as the seat of justice. In 1840 the population was 3,433 (*Reminiscent History of the Ozark Region*, 35-37).

Judkins, William (1788-1861). A well-known physician of Cincinnati. He began his medical practice in Jefferson County, Ohio, at the age of twenty-two and moved to Cincinnati in 1832. He contributed articles on his surgical cases to journals and eventually received an honorary medical degree from Transylvania University (*History of Cincinnati and Hamilton County: Their Past and Present, Including Early Settlement and Development* [Cincinnati: S. B. Nelson Co., 1894], 627-28).

Knox, James. A physician who came to New Paris, Ohio, in 1817 (*History of Preble County*, 270).

Lawrenceburg, Dearborn County, Indiana. The county seat, located in southeastern Indiana on the right bank of the Ohio River approximately twenty-two miles west of Cincinnati and eighty-six miles southeast of Indianapolis. In 1830 it boasted one thousand residents and had eight lawyers, four physicians, and several stores and taverns. The town was laid out in 1802 by Captain Samuel C. Vance, who named the town in honor of his wife, whose maiden name was Lawrence (Scott, *Indiana Gazetteer*, 104; WPA, *Indiana*, 364-65; *History of Dearborn, Ohio, and Switzerland Counties*, 241). Lindsay practiced for two or three years in Lawrenceburg (see Introduction).

Lewisburg, Conway County, Arkansas. An early port on the Arkansas River. When Morrillton was built in the 1870s and became the seat of justice, it absorbed Lewisburg (WPA, *Arkansas*, 245; *Historical Reminiscences and Biographical Memoirs of Conway County*, 11).

Liberty, Union County, Indiana. The county seat, located thirteen miles south of Richmond. In 1830 it had a population of five hundred, four physicians, and several stores and taverns (Scott, *Indiana Gazetteer*, 106).

Magazine Mountain, Arkansas. The highest mountain in the state, rising at its peak to 2,753 feet above sea level. It is located in northwestern, central Arkansas, in the Ouachita Mountains in Logan County.

Marion County, Indiana. A county located in central Indiana, bounded on the north by Hamilton and Boone counties, the west by Hendricks County, the south by Morgan and Johnson counties, and the east by Shelby and Hancock counties. The county was organized in 1821, with Indianapolis as its county seat and also the capital of the state. In 1830 the population was 7,181 (Scott, *Indiana Gazetteer*, 113).

Matchett, W. J. An Indiana physician who practiced in Abington in 1828 (Young, *History of Wayne County*, 450).

Milton, Wayne County, Indiana. A village located nine miles west of Centerville. Laid out by John Bell in 1824, it had a population of five hundred in 1830 (Scott, *Indiana Gazetteer*, 121; Young, *History of Wayne County*, 325).

Montgomery County, Ohio. An Ohio county located in southwestern Ohio, bounded on the north by Miami County, on the east by Greene County, on the south by Warren and Butler counties, and the west by Preble County. The principal rivers in the county are the southwest branch of the Miami River and the Mad River. In 1830 the county had a population of 24,252, and the major city was Dayton (Jenkins, *Ohio Gazetteer*, 310).

Mount, W. An Ohio physician who began practicing in Eaton in 1830 and several years later relocated to Hamilton (*History of Preble County*, 112).

Mulberry, Crawford County, Arkansas. An early settlement located below Fort Smith on the north side of the Arkansas River.

Nacogdoches, Nacogdoches County, Texas. A city located in the eastern part of the state. At the time of Lindsay's trip to Arkansas (1837-38), Nacogdoches was part of the newly independent Republic of Texas.

Natchitoches, Natchitoches Parish, Louisiana. The parish seat, located in the northwest central part of the state.

New Paris, Preble County, Ohio. A town located twelve miles northwest of Eaton and six miles northeast of Richmond. Platted in 1817, it was next to Eaton the largest town in the county. In 1830 the town had a population of 154. By the mid-1830s it had 400 residents, 3 physicians, and several businesses (Jenkins, *Ohio Gazetteer*, 332; *History of Preble County*, 265).

Newport, Wayne County, Indiana. A village located eleven miles northeast of Centerville. In 1830 it had a population of three hundred. The town was laid out in 1818 by Solomon Thomas and Redden Chance. Additions to the town were made in 1830, 1832, and 1844. The town was unincorporated until 1844 (Scott, *Indiana Gazetteer*, 132; Young, *History of Wayne County*, 298). Newport is now Fountain City.

Nisbet, R. P. A physician practicing in West Alexandria, Ohio, with William G. Lineaweaver. In 1854 Nisbet graduated from the Medical College of Ohio. He also received training in dentistry (*History of Preble County*, 328; George W. Hawes, *The Ohio State Gazetteer and Business Directory, for 1859 and 1860*, No. 1 [Cincinnati: George Hawes, 1859], 528).

Nixon, Samuel. A physician who came to Richmond, Indiana, in 1830. He practiced there for several years and then moved west (Young, *History of Wayne County*, 377-78).

Noble, Noah (1794-1844). A lawyer and Whig politician who served as governor of Indiana, 1831-37 (Shepherd, *Biographical Directory*, 1:294).

Northwest Territory. Known in the eighteenth century as the Old Northwest, it consisted of an area of approximately 248,000 square miles, formed from the cessions of western lands by Virginia, New York, Massachusetts, and Connecticut. It was organized under the Ordinance of 1787, and from this territory the states of Ohio, Indiana, Illinois, Wisconsin, and Michigan were formed.

Old Dwight Mission Ground. See Dwight Mission, Arkansas.

Otwell, Curtis. The first physician in Williamsburg, Indiana (Young, *History of Wayne County*, 227).

Ozark, Franklin County, Arkansas. The county seat, located on the north bank of the Arkansas River (*Reminiscent History of the Ozark Region*, 35-36).

Paddy's Run, Butler County, Ohio. The oldest settlement in Morgan Township, established in 1803 approximately ten miles southwest of Hamilton. The village (consisting of a few houses and a post office) was located near a small stream of the same name, that of an Irishman who drowned in it. When the town was officially platted, it was called New London. In the late nineteenth century, its name was changed to Shandon (Bert S. Bartlow et al., eds., *Centennial History of Butler County, Ohio* [Indianapolis: B. F. Bowen & Co., 1905], 352[12]).

Paramore, Jesse (d. 1857). An Eaton, Ohio, physician who settled in Preble County in 1820. In 1836 he served as the first mayor of Eaton (R. E. Lowry, *History of Preble County, Ohio* [Indianapolis: B. F. Bowen & Co., 1915], 321).

Percival, Jabez. A physician who practiced medicine in Lawrenceburg, Indiana. A native of New York, he settled in Indiana in 1801 (*History of Dearborn, Ohio, and Switzerland Counties*, 165-67).

Percival, John. A physician who practiced medicine in Lawrenceburg, Indiana. He began his Indiana practice in 1820 (*History of Dearborn, Ohio, and Switzerland Counties*, 165-67).

Pike, Zebulon (d. 1834). The father of Zebulon Montgomery Pike. He served in the Revolutionary War and remained in the army, rising to the rank of major. He served in the War of 1812 as a brevet lieutenant colonel (Francis B. Heitman, *Historical Register and Dictionary of the United States Army*, 2 vols. [Washington: Government Printing Office, 1903], 1:792).

Pike, Zebulon Montgomery (1779-1813). A soldier who explored the upper Mississippi region of the Louisiana Purchase, 1805-6, and the Southwest, 1806-7. He served as a brigadier general in the War of 1812 and was killed in 1813 during an expedition against York (Toronto), Canada.

Plummer, John T. (1807-1863). An Indiana physician who practiced in Richmond, Indiana. Plummer was a graduate of Yale University School of Medicine. He studied not only medicine but also natural history, horticulture, geology, meteorology, and chemistry. He also made several contributions to scientific journals (William DePrez Inlow, "The Indiana Physician as Geologist and Naturalist," *Indiana Magazine of History* 56 [1960]: 11-15).

Pope County, Arkansas. A county in northwest central Arkansas presently bordered on the north by Newton and Searcy counties, the east by Van Buren and Conway counties, the south by Yell County, and the east by Johnson and Logan counties. It was established in November 1829 with Dover as the county seat (the county seat is now Russellville). In 1830 it had a population of 1,483 and in 1840, 2,850 (*Reminiscent History of the Ozark Region*, 39).

Preble County, Ohio. A county located in the southwestern part of the state and bounded on the north by Darke County, the east by Montgomery County, and the south by Butler County. Established in 1808, it contains the towns of West Alexandria and Eaton (Jenkins, *Ohio Gazetteer*, 372-73).

Pretlow, Richard. A Richmond, Indiana, physician (*History of Wayne County*, 2:185).

Pritchett, John. A Wayne County, Indiana, physician born in 1803 in New Jersey. He studied medicine under Dr. Gustavus Allen of Fairfield, Ohio. In 1826 Pritchett moved to Wayne County, Indiana, and in 1843 he received a medical degree from Cincinnati's Ohio Medical College (*History of Wayne County*, 2:356).

Richmond, Wayne County, Indiana. A city located sixty-eight miles east of Indianapolis. In 1830 its population was 1,740. During this period it had six physicians, two lawyers, several tradesmen, a number of stores and taverns, and several industries. The town was founded in 1805, platted in 1816, and incorporated in 1818. Early in its history, a large community of Quakers settled in the city (Scott, *Indiana Gazetteer*, 104; WPA, *Indiana*, 338). Richmond was one of the larger cities (along with Indianapolis and Dayton) in which Lindsay practiced medicine. He remained there for ten years and during that time recorded most of the case histories in this book (see Introduction).

St. Joseph County, Indiana. Located in the northernmost part of the state between LaPorte and Elkhart counties. Organized as a county in 1830, its population was then 287, which within two years grew to an estimated 1,500 (Scott, *Indiana Gazetteer*, 164-65).

Salisbury, Wayne County, Indiana. A small village located three miles east of Centerville. It was formerly the county seat. In 1830 it had a population of thirty to forty (Scott, *Indiana Gazetteer*, 155). Salisbury is no longer in existence.

Salter, James W. A Richmond, Indiana, physician who published the newspaper, *The Telegram*, in the late 1860s (Young, *History of Wayne County*, 92).

Sebastian County, Arkansas. A county located in western Arkansas, presently bordered on the north by the Arkansas River, the west by Franklin and Logan counties, and the south by Scott County. It was formed in 1851, after Lindsay's visit to the region (*Reminiscent History of the Ozark Region*, 39).

Smith, Catharine (1760-1831). Lindsay's mother-in-law. Formerly Catharine Stout, she was born in New Jersey.

Smith, Peter (1753-1816). Lindsay's father-in-law. Smith was born in Wales and educated at Princeton University. He married Catharine Stout on December 23, 1776. From the 1780s until 1794, he moved frequently, living in Virginia, the Carolinas, and Georgia. In 1794 he moved to Ohio and settled in Columbia (now part of Cincinnati). While there, he preached, farmed, and practiced medicine, prescribing only roots and herbs. He then moved to Donnel's Creek in Clark County, where he published the first materia medica book in the Midwest, *The Indian Doctor's Dispensatory* (John Uri Lloyd, "Dr. Peter Smith and His Dispensatory," *American Journal of Pharmacy* 70 [1898]: 3-9).

Smith, William B. (1808-1856). A Richmond, Indiana, physician who was born in Washington County, Pennsylvania. He moved to Richmond in 1825 and began the study of medicine with Dr. John T. Plummer in 1828. He graduated from the Medical College of Ohio in 1831. Smith began his practice of medicine in Raysville, Indiana, but after two years returned to Richmond where he practiced until his death (*History of Wayne County*, 1:599).

Steele, John (1791-1854). A Dayton, Ohio, physician who was born in Fayette County, Kentucky, and received an undergraduate education at Transylvania University. He attended lectures at the Medical Department of the University of Pennsylvania. After completing his medical education, Steele moved to Dayton. He became a prominent member of the Montgomery County Medical Society and served as a member and president of the Dayton City Council (*History of Montgomery County, Ohio*, bk. 3, pt. 2, p. 243).

Stipp, George Winfield (1799-1879). Lindsay's partner in Indianapolis. Stipp was born in Winchester, Virginia, and began practicing medicine in Troy and Xenia, Ohio. In the early 1830s he moved to Indianapolis, and in 1846 he relocated to Bloomington, Illinois, where he not only practiced medicine but also speculated heavily in land. During the Civil War, he was a lieutenant colonel and served as a regimental surgeon and medical inspector of the army. Unlike Lindsay, he died wealthy; his estate was valued at over $150,000 (Bloomington [Ill.] *The Paragraph*, August 29, 1879).

Stratten, F. J. An Eaton, Ohio, physician who set up practice with Dr. Nelson Donnellon in February 1851. Their partnership, however, lasted less than five months (Eaton *Democrat*, February 27, 1851).

Tardy, R. An early physician of Liberty, Indiana (*1884 Atlas of Union County, Indiana to Which Are Added Various General Maps . . .* [Chicago: J. H. Beers & Co., 1884], 28-29).

Tom's Run, Montgomery County, Ohio. A small stream located in Perry Township in the western part of the county. The first gristmill in the township was located on this stream (Conover, *Dayton and Montgomery County*, 2:821).

Treon, John (b. 1791). A pioneer physician of Montgomery County, Ohio. He was born in Hamburg, Berks County, Pennsylvania, and relocated to Miami Township, Montgomery County, Ohio, in 1811. Treon served as a surgeon in the War of 1812. In 1818 he helped lay out the town of Miamisburg, Ohio. He continued in practice until 1872 (*History of Montgomery County*, bk. 3, pt. 2, pp. 423-24).

Trout,_____ . A physician who moved from Ohio to Germantown, Indiana, in 1834. He was Germantown's first physician, but remained in the town for only a few years (Young, *History of Wayne County*, 244-45).

Union County, Indiana. A county located in the eastern part of Indiana, bordered on the east by the state of Ohio, the north by Wayne County, the west by Fayette County, and the south by Franklin County. It was organized in 1821 and by 1830 had a population of 7,957 (Scott, *Indiana Gazetteer*, 175).

Vaile, Joel (1804-1868). A physician who was born and educated in Vermont. He began the practice of medicine at East Brookfield, Massachusetts. In 1839 Vaile moved to Richmond, Indiana, and remained there until his death. During the Civil War he served as a surgeon of the Forty-first Regiment of Indiana volunteers (*History of Wayne County*, 602).

Van Buren, Crawford County, Arkansas. The county seat in the northwest part of the state on the Arkansas River, six miles northeast of Fort Smith.

Van Buren County, Arkansas. A county located in north central Arkansas. It is presently bounded on the north by Searcy and Stone counties, on the east by Cleburne County, the south by Conway and Faulkner counties, and the west by Pope County. The county was established in 1833, with Clinton as the seat of justice. In 1840 its population was 1,518 (*Reminiscent History of the Ozark Region*, 35, 40).

Van Tuyl, Henry. A Dayton, Ohio, physician. An officer in the Montgomery County Medical Society, he platted part of Dayton in 1845, was elected to the board of directors of the Dayton Bank in 1845, and was director of the First District School of Dayton (*History of Montgomery County*, 492, 598, 601, 686).

Vicksburg, Warren County, Mississippi. The county seat located in the western part of the state on the Mississippi River, forty miles west of Jackson.

Washington County, Arkansas. A county located in the northwestern part of the state, presently bounded on the north by Benton County, the west by Madison County, and the south by Crawford County. The county was established in 1828 and in 1830 had a population of 5,182 and in 1840, 7,148. In 1846 and 1883 changes were made in the boundary lines (*Reminiscent History of the Ozark Region*, 35, 40).

Wayne County, Indiana. A county in eastern Indiana organized in 1810. It is bounded on the north by Randolph County, the west by Henry and Fayette counties, the east by the state of Ohio, and the south by Fayette and Union counties. In 1830 its population was 23,344 (Scott, *Indiana Gazetteer*, 190-91).

Webber's Falls. Falls located in the southeast corner of present-day Muskogee, Oklahoma. At the time Lindsay traveled to this area, it was still a part of the Cherokee Nation. The Falls was the head of steamboat navigation when the Arkansas River was low.

West Alexandria, Preble County, Ohio. A town located eighty-seven miles southwest of Columbus, Ohio. The town was laid out in 1818. Although the Dayton Turnpike passed through the town, its population remained small. By 1830 it had a population of 150, and it had only three stores (Jenkins, *Ohio Gazetteer*, 469; *History of Preble County*, 327). Lindsay practiced medicine in West Alexandria for a short period in the 1820s and returned there in 1849. He practiced in the town until his death in 1876 (see Introduction).

Whiteridge, John. A Preble County, Ohio, physician (*History of Preble County*, 270).

Whiteridge, Peleg. A Preble County, Ohio, physician (*History of Preble County*, 270).

Williams, D. D. An Arkansas physician practicing in Mulberry in the 1830s. A native of Wales, he was listed in the 1850 census.

Williamsburg, Wayne County, Indiana. A town located in Greene Township. It is located five miles southeast of Economy and eleven miles northeast of Richmond. William Johnson and John Frazor laid it out in 1830 (Young, *History of Wayne County*, 227).

Yell County, Arkansas. A county located in west central Arkansas. At present, it is bordered on the north by Logan County and the Arkansas River, on the east by Perry County, on the south by Garland and Montgomery counties, and the west by Scott County. The county was organized in 1840, after Lindsay's visit to Arkansas (*Reminiscent History of the Ozark Region*, 40).

Suggestions for Further Reading

Medicine and Health Care. Several studies provide a general overview of the history of American medicine. Richard Harrison Shryock's work *Medicine and Society in America, 1660-1860* (New York: New York University Press, 1960) is a concise account of the role of medicine and disease in American society from colonial times to the Civil War. John Duffy's *The Healers: A History of American Medicine* (1976; reprint, Urbana: University of Illinois Press, 1979) traces the history of American medicine to the twentieth century and contains discussions of surgery, medical practice, sectarian practitioners, medical education, and licensing legislation. William G. Rothstein's *American Physicians in the Nineteenth Century: From Sects to Science* (Baltimore: Johns Hopkins University Press, 1972) also provides a good survey of nineteenth-century American medicine. The best history of medical care during the Civil War is George Worthington Adams's *Doctors in Blue: The Medical History of the Union Army in the Civil War* (New York: Henry Schuman, 1952).

One of the most insightful analyses of nineteenth-century therapeutics is John Harley Warner's recent work *The Therapeutic Perspective: Medical Practice, Knowledge, and Identity in America, 1820-1885* (Cambridge: Harvard University Press, 1986). In his book, Warner examines the therapies employed by nineteenth-century physicians and notes that doctors often individualized their treatments based on a patient's age, gender, and socioeconomic position. Another very useful work is Irvine Loudon's *Medical Care and the General Practitioner, 1750-1850* (Oxford: Clarendon Press, 1986) which examines the type and quality of surgical care provided by the ordinary practitioner. Although Loudon's work concerns physicians in eighteenth- and nineteenth-century England, his observations on routine medical and surgical care raise interesting questions about the quality of ordinary health care in the United States.

201

During the 1800s a number of changes were occurring both in the medical profession and in society. By the end of the century, these changes had dramatically altered the practice of medicine. The most comprehensive book describing these changes is Paul Starr's *The Social Transformation of American Medicine* (New York: Basic Books, 1982). George Rosen's *The Structure of American Medical Practice, 1875-1941*, ed. Charles E. Rosenberg (Philadelphia: University of Pennsylvania Press, 1983) focuses on the changes occurring in medicine during the late nineteenth and twentieth centuries. This book, as well as Rosen's earlier work, *Fee and Fee Bills: Some Economic Aspects of Medical Practice in Nineteenth Century America* (Baltimore: Johns Hopkins Press, 1946), are also good sources for information on the economics of medicine.

Recently several medical historians have published collections of essays and original source material. These works integrate social and intellectual history with medical history. Judith Walzer Leavitt and Ronald L. Numbers, eds., *Sickness and Health in America: Readings in the History of Medicine and Public Health*, 2d ed. (Madison: University of Wisconsin Press, 1985) contains a number of essays on subjects as diverse as medical education, women and medicine, medical economics, and public health reform. Other collections of essays on various issues confronting physicians and the health care system include Susan Reverby and David Rosner's *Health Care in America: Essays in Social History* (Philadelphia: Temple University Press, 1979) and Morris J. Vogel and Charles E. Rosenberg's *The Therapeutic Revolution: Essays on the Social History of American Medicine* (Philadelphia: University of Pennsylvania Press, 1979). Gert H. Brieger's *Medical America in the Nineteenth Century: Readings from the Literature* (Baltimore: Johns Hopkins Press, 1972) contains essays by nineteenth-century medical authors which reflect the problems of the physician, student, and patient.

The most comprehensive source on the history of medicine in the Midwest, including Indiana, is Madge E. Pickard and R. Carlyle Buley's *The Midwest Pioneer: His Ills, Cures, and Doctors* (New York: Henry Schuman, 1946). Pickard and Buley's book covers all aspects of nineteenth-century midwestern medicine.

Medical Licensing and the Growth of Medical Societies. Most of the works mentioned above contain sections on medical licensing and the development of medical societies. Joseph Kett's *The Formation of the American Medical Profession: The Role of Institutions, 1780-1860* (1968; reprint, Westport, Conn.: Greenwood Press, 1980) focuses on the growth of medical societies and licensing legislation before the

Civil War and their effects on the medical profession. A brief, yet informative book on the history of medical licensing is Richard Harrison Shryock's *Medical Licensing in America, 1650-1965* (Baltimore: Johns Hopkins Press, 1967).

Medical Education. Although most histories of American medicine also contain discussions of early medical education, several books are devoted to the subject. One of the most thorough is William Frederick Norwood's *Medical Education in the United States before the Civil War* (New York: Arno Press, 1971). The book contains a history of most of the antebellum medical schools. Another good survey is Martin Kaufman's *American Medical Education: The Formative Years, 1765-1910* (Westport, Conn.: Greenwood Press, 1976). Kenneth Ludmerer's recently published *Learning to Heal: The Development of American Medical Education* (New York: Basic Books, 1985) also provides an overview of the early medical education system and its late nineteenth-century reform. William G. Rothstein's recent work *American Medical Schools and the Practice of Medicine: A History* (New York: Oxford University Press, 1987) shows how changes in medical science and in society affected medical schools and medical education.

The better-trained physicians in the early nineteenth century studied in Paris. Two books which focus on the Parisian educational system are: Russell M. Jones, ed., *The Parisian Education of an American Surgeon: Letters of Jonathan Mason Warren (1832-1835)* (Philadelphia: American Philosophical Society, 1978) and Erwin H. Ackerknecht's *Medicine at the Paris Hospital, 1794-1848* (Baltimore: Johns Hopkins Press, 1967).

Sectarian Medicine. Alternative medical systems abounded during the nineteenth century, and several works focus exclusively on that topic. Guenter B. Risse, Ronald L. Numbers, and Judith Walzer Leavitt, eds., *Medicine Without Doctors: Home Health Care in American History* (New York: Science History Publications, 1977) contains a collection of essays on home remedy books, Thomsonianism, homeopathy, and patent medicines. Joseph Kett's *The Formation of the American Medical Profession* (see above) contains an extensive and insightful discussion of Thomsonianism and homeopathy. Two exhaustive works on homeopathic medicine are Martin Kaufman's *Homeopathy in America: The Rise and Fall of a Medical Heresy* (Baltimore: Johns Hopkins Press, 1971) and Harris L. Coulter's *Divided Legacy: The Conflict between Homeopathy and the American Medical Association: Science and Ethics in American Medicine, 1800-1914* (1973; reprint, Richmond, Calif.: North Atlantic Books, 1982). Jane B. Donegan's latest publication, *"Hydropathic Highway to Health": Women* *and Water-Cure in Antebellum America* (New York: Greenwood Press, 1986), discusses the history of hydropathy and shows why this sect appealed to women as both patients and practitioners.

Surgery. Most histories of surgery examine the lives of well-known surgeons and their surgical innovations. Except for Irvine Loudon's study of medical care in eighteenth- and nineteenth-century England (see above), none of these works discuss ordinary surgical care. Many of the general histories of American medicine such as Duffy's *Healers*, Rothstein's *American Physicians*, and Brieger's *Medical America in the Nineteenth Century* contain discussions of surgery during this period. Jurgen Thorwald's *The Century of the Surgeon* (New York: Pantheon Books, 1956), based on historical facts but written in novel form, gives the lay reader an understanding of the hardships faced by surgeons and their patients before anesthesia and asepsis. Owen H. Wangensteen and Sarah Wangensteen's *The Rise of Surgery: From Empiric Craft to Scientific Discipline* (Minneapolis: University of Minnesota Press, 1978) is a lengthy volume discussing the many technological advances made in surgery, as well as the conditions under which surgeons operated. Frederick F. Cartwright's *The Development of Modern Surgery from 1830* (London: Arthur Barker, 1967) provides a more concise account of technological advances in surgery. Francis R. Packard in his *History of Medicine in the United States*, Vol. 2 (New York: Paul B. Hoeber, 1931) devotes several pages (1055-1118) to the achievements in American surgery. A. Scott Earl, ed., *Surgery in America from the Colonial Era to the Twentieth Century: Selected Writings* (Philadelphia: W. B. Saunders, 1965) contains excerpts from writings by American practitioners regarding surgical procedures and care.

A number of histories recount the events leading up to the discovery of anesthesia. One of the earliest sources for this history is Richard Manning Hodges's *A Narrative of Events Connected with the Introduction of Sulphuric Ether into Surgical Use* (Boston: Little, Brown, and Company, 1891). Martin Pernick's *A Calculus of Suffering: Pain, Professionalism, and Anesthesia* (New York: Columbia University Press, 1985) provides excellent insight into the history of pain and why after the introduction of anesthesia in 1846 doctors chose to use it only selectively.

Obstetrics and Childbearing. The two best works on the history of childbearing and obstetrics in nineteenth-century America are Judith Walzer Leavitt's *Brought to Bed: Childbearing in America, 1750-1950* (New York: Oxford University Press, 1986) and Jane B. Donegan's *Women and Men Midwives: Medicine, Morality, and Misogyny in Early America* (Westport, Conn.: Greenwood Press, 1978).

Conclusion. These secondary works provide an overview of the history of medicine and a framework in which to interpret that history. An understanding of early nineteenth-century medicine and health care can also result from reading the literature of the period. S. D. Gross's *History of American Medical Literature from 1776 to the Present Time* (1876; reprint, New York: Burt Franklin, 1972) provides an account of medical books published in the nineteenth century. Period texts provide a glimpse of state-of-the-art medical and surgical procedures; they do not, however, discuss the actual therapeutics and surgical techniques employed by physicians during this period. The best sources for this type of information are transactions from local and state medical societies and medical journals; diaries, account books, and journals of physicians; and letters and diaries of patients.

Index

DUE

	PRINTED IN U.S.A.